Climb along the Cutting Edge

An Analysis of Change
in
Religious Life

Joan Chittister, O.S.B.
Stephanie Campbell, O.S.B.
Mary Collins, O.S.B.
Ernestine Johann, O.S.B.
Johnette Putnam, O.S.B.

PAULIST PRESS
New York, N.Y./Ramsey, N.J.

Library of Congress
Catalog Card Number: 77-80802

ISBN: 0-8091-2038-0

Published by Paulist Press
Editorial Office: 1865 Broadway, New York, N.Y. 10023
Business Office: 545 Island Road, Ramsey, N.J. 07446

Printed and bound in the
United States of America

Contents

Convent Life Prior to Vatican II: Regularity—
Prayer Structure—Lifestyle—Practice of the Vows
—Need for Change

Convent Life After Vatican II: Early Changes in
Prayer Structure—Personal Decision-Making—
Interpersonal Relationships—Government Struc-
tures—Clothing Issue

Increased Representation at the General Chapter—
Pre-Chapter Sessions—Development of Committees
—Use of Consultants at Chapters—Expansion of the
Federation Council—The Conciliation Board—
Revision of Visitation Procedures—Interim Con-
stitutions—*Call to Life*

Implementation: Ecclesiastical Support Factors—
Social and Organizational Factors—Personal Involvement Factors—Eight Obstacles to Implementation—Seven Factors Which Did Not Obstruct—
Conclusions

Demographic and Personality Profiles of Chapter
Delegates—Conclusions

From Vatican I to Vatican II: The Papacy and
Catholic Identity—American Benedictine Sisters
Between the Councils—The Sixteen Documents of
Vatican II and Catholic Identity

Theological Issues in the Renewal of American
Benedictine Women: Ecclesiology: The Nature of
the Church—Religious Authority—Religious Life
—Person—Community—Eschatology: Ultimate
Truth Foreshadowed—Conclusions

Climate for Renewal in the Congregation, 1966-68—
Renewal Chapters, 1966-68—Opinionnaire on
Benedictinism, 1967: Analysis and Conclusions

Theological Concepts Developed 1968-74: The
Meaning of Monastic Community—The American
Benedictine Community in the Modern World—
Monastic Community as Prophetic—Elements of
American Benedictine Life

An Attitude Study: The Evaluation of Pre-Vatican
II Religious Life—An Evaluation of Post-Vatican
II Religious Life—Comparison—Conclusions

Behavioral Orientation: The Implications of Behavioral Choices—Spiritual Practices—Leisure—Human Relationships—Direction and Control—Identity—Current Questions—Conclusions

Motives for Change: Types of Change Agents—Impact Analysis—Conclusions

Belief Patterns: The Nature of Conformity and Belief—The Effect of Belief on Behaviors, Attitudes and Social Movements—Revaluation or Evolution

Emerging Issues: Ministry—Meaning—Cohesion—Survival—Prognosis for the Future

DEDICATION

This book is dedicated to all Benedictine Sisters of the Federation of Saint Scholastica because of whose past work and present commitment the future is possible.

It is also dedicated to Matthew Benko, O.S.B., monk of St. Vincent Archabbey and canonist of the Federation of Saint Scholastica, a man who believed that women could be self-reliant.

ACKNOWLEDGEMENTS

The writers want to acknowledge the generosity of the many individuals and organizations who provided financial support for the research and writing of this book: Mr. & Mrs. David McKinney of Chicago, Illinois; the Benedictine Sisters of Sacred Heart Convent, Lisle, Illinois; the Lewis Foundation of Chicago, Illinois; The Raskob Foundation of Wilmington, Delaware; Most Reverend Joseph Vath, Archbishop of Birmingham, Alabama; and the Ladies Catholic Benevolent Association of Erie, Pennsylvania. Some additional funds were received from the Federation of St. Benedict and the priories of the Federation of St. Scholastica.

Additional support for the work came in other forms from the Penn State University Department of Speech Communication Theory, where Dr. Robert Craig designed the computer program basic to the project, and the Institute for Ecumenical and Cultural Research at Collegeville, Minnesota, which awarded the team a research fellowship for the summer of 1976, during which time this book was written.

Research associate Maureen Tobin, O.S.B., Erie, Pennsylvania, coordinated the support services necessary to maintaining the project and the people who did it from start to finish. Other research associates who were directly engaged at critical points in the shaping of the project were Patricia McGreevy, O.S.B., Erie, Pennsylvania and Augusta Hamel, O.S.B., Cullman, Alabama. Readers and consultants who offered constructive advice and advanced it toward its final form include Mary Susan Sevier, O.S.B., Cullman, Alabama, past president of the Federation of St. Scholastica; Mary Austin Schirmer, O.S.B., past prioress of Mount St. Scholastica, Atchison, Kansas; Enid Smith, O.S.B., St. Joseph, Minnesota, president of the Federation of Saint Benedict; Dr. Robert Bilheimer, director of the Institute for Ecumenical and Cultural Research, Collegeville, Minnesota; Dr. Patrick Henry, associate professor of Religion of Swarthmore College; Martin Burne, O.S.B., St. Mary's, Morristown, New Jersey, president of the Council of American Benedictine Presidents; Dr. Sarah Pitzer, State College, Pennsylvania; and Sister Virginia Ann Gardner, C.S.J., Erie, Pennsylvania. The index for the work was prepared by Ellen Richardson, O.S.B., Atchison, Kansas. Mary Paul Ege, O.S.B., Atchison, assisted with the editing. Mary Alice Rettger, O.S.B., and Patricia Mowry, O.S.B. provided valuable assistance by preparing the manuscript for publication.

Last on this list but not last in their hearts, the writers acknowledge the support and encouragement of their own religious communities who smiled on this group as it undertook one more quixotic project.

In summary, the work was made possible by a number of people, but for the concepts and their presentation the writers hold no one responsible but themselves.

CONTRIBUTORS

JOAN CHITTISTER, O.S.B., Mount St. Benedict Convent, Erie, Pennsylvania, the director of this research has served as president of the Federation of St. Scholastica since 1971, and as president of the Conference of American Benedictine Prioresses since 1975. She is also currently president of the Leadership Conference of Women Religious. An elected delegate to the renewal chapters from 1968 and member of the preparatory committees on poverty and Benedictinism, she holds a PhD in Speech Communication Theory from Penn State University. She has lectured widely and conducted workshops on renewal of religious life since 1969. More recently, she has represented American Benedictine women at the 1974-77 Congress of Abbots and the Leadership Conference of Women Religious at the Sacred Congregation for Religious and the International Union of Superiors General. She organized the delegation of the LWCR at the 3rd Inter-American Conference on Religious Life in Montreal in 1977.

STEPHANIE CAMPBELL, O.S.B. is a member of the Benedictine Sisters of Severn, Maryland, a foundation made from St. Walburga's Convent at Elizabeth, New Jersey, during the renewal period. An elected delegate to the 1968-69 renewal chapter and chairperson of the Poverty preparatory committee, she was also a community-elected associate member of the 1971 and 1974 chapters. Author of the St. Walburga Convent community history, *Chosen for Peace,* she holds graduate and undergraduate degrees from the Catholic University of America. Currently, she is principal of Martin Spalding High School, Severn, Md.

MARY COLLINS, O.S.B., Mount St. Scholastica Convent, Atchison, Kansas, is currently first councillor of the Federation of St. Scholastica. An elected delegate to the 1971 and 1974 chapters, she served as consultant to the 1971 preparatory committee on Prayer and as chairperson of the Theology preparatory committee for the 1974 chapter. First president of the Atchison community senate, she served three terms helping to guide community renewal effort. She earned the PhD at the Catholic University of America, focusing in the area of liturgical theology, and has done research and writing on liturgical and ecclesial renewal since 1967. She now holds an appointment as associate professor of religion at the University of Kansas. She serves also as president of The Liturgical Conference and as director of the program for liturgical renewal at the Center for Benedictine Studies in Atchison.

ERNESTINE JOHANN, O.S.B., has been prioress of St. Benedict's Convent, Bristow, Virginia, since 1967. Earlier, she earned the Master of Arts degree at the Benedictine Institute for Sacred Theology, Collegeville, Minnesota, and served as director of novices for her community. A delegate to all the renewal chapters from 1966 through 1974 and a member of both the Formation and Theology preparatory committees, she has served on the Council of the Federation of St. Scholastica since 1968 and is presently Federation treasurer. At present she is a member of the Procedural Committee of the Leadership Conference of Women Religious and has also served that organization as chairperson of the Nominations and Elections Committee.

JOHNETTE PUTNAM, O.S.B., served as prioress of St. Scholastica Priory, Covington, Louisiana, from 1968 to 1975. A participant in the renewal chapters from 1968 through 1974, chairperson of the preparatory committee on Benedictinism and a member of the Juridic commission which prepared *Call to Life* for the 1974 chapter, she has also been a member of the Federation council since 1968. Currently she is completing graduate studies in theology at St. John's University, Collegeville. Throughout the renewal period, she has directed her energies to providing moral leadership for the southern civil rights struggle in her locale and to examining the sources for a contemporary Benedictine monastic theology and spirituality.

Preface

We began this work because history was slipping away from us. In the space of one decade, convent life had undergone momentous change. Volumes of position papers, meeting minutes and constitutional amendments marked the significance of the period but, other than letters, very few materials exist to enable the next generation to narrate the train of events which led to renewal or to describe the personal pressures which surrounded it. In fact, we realized, neither young women who are entering now nor outsiders who had known women religious before could really account for the situation either.

We thought first of simply identifying some people who had been key to the process and asking them to tape their recollections in order to leave an oral history of the renewal period. That might still be a good idea since it would flesh out from single points of view the environment and personal struggles of the era.

This work, however, took a different turn. A group of us, all of whom had special connections with the renewal Chapters by virtue of position or committee involvement created a survey instrument designed to bring information to the following topics:

1. How change occurred
2. What issues existed which prompted change
3. What delegates did to effect change
4. What was the purpose of renewal
5. What problems, if any, affected the implementation of renewal decisions
6. What kinds of people were the delegates
7. How the delegates now feel about the changes which have taken place in religious life as a result of renewal Chapter decisions
8. What is the future of religious life.

We asked every delegate to the Chapters of Renewal to respond. Then, using their responses as a guide we set about in interdisciplinary fashion to analyze renewal as it occurred in our single federation and to assess its effects. As a result, the book has two characteristics. In the first place each researcher is treating the same materials so there is a degree of repetition. Since the separate sections explain the materials from a different focus, however, we felt the reiteration of basic examples was necessary and even revealing to the reader. Furthermore, it seemed to us that because the material is treated from a variety of academic vantage points—history, theology and social psychology—some readers might prefer to read only those sections which dealt with their special interest. Consequently, we made the judgment to leave every unit whole rather than to deal with major issues from only one perspective.

Secondly, because the book is explanatory as well as historical there are overtones of apologia as well as narration for which the writers make no apology. We do not, however, intend to assert the superiority or rightness of present forms, only to explain the motives and values from which they have arisen.

Finally, reader-reactors who by their criticism have helped to shape this work have brought us to recognize that underlying the journey through renewal in the United States is feminism as well as democracy and personalism. In retrospect, it can be seen that there is a clear case to be made for this position. Unlike the other two principles, however, woman's rights were never argued on the chapter floor nor used to substantiate a position. For that reason, this explanation is not given in the text though the writers acknowledge the likelihood of the woman issue as a residual influence on community renewal programs, even as early as 1966. It should be noted, however, that most of the consultants to whom the sisters turned for direction or approval were men.

This is a significant period in the history of religious communities. What has happened in the last ten years will affect a number of sisters for a long time to come. In this work we ask ourselves what we hoped to accomplish as a result of renewal: what were our goals; what were our motivations; what are our feelings now. In this way we hope to provide a record of what we ourselves thought we did as we revised policies that deliberately reshaped religious life as we had experienced it.

Such a record can be a guide to future generations. It can also help us at the present time to identify the issues which are surfacing now.

It is easy to grow weary at a time like this. The old vision has been blurred and the new one is unclear. We sometimes wonder if there is present value or future hope in our own lives. We forget that a people chosen before us also wandered, wondering about the wisdom of their past decisions and the presence of God, but they went on anyway. Going on was their contribution. We may forget as we climb along the cutting edge of history that it can also be ours.

Joan Chittister, O.S.B.

Introduction

"I SEE THE FUTURE AS YET UNCHARTED . . ."

It may just be that the whole structure of religious life as we have known it in the past will be changed. The renewal brought about an intensification of a deeper prayer life and therefore new insights through the Spirit, and so I see the future as yet uncharted. We just have to be open to where the Spirit breathes.

Delegate's Response to Participant Profile, 1976

The sisterhood of the American Roman Catholic church has played a major part in the history of the church in the United States and in the development of the country itself. Religious communities of women have founded and administered schools, hospitals, and orphanages; they have worked with the poor, the oppressed, the working class and the wealthy; they have influenced—for good or ill —every generation of Americans and the institutional structures of the nation since its founding. They have worked for subsistence wages and been totally self-supporting. At the present time in history, there are over 125,000 Catholic religious women in the United States. These women, as an organized group with common values and distinct goals have a significant effect on society.

This book is about one segment of these women, those who make up the Federation of St. Scholastica, an association of Benedictine women from twenty-three North American priories located in sixteen states from New Jersey to California, in twenty dioceses and in the Republic of Mexico. There are 2200 Sisters in these twenty-three convents. The book records the story of the development of American Benedictinism in the Federation of St. Scholastica since the time of Vatican Council II in 1962-65, but is actually a microcosm of the pain and process of change in every community of women religious, Benedictine or not. It speaks to some large issues: What has really happened in communities of women as a result of renewal? Why did it happen? What are its results? What do these changes mean for the future of religious life and for the Catholic church in America?

Sometime between 1922—the time the first set of constitutions of the Federation of St. Scholastica was approved in Rome—and 1966, the period in which the deliberate renewal and reorganization began, things happened that brought religious communities of American

3

women to the point of change. This study identifies the factors that led to change and assesses the results in a single religious federation. In doing so, it may serve to explain to the public as well as to other Sisters the present state and goals of their religious life.

Five major topics have been developed in telling the story of the renewal period.

1. Religious life and community forms prior to 1966.
2. The dynamics of renewal in the religious institutions.
3. The theological and ecclesial milieu of the period of Vatican Council II.
4. The development of Benedictine monasticism for American women.
5. The social-psychological analysis of the attitudes and behaviors, motivations and beliefs of community leadership during renewal, the consequences of change and the emerging new issues in these religious communities.

Each of these topics is treated in a separate section by a writer specialized in that area. The data basic to this study of renewal in the Federation of St. Scholastica was gathered through a 453-item Participant Profile distributed to the 158 women who had been elected by their own communities as delegates to the renewal chapters of the period. One hundred forty-two women completed and returned the profile, a return of almost 90%. What is narrated here is essentially an account of what these women did and how they felt about it.

The work was designed to supplement the only previous research that had been done on the Federation of St. Scholastica. The *Benedictine Congregation of St. Scholastica—Its Foundations and Development: 1880-1930* by Sister Regina Baska, O.S.B., is a valuable description of the organization of the Federation, its purposes and historical problems. That history covers the implantation of the Benedictine houses of women in the United States and the efforts of the federation in the canonical structures of the Roman Catholic church during that era. The present deals with the second major period in the development of communities of Benedictine Sisters: the renewal and refounding of Benedictine religious life at a time of phenomenal structural, theological and cultural change. It also shows in what ways renewal and change have altered the character of women's religious communities in this country and have affected the relation of the American Sisterhood to the ecclesiastical network of the Catholic church at this time.

In the past decade, communities of American women religious and their members have personally undergone vast changes in lifestyle, work, and operating processes. These new responsibilities and behavioral patterns have taxed the faith, understanding, psychic energy and organization of the Catholic laity, the American church and the sisters themselves. Because this is such a crucial period in the existence of orders of religious women, the research was begun in order to collect and preserve the hopes, feelings, fears and explanations of the very people who have borne the weight of this historical period rather than to surrender to the insights of future historians alone the analysis of this era. Perhaps a full and honest description of these factors by the people who participated in this period will serve as a future model or guide to succeeding generations of sisters as they contemplate future changes or evaluate the present ones.

The book addresses itself to the cultural factors which led to major changes in religious life and the individual religious women themselves. In addition, it provides reflection on the present state of religious life and assesses the type of spirituality which is emerging from these new structures and from new theological understanding. In this way, it may serve primarily to explain to the American Catholic sisterhood, and interested clergy and laity the nature of contemporary women's community in the Benedictine tradition. Because the group under study is a Benedictine one, the work will describe to European Benedictines the evolution of religious life in contemporary America. Finally, it attempts to present an honest evaluation of the possible failures and the forseeable future of post-conciliar religious life.

Beyond these immediate audiences, the material ought to have increasing value to church historians, religious historians, students of contemporary spirituality, students of religion in America, students of women's movements in the contemporary church and society, and male seminarians whose future it will be to share the pastoral ministry of the Church with women religious. It documents significant developments in religious life during these years of renewal and reorganization. It gives an account of the present state of Benedictine life in communities of American sisters as the Order prepares to mark in 1980 fifteen hundred years of Benedictine influence in the church. It makes a contribution to the history of American Catholic spirituality.

Since there is reason to believe that the vocation crisis in religious communities may be at least partially explained by the fact that confusion, suspicion and uncertainty now affect the understanding of religious life, this work consciously addresses itself to the nature of the changes that have occurred and the intent of these changes in the present life-style of religious. As an actual evaluation of the events and the effects of renewal by the participants themselves, it highlights the values they sought to promote. In doing this it gives a public accounting to the Church and to other groups as well. Its purpose is definitely not to derogate the past or the strong, saintly women who lived it but only to analyze those factors which made it necessary to develop new ways to live religious life. In no way is this text meant to be an instrument of division or humiliation but rather one of understanding and compassion. The past produced the present, made it possible and saw it through. The past is past, however, and that very reality needs to be explained.

The need for explanation and assessment can obviously be met from a privileged point of view by the people involved, the sisters themselves. What is more, no other group of researchers is even attempting to preserve, analyze and synthesize the feelings and goals of the participants in the renewal process. Consequently, a valuable body of primary data from one of the most significant periods of religious history is being overlooked now and possibly lost forever, despite the fact that community after community is in the very process of seriously attempting to reorient itself within the developing church and society. Without the kind of information and analysis provided by a work such as this, the reorientation efforts may conceivably fail and multiple religious institutions with them.

Because the topic the book treats of is current and the method analytical, the work has both immediate and historical value. Its purpose is not to convince the reader about the worth of the developments that have occurred, but to make them intelligible and thereby open to understanding. Such understanding, when it comes, will be the strongest foundation for renewed commitment and a hopeful future for American religious women.

PART I
Benedictine Convent Life
Before and After
The Second Vatican Council

The purpose of this first essay is to give a brief description—
from lived experience as well as from the documents in use at the
time—of the lifestyle of American Benedictine Sisters before the Second Vatican Council and to compare that lifestyle with the one found
in Benedictine convents today. The elements perceived today as negative in the description of pre-Vatican II convent life have been
stressed because they caused tensions within the various communities,
and those very tensions precipitated the subsequent changes. However, it is important in reading about the heavy prayer and work schedules, the formality, and the antiquated customs, that we remember
that the sisters who established these communities in the 19th century
were women of their own day, staunch women of the Church, and
daughters of hard-working immigrants. The lifestyle that they established enabled them to form a substantial part of the backbone of
the Roman Catholic Church in the United States, especially through
the sacrifices they made on behalf of the parochial school system.

"WE . . . ARE ASKING FOR MORE VOICE"

... It seems that we are contradicting ourselves. We, as religious women, are asking for more voice in decisions and dialogue affecting our lives. On the other hand, we keep writing and looking for a more specific statement from a group of men—the Sacred Congregation—regarding our clothing, etc., after they have given us directives in the Decree on Adaptation and Renewal of Religious Life. . . . I fear disastrous results if we continually try to restrain rather than direct progress.

Letter from a Prioress to the Federation President, 1966

In order to understand the changes that have taken place in American Benedictine convents in response to Vatican Council II, and in order to understand the reactions of the sisters themselves to those changes, it is important to know how the sisters lived their religious lives in the days before the Council and how they are living now. A clearer perception of the cataclysm that has taken place may throw some light on the ensuing withdrawal from communities on the one hand, and the dearth of new recruits on the other.

BEFORE THE COUNCIL

In the years immediately preceding the Council, one of the most satisfying aspects of religious life was the high degree of certainty regarding moral values which it imparted to its members and, consequently, the sense that by living the life in harmony with the current interpretation of the Rule of the founder they would be assured not only of ultimate salvation, but also of an eminent degree of inner peace in this life.

This sense of moral security was supported by a life style and a prayer schedule which constantly reminded the sister that she was giving her entire self for the love of Christ. The moral security and the regularity of the daily schedule, reinforced in Benedictine houses by the rule of silence as an aid to prayerful union with the Lord, established an atmosphere of calmness and seeming serenity.

In addition to the apparently untroubled atmosphere and the moral certitude, the sisters' practice of the vows of poverty, chastity, and obedience made for strong-willed women accustomed to the habitual restriction of their natural desires, whose energies then poured out in a phenomenal amount of work for the church, and especially for those elements in the church who really needed their services—children and the sick.

However, these very elements which made convent life most rewarding planted the seeds for the revolution which erupted in the late 1960's. Regularity and peace can become ends in themselves when there is no system to ensure that changes can be made easily when needed.

In the two decades immediately preceding Vatican II, formalism threatened to undermine the basic meaning and purpose of Benedictine life as a commitment to the dynamic life of the original apostolic community at Jerusalem. A typical day in Benedictine priories of the 1950's and most of the 60's went something like this.

4:50 a.m.	Rising Bell
5:10	Lauds
5:40	Meditation
6:10	Prime
6:30	Mass followed by Terce, Sext, and None
7:45	Breakfast (eaten in silence)
8:30 - 11:45	Work (home or school)
11:50	Particular Examen
12:00	Dinner (with table reading) followed by Vespers
1:00 - 4:30 p.m.	Work (home or school)
4:45	Matins
5:30	Spiritual Reading
6:00	Supper (with table reading) followed by dishwashing, kitchen chores, etc.
7:00	Recreation
8:00	Compline followed by the Great Silence
9:00	Lights out for those who were neither teachers nor students
10:00	Lights out for teachers and students

Such a schedule was established originally for a life given over primarily to choral prayer. So much emphasis was placed on prayer in choir that if a sister's work in the classroom, hospital, or kitchen necessitated her being absent from one or more of the community's "spiritual exercises," she strove diligently to "make it up" on her own time. In addition to the prayers recited in common, the Declarations of the Congregation of St. Scholastica advised the daily recitation of the rosary, the Way of the Cross, and frequent private visits to the Blessed Sacrament.

The Declarations of the Congregation (1953 edition, pages 16-18), interpreting St. Benedict's sparse statement on "Reverence at

Prayer" in the Rule, read in part as follows:

> In addition to the Divine Office and vocal prayer the Sisters should devote themselves with special fervor to the exercises of recollection, or mental prayer. A half hour daily, therefore, is to be set aside for meditation and another half hour for spiritual reading. The particular examination of conscience should be made before the midday meal; the general examen of conscience after the last community exercise in the evening . . .
>
> Besides these ordinary exercises, let all each year enter upon the sacred Retreat . . .
>
> Candidates, Novices, and Sisters will prepare themselves well in advance for the reception of the habit or the profession of temporary vows by suitable exercises for at least eight full days. Having on the prudent advice of their Father Confessor made a General Confession, let them approach the Holy Table during the Mass of reception or profession.
>
> The Prioress shall designate a Sunday out of each month as a day of extraordinary recollection, of silence and pious exercises . . .
>
> We urge upon the members of the Congregation the most fervent devotion to the august Sacrament of the Eucharist, which, after due permission of the local Ordinary they may conserve in their churches and chapels and expose solemnly for adoration.
>
> We recommend in the next place devotion to the Sacred Heart of Jesus, a tender veneration for the most blessed Virgin Mary, as well as for St. Benedict and St. Scholastica, (the Patrons of the Order), and for other saints . . .
>
> After the midday meal and after supper let them visit the most blessed Sacrament of the Altar and recite in common the customary prayers . . .
>
> The Prioress will see to it that no one miss any of the religious exercises, except for a grave reason . . .
>
> The Sisters who are prevented by their various occupations from attending the exercises of the community are to be given an opportunity at another time wherein to do their spiritual reading, say their prayers, and above all, make their meditations.[1]

The Declarations concluded, "However, caution must be exercised against introducing too many community devotions . . . lest they come to honor God with their lips more than with their minds and hearts."

In addition to the Declarations of the Congregation, each priory had its own book of customs which were derived in large part from the customary of the founding community, St. Walburga Convent, Eichstadt, Bavaria. These customs books prescribed, for example, on what days the community was to have Benediction, what prayers were to be said while dressing and undressing, prayers recited before and after meals, prayers while unfolding the table napkin, prayers when the clock struck the hour . . . And the prescriptions were honored in detail.

From studying the daily schedule, reading the chapter from the Declarations on private prayer, and reading the customs books, it would be difficult to infer that the women following this regimen were also full time students, cooks, school teachers, housekeepers, nurses, or administrators. In most communities since school teachers, administrators, and nurses regularly missed some part of the community's spiritual exercises, a good part of their unscheduled time was given over to "getting in" the missed exercises. But there were also lessons to be prepared, students' papers to be corrected, professional reading to be done. Convent humor included stories about sisters sleeping during meditation and during spiritual reading. But the need for rest and relaxation was very real.

The tightly woven and crowded schedule was a distinguishing aspect of religious life prior to the Second Vatican Council. Another aspect, equally important from the vantage point of the subsequent changes, was the formality observed in almost every area of life.

When a young woman entered the novitiate of an American Benedictine house between the years 1946 and 1968, one of the first books given her to study was entitled *Choir Ceremonial for the Benedictine Sisters of the Congregation of Saint Scholastica.* In this book of sixty-one pages, she would learn that there was a correct procedure for every detail of the Liturgy of the Hours (then called the "Divine Office"). A few excerpts convey the degree and extent of the stylization of the sister's prayer life.

A. Entering Choir
1. When the Sisters enter the chapel in a body, they walk two and two, take holy water, genuflect, and pass on to their places according to rank, the youngest entering first.
2. When the Blessed Sacrament is exposed, the genuflection is made on both knees, accompanied by a moderate bow.
3. When passing before the side altars, the Sisters make a moderate bow.
B. Leaving Choir
1. When the signal is given to leave the chapel, all rise together, observing the same reverences made on en-

tering the chapel, the seniors leaving first.
2. On entering or leaving the choir by herself, a Sister
   first genuflects towards the altar and then bows to
   both sides of the choir.

. . .

IV. Various Liturgical Bows
There are three kinds of bows, namely, the simple, with
the head alone; the moderate, with the head and shoulders
somewhat inclined; and the profound, with the head bent so
that the knees can be touched with the extremities of the
fingers.

There followed five and a half pages listing the exact occasions
on which each type of bow was to be made, and when no bow was
called for. Among the rules laid down were such prescriptions as the
following:

A minor reverence is always included in a major one;
hence we do not add a bow of the head when making a
profound bow. There is no bow of the head at a simple
genuflection.
When one is already bowing, one should not bend the
head still more at the names of "Jesus," "Maria," etc.
When one is kneeling, the inclination of the head or
simple bow is not omitted, but the profound bow is never
made when one is in a kneeling position . . . [2]

The emphasis on the external perfection of detail may ring of
caricature to those who did not experience it. But those who did,
know that although the rigid uniformity of the choir ceremonial was
somewhat unique, the twin characteristics of formalism and perfec-
tionism tinged almost every aspect of convent life in the pre-conciliar
period.

One practice which illustrates these traits and also illustrates the
almost complete deterioration of a wholesome monastic exercise was
the chapter of faults or culpa chapter. From its original intention—
the public acknowledgment of genuine offenses against the community—the culpa chapter had become a routine recitation of failure
to adhere to the customs. For example, a sister would accuse herself
publicly of having allowed her scapular, a part of the religious garb,
to trail on the stairs, of failing to kiss her religious clothing when
dressing and undressing, of sitting with her knees crossed, of visiting
another in her "cell," and so on.

Even the evening recreation tended to be formalized and stiff.

The wording in the 1953 Declarations provides for recreation, but with some reluctance.

> That the minds of the Sisters may be refreshed and united, the custom of recreation and intercourse has been received down from the very beginning of the monastic life. This custom is permitted after dinner for about an hour—or with the discreet permission of the Superioress, once in a while a little longer—and for about the same length of time, also after supper . . .
> All the sisters are to be present in the recreation room, no one without the permission of the Superioress being permitted to separate herself from the others. Visiting or taking recreation in private rooms without the express permission of the Superioress is especially forbidden. When the weather permits, recreation may be taken in the open air; otherwise all assemble in the common recreation room. The Sisters who have not yet made perpetual vows—Scholastics, Novices, Candidates—all take their recreation separately with their respective Mistresses.
> Let the Sisters take special care not to be forward, ill-tempered, bitter, overbearing or personal in speech, so that no injury is done to the family spirit, to godly reserve and urbanity, and to that peace which is the legacy of our Holy Father, St. Benedict, and a most agreeable spectacle to angels and to men.[3]

The tone and language of this passage, which had been thoroughly acceptable in 1930, by 1960 was unacceptable to many, even amusing to some.

In addition to this, the sisters all took their "recreation" in one room, at one time, and with the same people with whom they had been praying and working all day long. It is little wonder that many of them regularly came to the common room with students' papers to correct or with sewing to be done, because "recreation" had become just one more chore.

In addition to the highly structured life, the hecticly paced schedule, and the formality already mentioned, there was in convents a deep distrust and fear of outside influences. This is attested to by many practices which, while not universal, were experienced by many sisters in the various priories. The sisters' personal mail—both incoming and out-going—was subject to inspection by the superior. The use of the telephone was restricted. The sisters were allowed in their own homes only at the time of the death of a close relative. Mingling with other people outside the convent was restricted, and the restriction was reinforced by the regulation which required a sister always to have a companion (another sister) when going outside the convent. Reading material and the use of the media were regulated. It was as if all of life were separated into two antagonistic spheres—the sacred and the secular—and as if the sister must live as exclusively as possible in the sacred.

In an attempt to reinforce the sense of the sacredness and apartness there was an attempt to "sacramentalize" every aspect of convent life. Many actions were made religious acts by relating them, however remotely, to the life of Jesus. At meals bread was to be broken in three or five pieces before eating in memory of the Trinity or the five wounds of Jesus. The arms were crossed at the wrists when walking in honor of Jesus bound. Requests were asked for "For the love of Jesus." Thus, the sisters' spirituality was nourished on a kind of piety which was understandable in a milieu which was largely deprived of education in scripture and theology, as well as in the history of early monasticism.

In the name of chastity the religious garb, which was made to very exact specifications, obliterated every suggestion of the female figure. The sister's hair was clipped short or shaven, her head swathed in linen, then covered with a veil. Her dress had to be approved by clerics in Rome, and once approved as the standard garb it was to be worn at all times.

Obedience is perhaps the oldest of the vows, being mentioned specifically even in pre-Benedictine monasticism. The early nun and monk vowed to live as completely as possible in accord with the will of God. In order that they might not be deceived in discerning the will of God, it became the practice to test their own discernment with that of an older and more experienced religious—usually the abbot or abbess, the charismatic leader of the monastery. But the original intent of the vow was obedience to God's Holy Spirit. However, since the virtue of humility was highly prized as the sign of a truly God-fearing person, discernment in conjunction with the leader of the monastery became the practice.

By the twentieth century, in Benedictine convents, the idea of obedience to the superior had become so pervasive that the sister made few, if any, decisions on her own. She was expected to ask permission of the superior to do such things as use the telephone, receive visitors, write to anyone other than her family, or even to write to her family during Lent, to make a dental or doctor's appointment, and so on. These were not simply routine "permissions." In some cases superiors were not hesitant about refusing permission when they deemed it prudent or when they thought that the sister's virtue needed testing.

Most often, the superior posted work or professional assignments on the community bulletin board one day in August. Then the sister would know whether she was to teach 2nd grade or 7th grade and at what school. Only a few knew about their assignments before they were posted. Naturally, the superior had to take into some consideration the sister's talents and abilities before making the assignments, but the sister herself was seldom consulted. Then to symbolize complete immolation on the altar of obedience, the sister, having read her assignment, would go to the superior, kneel, and beg the superior for patience while she carried out the assigned task.

Kneeling to the superior was not confined to begging her patience. The sister knelt when asking a permission of any kind; she knelt when being admonished by her superior; she knelt when she asked for whatever she needed—clothing, toilet supplies, in some places even pins, needles, and shoelaces; she knelt when she took to the superior gifts given her by family or friends.

The woman kneeling to the superior in the enclosure of the convent might within the next few minutes sit at her own desk as a college president, a hospital administrator, an elementary or high school teacher and so had opportunity to learn humility in more effective ways. For an earlier generation, the mystique of the lifestyle based on a popular spirituality chiefly characterized by self-abnegation had a fascination and an attraction. But by the 1960's another generation of American women, touched by other influences and developing a different spirituality, were becoming restive with what they perceived as the childish role of the sister within the convent. Many of the young women who came to the convent in the 50's and 60's were simply amused at regulations which required them to ask permission to do things that they had been doing quite freely since childhood. For this generation, the idea of wearing special convent-style underwear and night clothes seemed ridiculous. Even the practice of the entire community sitting down together for three meals a day was foreign to some. Consequently, many of the more free-spirited young sisters either ignored the regulations altogether or made a game of circumventing the customs of the house.

In the name of "holy poverty," it was customary for the sister to ask either the prioress (superior) or the procurator (purchasing agent) for her every need—soap, toothpaste, sanitary napkins, thread—everything. Often these busy women waited for an hour or more in line with others who had similar needs. The idea of a common supply room where sisters could take what they needed was bitterly resisted by some because the exercise of asking for what one needed was considered necessary to the development of humility and a safeguard against stockpiling possessions.

One added characteristic of Benedictine convent life prior to the Second Vatican Council made change inevitable—the over-emphasis on rank. According to St. Benedict's Rule, for the sake of order each person sat in the chapel and at table in the rank of her entrance into the community, except for the prioress and the officials who took precedence over the rest. From the original intention of orderliness, the notion of rank in some women's communities had developed into a caste system which bred resentment. Instead of following St. Benedict's admonition for the community members to vie with one another in serving the needs of all, it had become frequently understood that the younger sisters were to be at the disposal of those of greater rank. In some places the ideology of rank was so valued that postulants, novices, and younger sisters could be treated with less than common courtesy, and when a sister had been professed for 25 years and celebrated her silver jubilee, although she might still be youthful and vigorous at 45, she was no longer expected to wait on the tables and perform certain other household tasks. Seniority took the meaning of privilege. It was a far cry from the ideal in the gospels and in St. Benedict's Rule.

In short, the lifestyle in American Benedictine convents by 1960 was pervaded by a crippling rigidity and formalism which tended to hamper the development of the sisters instead of enhancing it. This is not meant to imply that there were not in every community large-hearted women with free spirits who accomplished outstanding tasks for the church and for society, or who were simply liberating influences within their own communities, schools or hospitals. But many of them had begun to sense that much of what they could accomplish was limited by an archaic lifestyle.

One group which was among the first to feel the stress brought about by outmoded customs was composed of those sisters charged with counseling and guiding the newest members of the communities —postulants, novices, and young sisters in temporary vows. These sisters, directresses of formation as they were called, had the task of explaining community customs to the new recruits. It was also often their task to explain the young women's reactions and behavior to the more seasoned members of the community. In this unenviable position, the directresses were among the first in each community to push for changes. They were supported in their recognition of the need for change by the fact that the directresses in all of the communities of Benedictine Sisters in the United States, Canada, and Mexico had begun meeting annually in the 1950's to discuss mutual goals and problems.

In addition to this, the establishment of the Benedictine Institute of Sacred Theology at St. John's University, Collegeville, Minnesota, in 1957 was intended originally to give directresses adequate academic training in scripture, theology, and spirituality as an aid to their work with the young sisters.

The annual workshop for directresses and the theology institute were simply the Benedictine version of what had become the Sister Formation Movement in America, a movement initiated largely in response to Pope Pius XII's call for more professionalism in the schools and hospitals staffed by religious sisters.

Pope Pius was a staunch supporter of American sisters. It was his recognition of the indispensable role of the sisters in the history of the American Church which prompted him to point out that their work in education and in health care would come to an end unless they maintained adequate professional standards in their work. The sisters' response to the pope's advice unwittingly helped to lay the groundwork for other changes in their lives. Being sent by their communities to colleges and universities for better academic preparation brought them into closer contact with the forces which were shaping modern American society. That movement away from the more protected atmosphere of the convent had an inevitable effect.

CONVENT LIFE TODAY

From the viewpoint of American Benedictine sisters who entered the convent before 1960, the word "cataclysm" is not too strong to describe the changes brought about in response to the mandate of Vatican Council II in the document On the Adaptation and Renewal of Religious Life. The Council Fathers in this document directed religious communities to make the Gospel their supreme rule; then to examine the spirit of their founders and study the sources of their own spirituality; and, finally to see to it that their manner of living, praying, and working was in harmony with the present-day physical and psychological condition of their members, and in harmony with the needs of the apostolate.

The Benedictine sisters needed a mandate from a higher authority to begin actually making the changes which brought about a veritable revolution in each priory. The essence of religious life was so closely interwoven with the forms and structures that each change in form was seen by some members as a desecration and destruction of the life itself. Even those members who were speaking out and actively leading their communities to make changes suffered from ambiguous feelings and wondered whether or not they were, indeed, destroying the essence of Benedictine community life.

Thus, the changes have not come about easily. They have caused dissension, some bitterness, and for varying lengths of time, distrustful polarization among the members. For two communities of the Federation of St. Scholastica the polarization was so severe that the communities divided, those members opposed to what were perceived as radical changes remaining at the priory, and those in favor of a new lifestyle forming a new community. But friction has been very much in evidence also in those communities which did not separate. There has been a tendency in each community to divide into two camps—each side convinced that it is preserving religious life and Benedictinism. This dissension within the communities may certainly be a contributing factor in their failure to attract new members during this period.

What then has been the nature of the changes which some see as essential to the vitality of the life, and others see as utterly destructive?

The first changes made in most communities had to do with the prayer structure and the daily schedule. The changes were made cautiously and, at first, simply by way of experimentation. For example, under the influence of Paschal Botz, O.S.B., of St. John's Abbey, Collegeville, Minnesota, in 1966 the prioresses tried doing away with the scheduled periods for meditation and spiritual reading, leaving it to the individual sister to read and meditate privately according to her own need. The elimination of these two scheduled periods was accepted rather easily by all but the most inflexible because the sisters realized that meditation and reading were not scheduled in detail in St. Benedict's Rule.

However, the structure of the sisters' choral prayer was the same prayer structure prescribed in detail by Saint Benedict in his Rule for Monasteries written in the 6th century. Therefore, when some sisters began to question the structure of the choral Office and its compatibility with the lives of modern American Benedictines working in schools and hospitals, there was immediate resistance. The sisters' identity as Benedictines was so enmeshed with the choral prayer forms that any change was perceived as an abandonment of something essentially Benedictine. Despite the moderation and flexibility of the Rule itself (Saint Benedict specifically mentions that his structuring of the Office or Liturgy of the Hours should be rearranged by anyone who saw a need for it), Benedictine convents had prided themselves on a literal interpretation of the Rule in regard to their common prayer life for so long that any attempt at restructuring the form or abandoning Gregorian chant met with varying degrees of resistance, even to the point of rancor and bitterness. It was the first real issue over which many communities tended to polarize.

Today it would be difficult to give a typical daily convent schedule because the schedule differs from convent to convent according to the circumstances and needs of the community. However, it is safe to say that most communities gather at least three times daily for prayer —Morning and Evening Praise, and Mass—and that psalmody and readings from Scripture form the basis of their prayer together.

Rather than list a series of prayers to be said, the 1974 Constitutions of the Federation of Saint Scholastica, entitled *Call to Life,* gives a brief theology of prayer, emphasizing the centrality of the Eucharist, and reminding the members of the importance of holy reading and reflection as a preparation for the liturgy, both of the Word and of the Sacrament. Gone is the impression that one received from the 1953 Declarations that the Federation (Congregation) had as its duty to prescribe specific behaviors for the various priories. Instead, the Federation lays down basic principles and leaves their implementation to the local community. And in most communities there is a growing trust in the ability of the sisters themselves to risk making their own personal decisions and abiding by the consequences of those decisions, not only in the area of prayer but in most areas of life.

The drastic change in lifestyle from one in which the sister needed the approval of an authority figure for almost every action—by means of "permissions"—to the freer atmosphere of personal decision-making has not been accomplished without many mistakes. Prioresses and others in positions of authority sometimes exercise their authority in such a way that the sisters feel insecure and unsupported. And the sisters themselves from time to time act irresponsibly in exercising their newly-acquired adult freedom.

In this whole area of personal freedom—freedom to use the telephone, to correspond with friends, to drive out alone in a car, to use the media, to visit home—the practice in the past differed widely between Benedictine monks and Benedictine sisters. In the 19th century society in which most of the American Benedictine houses had been founded, most women led a sheltered kind of life, protected and taken care of; although the sisters worked long and hard to support themselves and their various charitable institutions, paradoxically, they were considered too fragile to be exposed to the "dangers of the world." Men, on the other hand, were expected to be fearlessly independent, self-motivated, and self-reliant. This view of the role of women and men in society was formalized in the lifestyle of convents and monasteries. Thus, Benedictine men in America—though they followed the same Rule—were never restricted to the extent that the women were. When a young monk completed one year as a novice in his community, it was normal for him to go home for a visit with his family. When a young woman entered the convent she understood that she would never again go home except at the time of a death of a member of her immediate family. American monks have normally viewed themselves as adult and responsible members of their own communities; the sisters too often have allowed themselves to be taken care of by those in authority.

As a result, the monks, who also in the past usually had better opportunities for education in theology and church law, had a clearer perception of both the extent and the limits of their vow of obedience. The sisters, on the contrary, assumed that every request or even suggestion of the prioress or local superior, as well as such restrictions as asking permission to use the telephone, and other trivial matters were subject to the vow of obedience. Consequently, during the renewal period when the sisters began exercising their freedom of choice in such matters—and especially when prioresses began consulting members about the kind of work they would like to do, or even encouraging the sisters to seek the positions they wanted—some members cried out that there was no more obedience in the priories. But actually the various facets of obedience have been heightened so that the sister is more aware than formerly of her responsibility for her total community under the vow of obedience. She strives to be obedient to God as her conscience directs, she is obedient to decisions made in community, she is obedient to the prioress when the prioress speaks as the elected leader of the community, and she is obedient to the local bishop in matters over which he has jurisdiction.

The greater emphasis on personal decision-making has brought with it an inevitable change in the sister's relationships among themselves. Most of the old formalities have given way to a less formal and more natural type of interpersonal relations. For example, there is no more kneeling to superiors, the sisters sit wherever they like and with whomever they wish at meals and on other occasions. They may go out alone if they so desire; the regulation which required them to take along a sister-companion is no more. Since they use the telephone freely, they make their own appointments and arrange for their own transportation. Recreation and relaxation are seen as a personal responsibility, as are private prayer, reading, and professional updating.

Many of the frictions which are inevitable when numbers of people live together had been at least partially avoided by the old formalities, rules, and regulations. So the new freedom has brought with it new frictions. At first there was a kind of unreal expectation that once adults were free they would consistently act lovingly and unselfishly toward one another and toward the group. But time and human nature soon brought about more realistic expectations. The sisters are having to learn to assert themselves and to confront one another rather than expect the superior to mediate their differences. For many of them this new mode of living has required far more discipline in the way of give and take than they experienced under the old structure. They are having to learn to recognize their own anger and sense of competition. But most frightening of all, some are having to learn to deal forthrightly with their affection for one another and their own needs for intimacy. Formerly the sisters were very much on their guard against what were called "particular friendships," and the regulations such as that which forbad visiting another sister in her room, the rule of silence, and the practice of all taking recreation in common, tended to discourage the forming of close friendships. Today there is a recognition of the fact that healthy friendships not only enrich the lives of the sisters involved, but also often form the base of many of the works that the community performs. This has led to the recognition and acceptance of sub-groups within the community, based on friendship and preference rather than simply on the type or place of work.

Another area of change which has meant growth and development for the sisters is that of "temporalities," or possessions and the use of money. When the priories were founded in the 19th century, they were poor foundations established to serve the needs of poor immigrants. But by the 1960's each priory, through the unstinting labor of its members, had acquired land and buildings which gave them an image of corporate wealth. The sisters personally were vowed to "poverty" by which they meant communal ownership of capital possessions and living a life of personal frugality. In the name of poverty, the sisters did not possess any money, but looked to the superior to supply all of their needs. In this way, the practice of the vow of poverty achieved a rather high degree of uniformity among the members. In an agrarian economy this mode of frugality was understandable, but in 20th century America it was impractical and tended to keep the sisters in a child-like type of dependency. In an attempt to give the sisters a more realistic notion of the value of material things, as well as more responsibility for themselves, the General Chapter of the Federation of St. Scholastica in 1969 suggested that the priories experiment with allowing each sister to receive a fixed allotment of money out of which to buy her clothes and supplies. This is one of the changes in convent life that has gained wide acceptance among many active sisters who prefer to live on a personal allowance rather than get all of their supplies from a common supply room.

But this attention to the sisters' personal needs is a relatively minor result of the renewal period. A more important result, perhaps, has been an increased awareness on the part of the sisters of the social and economic ills of society and an increased concern that Benedictine communities address themselves to those ills. Concomitant with an increased awareness of needs has been an awakening to the responsibilities of stewardship. The sisters' most immediate response to society's ills was a sense of guilt: "Look at all that we have, while they have so little." Only later did the sisters begin to realize that their buildings and, in some cases, their land were not necessarily signs of a deterioration of the Christian ideal, but were rather responsibilities and means which they could and must use for the betterment of their own localities. The 1969 General Chapter urged each priory to make its facilities available to the more disadvantaged in the neighborhood.

In the area of priory and local convent government the changes have concentrated on the responsible participation of all of the members in those decisions which affect the whole community. This had always been the Benedictine ideal in accord with St. Benedict's Rule, but the American priories had modeled their notions of government on that of 19th century Europe and the hierarchical Church. It took the Vatican Council to bring the convents back to the conscious practice of delegation of authority and shared decision-making.

Involving the sisters in their own government was not an easy task. Long years of having sat silently through community chapter meetings had hardly prepared the sisters for expressing their own views, much less for the task of publicly debating controversial issues. Added to the fact that a majority of the sisters were inarticulate, many of them were relatively content with their lives and felt no need for change. Others, some of whom would have welcomed change at an earlier point in their lives, felt personally threatened by changes which seemed to deprive them of the status attained by seniority.

But there were also in each community those who were impatient and for whom the changes came about only too slowly. These could no longer tolerate what appeared to them as a state of over-dependency on the will of those in authority and excessive restrictiveness in most areas of life. Because of their inner pressures, these sisters became most articulate.

Community leadership, which was focused primarily in the prioress and the delegates to the general chapters, felt themselves mandated to introduce those changes called for by the renewal chapters. But, lacking in communications skills and without the government structures which would enable all of the sisters to be heard, they found themselves in a difficult position—distrusted by the hardliners on both ends of the spectrum. Eventually, with the help either of Federation personnel or of those sisters within the community with some professional training either in communications skills, psychology, or modern managerial techniques, they learned to involve more and more of their membership in the formation of community policy. Today almost every priory in the Federation has some type of "grassroots" organization which channels ideas and suggestions from the membership to the prioress and her council or to the entire community chapter; and, in addition, both the priory chapter and the priory council have learned the value of having committees research the pros and cons of new issues before they are brought to the membership for decision. Rather than a one-sided stress on obedience to the prioress, there is a recognition of the presence of the Holy Spirit also in the membership. This new view does not presuppose a members-versus-prioress attitude, but rather sees the prioress as the spokeswoman and elected leader of the membership as they discern together the will of the Lord.

One change in religious communities of women in response to the mandate to adapt their mode of living to the psychological and cultural needs of their members—*the* one change recognized by everyone and the most controversial of all the changes—has been that of the religious dress. Ninety-seven percent of the delegates to the renewal chapters admit that this was at one time an important issue in their communities, and even a decade after the first renewal chapter, thirty percent of them see the issue of clothing as one of continuing importance. This concern about clothing may also explain why thirty percent of the delegates think that religious life has become "somewhat secularized."

Clothing is, of course, symbolic and symptomatic. The fact that the sisters in each priory seem to have divided into three categories of dress—the traditional garb, the modified habit, and contemporary dress—seems to point to varying understandings of the function of religious dress and of the nature of religious life. Thirty-four percent of the delegates to the renewal chapters believe that sisters are called to special holiness because of their vows, while sixty-six percent reject this belief. This disparity of belief in regard to the theology of religious life may be at least partly the basis for the differing responses to the issue of dress, but there are also other reasons of a more subjective nature.

For some sisters the movement to contemporary dress has been an attempt to reject the notion of prestige and privilege which is suggested by a belief that members of religious communities are called to a higher way of life than the rest of the laity, that they are in something called "the state of perfection." For other sisters, the old outmoded habit was simply impractical and inconvenient, and the change to contemporary dress was a pragmatic decision. Still another group was convinced to change their clothing by the argument that the habit had originally been the ordinary dress of a former day, but was now imposed as a uniform. However, underlying all of these reasons was a discomfort with what was perceived as the image of the sister. There was an uncomfortable feeling that the sister's life was in danger of becoming totally obsolete, irrelevant to a new generation. Yet many of the sisters themselves were convinced of the value of their lives, not only for the present but also for future generations. The change then to contemporary dress has for some been an attempt to speak as graphically as possible to the abiding nature of religious vocation—a way of saying to the world: "We are a part of you. Our lives, committed to a celibate community life in union with Christ and dedicated to serving His people, are as relevant today as they were yesterday, and will be tomorrow."

It is the purpose of this text to tell how the delegates to the renewal chapters of the Federation of St. Scholastica attempted to preserve their Benedictine monastic heritage for the present generation, and so assure it for future generations.

PART II
The Change Process

The section which follows begins with an historical treatment of the Renewal Chapters from 1966 through 1974, the process by which each was developed and a description of the new structures which were created to make their work more effective. This is followed by an analysis from the Participant Profile of the factors which either helped or hindered the delegates in their work of implementing the General Chapter decrees. The section concludes with the demographic and personality profiles of the Chapter delegates in order to give a clearer picture of the women who shaped renewal in the Federation of Saint Scholastica.

"ALL THEY NEED IS COURAGE"

... your problems are many but not beyond solution because the Sisters are working hard at them and, may I say, manfully. Once they overcome their fear of the law and fear of making mistakes they are on their way. They possess sufficient knowledge and all they need is courage to trust their knowledge and put it into practice.

A Canonist to the Federation President, 1967

In the course of adaptation and renewal from 1966-74, the Federation of St. Scholastica created several new means to facilitate the ongoing work of the General Chapter itself.[1] Among these were: 1) the increasing of the number of delegates from each priory, 2) the creation of pre-chapter sessions to generate the chapter agenda, 3) the development of committees to research and present agenda items, and 4) the use of consultants at each session of the Chapter.

Other changes were effected as a consequence of chapter deliberations. These include: 1) the expansion of the federation council, 2) the creation of a conciliation board, 3) the change in the mode of visitation, 4) the publication of interim constitutions and 5) the latest edition of the declarations and constitutions, *Call to Life*.

Structural Changes

The creation of new structures reflects a whole new way of looking at the practice of obedience for the Benedictine sister. Formerly she simply submitted her will to the prescriptions of her superiors, both on the local and congregational levels. There was little opportunity for her own input through approved channels. The machinery generated by the renewal chapters opened up to her a whole new way of approaching the problems confronting religious life in the 1960's and finding valid solutions to many of them. The new structures were true to the concepts of collegiality and subsidiarity inherent in the Rule of Saint Benedict and advocated by Vatican II as well as consistent with the development of persons called for by contemporary consciousness and new insights of social psychology.

Each of these nine structural changes will be examined here in turn for its genesis, development and impact.

Increased Representation at Chapter

Prior to the 1968 Chapter, the attendance of only one delegate from each priory in addition to the prioress had been legislated by the

Constitution under Article 128.[2] This delegate was elected by the local chapter by secret ballot and majority vote. An alternate was also elected in case the delegate should be prevented for any reason from attending the Chapter.

In August of 1967, the Erie community sponsored a symposium to which they invited the president of the federation, the prioresses, delegates and alternates of six communities. At the close of this symposium Sister Mary Susan Sevier, the president, called a meeting of the group to discuss several matters concerning preparations for the General Chapter. Among these were the requests she had received to consider also seating the alternate delegates as voting members of the Chapter and further increasing the size of delegations according to community population.

A motion was passed to appoint a committee to poll the communities on the questions. The members of the committee, Sister Bernadine Hemberger and Sister Demetria King of Pittsburgh and Sister Rita Pruchniewski of Erie, sent out a questionnaire to be answered by all professed sisters. It asked whether the current practice of delegations as found in Article 128 should be maintained or, if not, which of the following plans was preferred:

(1) numerical representation with two delegates from each community regardless of size
(2) one delegate for each 100 sisters and each group of 50 or more over the even hundreds
(3) delegation according to the years of profession: e.g., one delegate for those professed 1-25 years; one delegate for those professed 26 or more years.
(4) delegation according to apostolic works: e.g., teachers and school administrators, non-teachers, nurses working outside or caring for the community's own sick and infirm.[3]

The question was pursued in the September meeting in Chicago before the data from the questionnaire became available. The rationale given for the request was that the added numbers would enhance the liaison among communities; there would be more people to share the work load of the committees and there would be a greater chance that diversity of opinions would be represented. Reverend Ambrose Clark, OSB, canonist, advised that the delegates act immediately as Rome stated that any change in delegation which was passed by a two-thirds vote would be sanctioned before a General Chapter took place. Pending the outcome of the questionnaire, the decision was deferred. It was recommended that the other American Benedictine congregations be asked their views. However, the motion was made and passed that the alternate delegates be present at the General Chapter and that the first business of the agenda be the question of seating them as voting delegates.

The report on the increased number of delegates was made by the government committee at the Atchison pre-chapter in January, 1968. More than half of all the professed sisters in the Congregation had chosen a modification of plan 2 of the questionnaire: to have their delegation consist of the prioress, two delegates and an additional delegate for each 150 sisters in the community. By an 85.8% majority, the sisters agreed to name their alternate delegate as their second delegate if the General Chapter voted in favor of increased representation.

When the Chapter met in June, its first business was to consider these two matters. The motion to seat the alternates as voting delegates met with little or no discussion and was passed unanimously by secret ballot. The matter of additional delegates based on community population was not quite so easy; a prolonged discussion on the floor made it obvious that there was some fear of a potential power bloc on the part of those communities with large delegations. The delegates were chided by some for their lack of trust in the Holy Spirit.

When the vote was finally taken, the motion passed 55-7. This proportion agreed well with the 92.2% of the delegates who responded in the Participant Profile that life in a democratic society contributed to the acceptability of a broadened base of decision making. And 86.4% agreed that the increase in the number of delegates made the work of the Chapter representative of more views. Yet almost 60% felt that this enlargement of representation of delegates was of continuing importance to the Chapter; 33% felt it was still of continuing importance to both their communities and to themselves personally, evidence that for some the notion of the size of a delegation was still an issue.

The immediate effect of this decision was almost to double the number of forty delegates present at the 1966 Chapter only two years earlier; there were now 72 voting delegates (21 prioresses and 51 sisters). The base of the decision making process being thus dramatically broadened, member priories were able to make a greater impact than ever before at the congregational level. Furthermore, it became possible for communication at home to become more effective as several delegates, not just the prioresses, reported on their chapter experiences with varying points of view. In some cases such divergence led to polarization within the community on issues under consideration, but such was the reality of renewal. The statistics on this point are revealing: 16% of the delegates experienced increased polarization in their community to a great extent; 12% usually and 60% somewhat. Only 10% did not experience polarization at all.

The idea of receiving input from the younger members of each community had come up in the 1969 session as a floor comment and its implementation was left to the Congregation Council. Accordingly, when the Council met in March of 1970, the members came up with a plan of representation from geographical areas. Every community was to have its sisters under thirty select one from the group to represent them; then the area groups would meet to elect one from the group to attend the pre-Chapter. The areas were the following:

Group I—Glendora, Boerne, Mexico City, Tulsa, Atchison
Group II—Chicago, Benet Lake, Lisle
Group III—Tinley Park, Warren, Kentucky
Group IV—Elizabeth, Bristow, Ridgely
Group V—Florida, Louisiana, Alabama
Group VI—Erie, Pittsburgh, St. Marys

This group of six sisters was to come to the 1971 pre-Chapter as a panel of reactors to the position papers of the General Chapter of Renewal. It was felt that such a plan would have two benefits: the delegates would hear the views of the younger sisters and the attention of each priory would focus on this age group, with the hope that more from this age group would be elected delegates to the 1971 Chapter.

A later rearrangement of Group I into two groups to include Colorado Springs (which had been omitted through an oversight) brought seven young sisters to the panel at the pre-chapter in Kentucky in January of 1971; one each from Glendora, Atchison, Lisle, Covington (Ky), Elizabeth, Cullman and Erie. They agreed generally that the contents of the "Blue Book" were positive and to the point, but indicated that there were other areas that needed attention: the priority of prayer, a need for involvement with the poor, the role of femininity, greater treatment of the celibacy issue, and radical witness.

Later in the session a motion was made that the under-thirty reactors be invited to the Chapter in June as non-voting observers on condition that they consult their own group. Floor discussion brought out that these sisters had been eligible to be elected as delegates from their communities and for the Chapter to invite them would be to interfere with the autonomy of the community. It was felt that since no other age group had special representation, a precedent should not be set here. The motion was defeated with 26 in favor and 44 opposed.

This left the problem of how to incorporate their ideas and suggestions in the chapter. A motion was passed that this be the responsibility of the committees whose papers were to be presented.

A final adjustment to equalize representation was made at the 1974 Chapter when the constitutions committee brought the matter to the floor. Two factors figured in the rationale: larger communities needed more delegates in order to accomplish the tasks of communication called for by pre-chapter assignments, and yet the total size of the chapter had to be kept within some reasonable number so that housing and meeting facilities would be readily available.

Three plans for changed representation were offered based on the size of communities. The current delegation consisted of the prioress, two delegates and an additional delegate for each 150 sisters in a priory (Plan A). Plan B changed this last base to 100 sisters, Plan C to 75 and Plan D to 50. After discussing the advantages and disadvantages of each plan, the Chapter voted to accept Plan C. This increased the number of delegates from 67 to 80; when the eleven members of the Federation Council were added, the Chapter numbered 91 voting participants.

Introduction of the Pre-Chapter Session

A review of the minutes of the general chapters of 1944, 1956, and 1962 reveals a structured pattern which carried over from one chapter to another. It was a three-day meeting of the prioresses and one elected delegate from each motherhouse of the congregation. The first matter of business was the election of the mother president; in each of these three chapters it was conducted by the abbot of St. Benedict's Abbey, Atchison, Kansas, who was officially delegated by the local bishop to preside. Following this election, the abbot withdrew and the mother president conducted the election of the two visitators and the secretary general who comprised the congregational council.

Next were elected three definitors whose task it was to "prepare, under the president's direction, the matter received from the delegates to be laid before the group in later sessions." Each community was required to present a report on its financial condition and a statistical summary of the number of sisters, novices and postulants. The financial statements were audited during this session by three delegates appointed by the president and this committee reported its findings to the chapter on the last day of the meeting.

The agenda for the chapter consisted of the topics submitted to the definitors by the delegates. Many of them dealt with questions of interpretation on the declarations and constitutions; a priest-canonist was usually present to deal with these questions.

At the final session of the chapter, the secretary-general gave a financial report on the congregation, the auditors' report was accepted and the time and place of the next chapter were determined.

The structure that had the most far-reaching effect on both the agenda and process of each of the general chapters since 1966 was undoubtedly the pre-chapter, a preliminary meeting of all prioresses and delegates some six months before the chapter itself met in legislative session. When asked if the pre-chapter facilitated renewal, 99% of all the delegates to chapters between 1968 and 1974 agreed that it did. At these meetings organizational procedures were recommended and an agenda created, two steps which would facilitate the major work of renewal with which the delegates were faced.

The pre-chapter evolved in a gradual manner and was given its first impetus in a letter to the prioresses from Mother Mary Susan following the April 1966 Chapter and before a meeting of the prioresses in August in Milwaukee, where they would be attending a meeting of the Conference of Major Superiors of Women.[4] She wrote:

> A suggestion from Father Paschal (Botz, O.S.B., of St. John's, Collegeville, Minnesota) to Mother Mary Austin and some of the questions in the recent questionnaire sent by the Research Committee of CMSW lead me to propose for discussion the formation of a permanent committee of Mothers and/or Sisters whose function would be to carry on a continuing process of study and revision. I ask you to give this matter some thought, please; discuss it with whomever you will and come to Milwaukee prepared to speak your ideas on details concerning the following:
>
> (1) Who and how many should comprise the committee?
> (2) How should they be selected?
> (3) Topics that would fall within the competence of the Committee—e.g., effects on monasticism of changes in canon law and revised theological thinking; implementation of decrees from SCR, etc.
> (4) The manner in which all Congregation membership would have the privilege of contacting the Committee;
> (5) Any other point of consideration that would enter into the formation of such a committee.
>
> The proper functioning of the Committee would constitute one means of preparing for the next General Chapter.

The idea of such a committee was initially well received at the Milwaukee meeting and a committee of three prioresses, Mother Marie Denise Mohr, Tulsa; Mother Cornelia Boyle, Elizabeth; and Mother Mary Austin Schirmer, Atchison, devised a pyramidal plan which involved the formation of

> . . . four or five small committees consisting of several representatives from communities in the same geographical area. The geographical committee would have few members but the total membership of these basic committees would be rather large. This was designed to give ample representation to all communities and representation was based on membership. The manner of selecting members was to be left to each community and the number of Mothers and Sisters was regulated. These committee members were to select from their own membership those who would comprise the top Committee.

This plan was not adopted at this meeting because of expressed apprehension that it proposed a threat to the autonomy of individual houses. Instead, all communities were to inaugurate discussion on matters pertinent to their lives as religious in the latter half of the twentieth century. It was at this point that the president requested assistance from Father Paschal, the "officially adopted advisor" to the Congregation, asking him what guidelines he could suggest and whether the abbots' congress should not produce direction and leadership for the sisters. The continuing dependence for guidance from Benedictine men was still very much a part of the American experience.

A few months later, in January of 1967, the Southeastern Regional meeting of the Canon Law Society convened in Bethesda, Maryland, and its chairman, Rev. Matthew Benko, O.S.B., of St. Vincent's Archabbey, Latrobe, Pennsylvania, invited Mother Mary Susan to attend. The topic for discussion was sections 1-11 of *Ecclesiae Sanctae*, "Norms for the implementation of the Decree of the Second Vatican Council *'Perfectae Caritatis.'* " These sections dealt with the call for special general chapters and the norms for their preparation and execution.

Mother Pauline of Pittsburgh, Mother Cornelia and Mother Anselma of Ridgely attended with the president and as a result of the papers and discussions they heard, all four drew up a plan to prepare for their own 1968 Renewal Chapter. It called for the communities to elect their delegates before Easter of 1967. Criteria for selection of delegates were offered by the Congregation Council:

(a) one who has responded to the spirit of genuine renewal of the "open Church"
(b) one who understands the need to reanimate the traditions of St. Benedict which are directly rooted in his Rule or have been legitimate developments
(c) one who is convinced that there must be a consistency between theory and practice of the vows that is evident to a materialistic and ego-centered society
(d) one who knows her religious community is a portion of the People of God which contributes to the life of all the People in the measure that each member allows Christ to grow in her; one who takes Him to others in the apostolic works of the community.

The community-elected delegates were mailed a list of categories to be studied, each on separate color-coded paper. These categories were Temporalities, Formation, Apostolate, Community Life, Evangelical Counsels and Religious Government. Suggestions on these topics were to be solicited from community members by the delegates who would bring them to the proposed meeting where appropriate commissions would be formed to receive and study them. As some of the communities felt that an Easter planning meeting was too early to allow time for the election of their delegates, the Congregation Council scheduled the meeting for September to be held between the sessions of the CMSW meeting in Chicago.

The next influencing factor was the meeting of the Canon Law Society in June 1967 at Rosary College in Chicago. This three-day workshop on the subject of "Renewal Through the General Chapter" was attended by representatives from the communities of Pittsburgh, Erie, Chicago and Tulsa who communicated to Mother Mary Susan their concern that a one-day meeting in September would not be sufficient to deal with the questions and format of the 1968 chapter. They also asked to be allowed to submit the names of two Benedictine canonists to be invited to attend the September planning meeting. The president sent a poll to all prioresses, delegates and alternate delegates on these questions. The result was that the September meeting in Chicago was expanded to three days. The canonists, Father Matthew and Rev. Ambrose Clark of St. Mary's Abbey, Morristown, New Jersey, opened the session with a panel on "Theological Concepts of Renewal and Experimentation for Effecting Their Reality."

At this meeting Mother Mary Susan finalized the composition by priories of the topics to be studied, and each community gave the results of its study on each topic to the appropriate person. Committees then met during these three days to collate the input given them and to prepare a preliminary report for the final day of the meeting. The question of increasing the number of delegates to broaden the base of the chapter was discussed but no decision was reached at this time.

The assembly agreed that another planning session would be held in Atchison, Kansas, on January 5-7, 1968, to continue the preliminary processes. It was also agreed that the Chapter would open on June 19 at a place yet to be determined.

This September meeting was important because it sanctioned a distinct departure from all previous chapters, set up the committee approach to presentation of materials and gave the delegates the opportunity to contribute to the agenda. It marked the first of the pre-chapter planning sessions which were to facilitate greatly the work of the chapter itself.

When the delegates came together again in Atchison in January, 1968, they had had sufficient time to study the work at hand and had determined that it could not all be treated at one session. They therefore limited themselves to a consideration of only three topics for the June General Chapter: Religious Government, Community Life and Temporalities. The manner of approach was also defined: position papers with specific proposals attached were to be prepared by the committee for presentation on the floor. Each community committee was to submit its ideas on the topics to the appropriate congregation committee by March 1; the committee would use this material to write its position paper and submit it by mail to all delegates by May 1. This would provide time for the delegates to distribute copies to all members of their communities and to ascertain their reactions. The president impressed the delegates with their responsibility to circulate the papers, encourage their study and elicit response.

The timetable for presentation of the paper on the floor was spelled out: each topic was to be alloted two consecutive days for presentation with the proposals given in the afternoon, revisions in the evening and only voting on the following morning. The last organizational detail handled at this meeting was the determination of time and place for the General Chapter. It was set for June 19-26, 1968, at the Cenacle in Chicago.

The Renewal General Chapter was carried out according to the procedures cited and recessed for a second session to be held in June of 1969. Because the process had met with general approval, the pre-chapter held in Chicago in January of 1969 did not alter the format of the chapter to any great extent. Two additional features were adopted, however: first, a panel of reactors chosen from among the delegates would respond to each paper prior to general floor discussion and second, a different member of the Congregation Council would preside each day to give the council members more exposure to the chapter delegates.

As the Constitutions called for a general chapter every three years, 1971 was the date for the next chapter. Because the committee process had functioned so well at the two sessions of the 1968 Chapter, there was no need to devote much time to process at the next pre-Chapter meeting held at the Martin Luther King Center in Nazareth, Kentucky, on January 1-4, 1971. The agenda included a study of prayer. The Congregation Council met in Cullman, Alabama, on March 14, 1970, to discuss how this should be done. A paper on Benedictinism had already treated the subject in a limited way but the length of the paper had kept it out of the published proceedings. Besides, another paper on liturgy and private prayer was felt to be still needed, so the Council decided to create two committees at this time, one to edit the Benedictinism paper and the other to prepare a paper on prayer for the pre-Chapter.

The advantage of such pre-chapter meetings became obvious as the members met one another in the planning stages. It gave them the opportunity to know one another at close hand in the earliest stages of the chapter work. Latitude was given for the organizational skills of those delegates who possessed them to come to the fore, thus expediting the work of the chapter itself. Once the process had been established at the 1968 Chapter, it became more comfortable for the delegates to function within its framework. Group cohesion developed more rapidly as the process became familiar. The intensity of the purpose of the delegates is indicated by the 98% who characterized their basic attitude as serious.

The interim period between the pre-chapter and chapter sessions gave each delegate time to define and research the issues for herself as well as to inform and consult with members of her community in order that she might attempt to represent the views and concerns of the sisters who had elected her. The local community became informed on the issues under consideration and were able to feel involved to a higher degree than had been previously possible. This may certainly have varied from one community to another, depending on the energies and dedication of the delegates themselves. Lastly, the pre-chapters gave the delegates more time at the chapter itself to work on resolving the issues since the agenda had been prepared in advance, effecting a wiser use of time. This was a marked contrast to earlier chapters in which the agenda was drawn up at the chapter itself only after the delegates had presented the items the communities wanted discussed to a committee of three definitors who then prepared them for discussion on the chapter floor.

Development of Committees

Concurrent with the development of the pre-chapter session to create an agenda for the upcoming general chapter, the committee approach for dealing with the agenda items came into focus. The plan originated at the regional meeting of the Canon Law Society in Bethesda, Maryland, already alluded to. The Sisters of Mercy who hosted the meeting were already engaged in plans for their own General Chapter. The president and three prioresses talked to them and borrowed the idea of the commission approach for specific topics which they later expanded at a meeting of the entire Congregation Council in Birmingham, Alabama.

The allocation of topic to specific communities grouped geographically was handled through the mail by the president. Some showed preference for a specific committee and this was allowed. The plans were completed at the September 1967 meeting as follows:

Temporalities

Saint Lucy Priory, Glendora, California
Saint Scholastica Convent, Boerne, Texas
Benet Hill Priory, Colorado Springs, Colorado

Sister Formation

Saint Gertrude Convent, Ridgely, Maryland
Saint Benedict Convent, Bristow, Virginia
Saint Walburga Convent, Elizabeth, New Jersey

Apostolate

Holy Family Convent, Benet Lake, Wisconsin
Saint Scholastica Convent, Chicago, Illinois
Sacred Heart Convent, Lisle, Illinois
Our Lady of Sorrows, Tinley Park, Illinois

Community Life

Saint Benedict Convent, Erie, Pennsylvania
Holy Name Priory, San Antonio, Florida
Sacred Heart Convent, Cullman, Alabama
Sacred Heart Convent, Lisle, Illinois

Evangelical Counsels

St. Walburga Convent, Covington, Kentucky
Mount St. Mary's, Pittsburgh, Pennsylvania
St. Joseph Convent, St. Marys, Pennsylvania

Religious Government

St. Benedict Convent, Mexico City
Mt. St. Scholastica, Atchison, Kansas
St. Joseph Convent, Tulsa, Oklahoma
Sacred Heart Convent, Cullman, Alabama

Benedictinism

St. Scholastica Priory, Covington, Louisiana
Mount St. Mary's, Pittsburgh, Pennsylvania
Sacred Heart Convent, Cullman, Alabama

The first advantage of such an approach was the deep and immediate involvement of the delegates almost a year before the chapter itself met. As the committee members came together to work out their
ideas in a position paper complete with resolutions to be debated on
the chapter floor, it became clear that they must claim ownership of
the proposals they were advancing in order to speak from conviction.
They were required to substantiate their ideas with documented
sources in order to present sound and cogent reasons for their proposals. They thus became the internal experts on the subject they were
presenting to the delegates. The draft version of their paper was
readied in sufficient time for all delegates to receive a copy in advance of the chapter, making possible serious consideration of the
proposals so that they brought informed opinions to the discussions.

From the strength which committee work engendered among the
members, the level of belief in the final product was raised. The sense
of involvement was high: 47.2% of all delegates served on at least one
federation committee, 6.3% served on two committees and an additional 4.9% served on more than two, bringing a total of 58.4% of the
delegates committed to the process of formulating position papers
and bringing them to the floor for debate.

In these floor discussions issues were laid open and data flowed
freely to support or refute these issues. Sometimes it became necessary to refer the matter back to committee for clarification before
consensus could be achieved.

The committee approach received its justification when it was
agreed that subsequent chapters of this period should operate in this

manner. It was agreed by 97% of the delegates that the development of committees at the General Chapter facilitated renewal. Again, 94% felt that the influence of easy mobility in transportation resulted in greater exchange of ideas, a factor that figured largely as members traveled from one community to another for committee meetings. Ninety-two per cent thought that the influence of democratic principles in educational methods generated independent thinking among the delegates. And 96% believed that committee structure fostered greater involvement in the decision-making process.

Consultants to the Chapters

From the very beginning of the Congregation there had been a regular practice of having one consultant present at general chapter, usually a Benedictine priest who was a canonist. In preparing for the 1968 Chapter, the concept of *"periti"* as used at the Vatican Council was seen as practical for making experts available in various fields who could lend their knowledge and expertise to provide an in-depth background to the discussions of the Chapter. In addition to being present for questions and/or comments, consultants were called upon to make a formal presentation in their fields as they related to the topic under discussion. At the pre-Chapter, delegates had been invited to recommend qualified persons to the president.

Consequently, at the 1968 session fourteen consultants were present at one time or another; in 1969 there were fifteen. These consultants were men and women; priests, religious and laypersons; Benedictines and members of other religious orders. They included canonists, theologians, scripture scholar, philosopher, anthropologist, sociologist, psychologist, attorney and parliamentarian. For the first time, delegates saw a need to call upon disciplines other than canon law to assist them in their deliberations. They came to recognize that the social sciences could tell them much about themselves as persons and as community. This integration of disciplines gave a wholeness to their approach to renewal which might well have escaped them without consultants to facilitate this view.

By contrast, however, at both the 1971 and 1974 Chapters there were only three consultants present, evidence that by this time the Chapter had developed sufficient internal expertise to have confidence in itself without undue reliance on outside sources. This fact is borne out by the fact that 85.8% of the delegates subsequently agreed that they had the competence to make decisions in matters which affected their lives. Seventy-one point six per cent felt that their competence in the humanities and social sciences affected the agenda, process and results of the Renewal Chapter to a considerable degree; 73% felt that their educational level in scripture and theology had the same effect.

Despite this internal competence, the affirmation which consultants who had worked with the communities prior to and during the chapter brought to the chapter deliberations cannot be underestimated as the delegates found their views supported by some of the best witness possible. The secrecy of chapter discussions as formerly required by the Constitutions plus an inbred tendency fostered for so long by a cloister mentality were forced to give way to an openness hitherto little experienced as the problems of renewal were laid bare. The delegates found their horizons being stretched as they listened to the challenge of the consultants to explore new vistas. Moreover, a sense of security came through as these experts substantiated and documented what the delegates' own experience and thought had brought them to. When asked whether the use of consultants provided an in-depth perception for the background of agenda items, 95.8% of the delegates agreed that it had.

Expansion of the Federation Council

Until the Chapter of 1968 the federation council had consisted of the president, three visitators and a secretary-treasurer, all of whom had to be prioresses with the exception of the last named. Their duties were largely canonical: visitations, dispensations, transfers and financial matters.

The committee on religious government for the 1969 chapter proposed that this be expanded to an eleven-member council constituted as follows: a president and four councilors elected by the chapter delegates and six additional elected by and from the member priories in rotation according to size and geographical location. These offices were open to every perpetually professed sister in the federation with one stipulation: the president and first councilor (who might have to succeed her) should not be prioresses because it was felt that the double office was too burdensome for one person. The services of the council were to be expanded considerably beyond those of the past; in addition to the canonical duties mentioned above, a list of twelve other kinds of service formed part of the committee's recommendations. Among these were encouraging experimentation, improving communication on all levels, aiding in personnel exchange, and sponsoring in-depth studies on pertinent topics. All of these activities stressed the fact that the council was to be a service-oriented body for the autonomous priories.

The discussion on the chapter floor produced both objections to and support of the proposal. Those in favor spoke of the advantages to the Federation of more leadership and insights, the fact that an enlarged council would be more representative of the entire Federation with the possibility of encompassing more points of view. It was pointed out that the enlargement of services would require more people to perform effectively. One of the consultants observed that considering the wide geographical dispersion of the member priories, the expanded council would represent the richness of such a dispersion and that eleven members was not a large body for a federation of twenty houses and 2400 members.[5]

The recurring question in objection to the proposal was what would such a large body do, how would they spend their meeting time profitably? The difficulty of getting so many people together when a crisis situation arose was also of concern. Mother Mary Susan as president was asked her feelings on this matter and she agreed that it was sometimes necessary to make a decision quickly; could a quorum be allowed instead of assembling the entire council? The use of the telephone conference call was suggested to resolve such situations. It was also suggested by a consultant that the plan could be experimental for a few years and abandoned if it did not prove viable.

When the vote was taken, the proposal passed 69-3. In being asked to reflect on the efficacy of an expanded council, 97% of the delegates responded that it definitely provided a broader base of opinion at the executive level of government.

Conciliation Board

The committee on government for the 1968 General Chapter had incorporated into its paper a discussion on the executive, legislative and judicial functions of monastic government and recommended that a new arm of government be created by the addition of a board of conciliation. Previously there had been no stated means by which a sister could resolve on the federation level tensions created in a local situation. Article 149 of the 1966-68 Revision of the Constitutions stated that a prioress should seek the advice of the president if serious difficulties arose in her community and should accept the decision of the president "in a spirit of loyalty and cooperation." But there was no machinery set up for the ordinary sister to deal with conflicts that might arise within a given community or in the life of the individual sister.

The government committee sought to provide such a vehicle. One member from each priory was to be elected by her community to serve on a conciliation board. When a given case arose, the council would send a list of all members of the conciliation board to the parties concerned, asking them to indicate all those who would be acceptable to them. From this approved list, the president was to select five on whom the parties had agreed to hear the case. The board was to be experimental for a three-year period. The rationale for such a board was based on the fallibility of both community authority and members, leading to the possibility of error in decision-making. Such situations had arisen in the past in the Federation and there were those delegates who could appreciate the concept of a board almost immediately.

The floor discussion included the suggestion to consider such a board as analagous to the jury system whereby persons were judged by their peers rather than by a person in authority. Initially, some had referred to the new body as an arbitration board, but the term conciliation was suggested as having a broader scope. It was recommended that its function be to "listen with the heart" rather than to take a strictly juridical approach. Mother Athanasius Brugelman, president of the Congregation of St. Benedict, who was present as an auditor commented that the proposal was a very good idea; since there were no longer "infallible superiors," it would make a prioress more cautious in her judgments. Those who suggested that a board would have nothing substantial to offer were answered with the recommendation that each community take measures to see that they elected a qualified person for membership.

The vote taken was practically unanimous: 69-1 in favor of the addition of a board of conciliation to the federation government, 70-0 on its purpose, "to conciliate grievances according to the principles of charity and natural justice," and 70-0 on its membership as a pool from all communities. Only on the question of procedure was there variation from unanimity. The principle of subsidiarity had been carefully included in the proposal: a given issue was first to be handled on the local level, then referred to the federation council and finally to the conciliation board. On this point the vote was 66 in favor, 3 opposed and 2 abstaining.

The psychological value of having such a board available to any member of the Federation more than justified its existence. It has been requested only once in the eight years of its existence but the difficulty was resolved without an actual meeting of the board. When asked if structurally the conciliation board was an effective way to deal with individual grievances within the federation membership, 86% of the delegates responded positively.

Visitation Procedures

Historically, the bishop of the diocese was the visitator of religious communities at a time when monasteries were diocesan institutions without any kind of monastic congregation. Benedict himself makes allusion in his Rule to circumstances when the bishop is to be called in to intervene in monastic affairs. When the Council of Trent approved the system of congregations of monks, Benedictines became exempt from diocesan vistation and were allowed to have the president or general chapter appoint the visitators.

Such had been the practice of the Congregation of St. Scholastica from its beginnings; the three assistants to the president were in fact known as "visitators" and conducted an official visitation of the member priories every six years to insure that religious life was being observed as set down in the canons and the constitutions. The four members of the Congregation Council would decide among themselves which two would visit a given priory whose visitation was due. Two-thirds of the professed sisters of the priory were expected to present themselves to the visitators for a private interview in which questions of the following nature were asked:

1. Sister, what do you see as the most commendable characteristic of your community?
2. Do you feel that there is a spirit of charity in the house?
3. How is the common life observed? Do the sisters come regularly to prayers? to meals?
4. How is poverty observed here? Are your meals adequate? not lavish? Do the sisters keep such personal items as books, radios?
5. Are the sisters in general obedient to Mother? to the local superior? Are you concerned about the observance of the vows?

In preparation for the 1968 Chapter, the committee on religious government had sought comments from the member priories on their estimate of the efficacy of this mode of visitation. The returns were generally negative in tone: it was a waste of time and money, it was not productive of much good. Consequently, the position paper of the government committee had gone so far as to suggest asking for a rescript from Rome to eliminate visitations entirely but this was set aside by the delegates. Instead, they voted unanimously on this resolution: "The traditional visitation procedure is to be modified and the ends of visitation sought by experimental means to be determined by the Council in consultation with the priory to be visited . . ." Prior to the presentation of the Council's proposed plan at the 1969 session, the delegates heard a talk by Rev. Eugene McClory, Vicar of Religious for the Archdiocese of Chicago, who had recently served the Congregation on a visitation to a member priory; there had been a team of visitators consisting of two priests, a layman and a laywoman, each of whom came from a different background. In his talk he cited these criteria for a visitation: 1) the community should want a visitation; 2) the community should decide together on who the visitators should be; 3) prior to the visitation the community should make a self-study, determining their strengths and weaknesses; 4) there should be a report to the community at the end of the visitation. Father McClory spoke encouragingly of this approach and indicated it had been of considerable profit to the community involved.

The federation Council then presented its plan which called for a team of two to four persons selected by the community to be visited either from the federation Council, the council plus consultors or consultors alone. The visitation was to be preceded by a community self-study using evaluative criteria, a device familiar to many sisters by its use in schools for some time. The team was to receive these criteria as well as a profile of the community in advance of their visit. At the opening of the visitation itself, the community was to present its self-evaluation. The team would then tour the motherhouse and missions, interview groups or individuals who requested such interviews and observe the lifestyle and works of the community. At the conclusion of the visitation, a report would be made to the community on the team's findings.

The only point debated on the chapter floor was the frequency of visitation. As all former declarations regarding visitation had been suspended at the 1968 Chapter and canon law did not specify the intervals, it was necessary to legislate on this point. A motion was passed that visitation be held in each priory every five years. The vote was then taken on the Council's proposed method of visitation which was merely suggested and subject to changes by the local priory. It passed unanimously.

In 1975 the federation Council published a manual which outlined specific procedures for the preparation of a visitation, the role of the community as well as that of the visitators.[6] At this time it was specified that at least one of the visitators had to be from the federation Council.

These new procedures clearly put the emphasis of a vistation where it belonged: on the community itself who must seriously consider together its areas of strength and weakness. The preparation of such a report for the visitators prior to their arrival would engage the attention of every member for some time; such a period thus became a learning experience for the community as it came to grips with its actual situation. The interaction of community members as they made the study together resulted in evidence of positive growth in morale and development.

The role of the visitators shifted from that of inquirers to supporters, a team who corroborated the community's findings and encouraged them in positive commendations and recommendations. The entire process took on a healthier and more rewarding tone than had previously been possible to achieve. When asked if the community self-study prior to visitation contributed to the implementation of the decrees of the General Chapter, 58.6% of the delegates responded that it contributed greatly, 37.9% to some degree, a total of 96.5% positive response.

Interim Constitutions

The Chapter of 1966 had devoted almost all of its agenda to an overall revision of the Declarations and Constitutions. Actually, a study of the minutes shows that the revision was mainly confined to textual changes as the Chapter reviewed the declarations one by one. The chapter did vote to omit Prime from the recitation of the Divine Office, to remove the Wednesday abstinence, to consider modification of the religious habit and to hold general chapters every three instead of every six years. It was a two-day meeting facilitated by having had a committee of three prioresses prepare the revisions for presentation.

At the conclusion of the 1968 Chapter, it became necessary to examine this latest revised edition and to update it so that it would accord with actual practice during the period of experimentation provided for by the chapter. A committee was appointed by the president to perform this task before the Chapter concluded, indicating which declarations were to be considered still operative and which had become obsolete by virtue of 1) the adoption of specific resolutions and/or position papers by the Chapter, 2) the fact that they were covered by canon law, or 3) the fact that they were no longer contemporary.

The remaining declarations and constitutions were then assembled and printed in a volume designated later by the membership as the Blue Book which also included the minutes and position papers of both sessions of the General Chapter.[7] Those declarations in which experimentation was recommended until the next chapter were indicated by an asterisk. Authorization for experimentation had been established in *Ecclesiae Sanctae II*, 8, when it gave permission for renewal chapters to alter certain prescriptions of their constitutions. Thus the standing rules of the Chapter stated that the acceptance of a proposal in conflict with the present constitutions would imply the suspension of the corresponding part of the constitutions. Furthermore, all proposals adopted would form an experimental agreement available to those communities wishing to participate.

The definition of experimentation was unanimously approved by the delegates as "an attempt to seek new ways of doing things which juridically are contrary to or beyond existing law." The competent authority to initiate experimentation was the General Chapter or, on the local level, the prioress, the prioress and her council, and the chapter of the priory. Between the 1968 and 1969 sessions of the General Chapter, the federation Council had the faculty to initiate or expand experimentation as well as to rescind it upon the request of more than half the delegates of the previous chapter.

The areas for experimentation allowed by the Chapter were: government, local chapter meetings, local council membership and functions, retreats, the monthly retreat day, election of local officials, funeral masses, penance, postulancy and novitiate, temporary professions and the title given to the prioress.

The effect of the publication of these interim constitutions was to provide time for new experiences as allowed by the period of experimentation and to show that renewal was an ongoing process. In retrospect, 97.2% of the delegates felt that the Blue Book facilitated renewal in their communities. The freedom inherent in such a period was not without an overtone of ambivalence as local priories struggled to find new ways to adapt practices of the past.

Proof of this ambivalance can be established by citing that polarization increased to a great extent for 16% of the delegates and usually for another 12%; a lack of community cohesion was experienced to a great extent by 9% and usually for 14%. The existence of interim constitutions provided a degree of approval for the experimental patterns yet to emerge.

Call to Life

The 1971 Chapter had passed a resolution to "review, clarify and update" the interim constitutions of the Blue Book but it was left to the Congregation Council to decide how this was to be done. There had been problems with these constitutions almost from their publication. Many points were not clear, there were contradictions from one place to another in the text, it was not always reflective of the position papers. The inclusion of the minutes of the 1968 and 1969 sessions of the Renewal Chapter only muddied the content of the constitutions; the Blue Book had been only casually introduced into most communities and even though every sister had her own copy, its contents were not generally well known.

These and other arguments had been discussed in several council meetings in an attempt to decide how to proceed, but no clear direction emerged. Some felt a new document would only be a rehash of what had already been written. Finally, in August 1973, Sister Joan Chittister, federation president, called for the creation of a constitutions committee to produce a document and after considerable hesitancy and questioning, the council passed a resolution to this effect. The next question dealt with the membership of the committee. It was considered important by some that a member of the Federation council be on the committee to keep a close eye on the work; others were insistent that the members be delegates to past chapters who would thus be attuned to the evolution of the contents of the Blue Book. The president asked for recommendations and from the names given selected five sisters to form the constitutions committee which had as its task the "clarification of existing ambiguities and review of operational procedures" in the interim constitutions.

The committee was instructed to have its findings ready for the June 1974 Chapter. At the pre-chapter in November, 1973, Sister Joan asked the delegates to meet in their respective priories to determine any portions of the constitutions or any living situations which might have arisen since 1966 that they might want the constitutions committee to consider in their revisions and to send them to the committee c' airperson, Sister Patricia McGreevy of Erie.

The document which the committee presented to the Chapter in June 1974, *Call to Life*, had a totally new look.[9] Its sequence was

modeled on the Rule of Benedict and its content consisted of a precis
of each of the chapter position papers highlighting its theological
principles which undergird religious life. Each of the topics treated;
e.g., community, authority, vows, etc., was followed by policy statements which each priory was to implement in its own manner. A second section of the book contained the constitutions of the federation.

With the acceptance and publication of this work, an affirmation
of the entire period of renewal since 1966 was achieved. An element
of stability was restored as the period of experimentation drew to a
close. However, these constitutions were not to be seen as a final
work; there would be a constant ongoing evaluation by a permanent
juridic commission so that a static condition would not develop. But
as a spiritual document, *Call to Life* gave the religious rationale for
the new directions Benedictine life had taken in the Federation of St.
Scholastica and thus became an instrument valuable not only to current members but also for those to be trained in formation programs.
It is not surprising that 97% of the delegates agreed that the publication of *Call to Life* facilitated renewal.

IMPLEMENTATION OF CHAPTER ACTS

It was one thing for the General Chapter to pass resolutions
decreeing change in the mode of religious life; it was admittedly
another for those decrees to be implemented in the local priory at the
grass roots level. There were many factors operating both within and
without the communities that had a direct effect on their ability to ac-
tualize the decrees of the chapter. In this section of the participant
profile, delegates were asked to respond to a list of twenty-four factors that might have contributed to the implementation of chapter
decrees and twenty-three factors that might have been obstacles to
this implementation.

Contributions to Implementation

Fifty per cent of the respondents selected thirteen factors that
they felt contributed greatly to the task of executing chapter decrees
on the local level. These factors group themselves into three categories: those which evidenced ecclesiastical support, those which gave
social and organizational support and those which showed personal
involvement.

The ecclesiastical support for implementing change came from two sources, the Rule of St. Benedict and the mandate of Vatican II. Of the delegates, 71% felt that the flexibility of the Rule was an enabling factor in bringing about change. After all, Benedict himself had said after devoting eleven chapters of the Rule to the manner of reciting the Divine Office that if anyone found a better way, he should not hesitate to use it. He called his Rule a beginning, told the abbot he must "adjust and adapt himself to all," admonished the monks to follow the scripture: "Distribution was made to each according as anyone had need." He showed special consideration for the old, the sick and children. After legislating the kind and amount of food and drink for the monks, he leaves it to the abbot's discretion to add to these whenever circumstances warrant. Throughout the Rule there are other allusions to the authority of the abbot to change or modify the prescriptions as set down; in Chapter 64 St. Benedict advises the abbot to "so temper all things that the strong may have something to strive after and the weak may not fall back in dismay." The flexibility of the Rule has been acclaimed by its admirers down through the ages. Community members were familiar with the declarations to the Rule, those changes and adaptations made by previous general chapters which updated the interpretation of the Rule as times required. Consequently, they were predisposed to the whole concept of changes sanctioned by legitimate authority, in this case the Renewal Chapter. The delegates themselves believed in their authority to make changes, an authority based on the principles laid down in the Rule.

Vatican II was the other source of support for changes in religious life. The decree on the Appropriate Renewal of Religious Life, *Perfectae Caritatis*, was quite specific:

> The manner of life, of prayer and work should be in harmony with the present day physical and psychological condition of the members . . . . the needs of the apostolate . . . the requirements of the culture and with social and economic circumstances.
> The mode of government of the institutes should also be examined according to the same criteria.
> For this reason, constitutions, directories, books of customs, of prayers, of ceremonies and such like should be properly revised, obsolete prescriptions being suppressed, and should be brought into line with conciliar documents.[10]

Furthermore, in the norms for implementing *Perfectae Caritatis*, Paul VI had said that:

> It is the institutes themselves which have the main re-

sponsibility for renewal and adaptation. They shall accomplish this especially by means of general chapters . . .
    The cooperation of all superiors and subjects is neces-
sary for the renewal of their own religious lives . . ."

With such a clear call from the Holy Father himself, it is not
surprising that 63% of the delegates believe that Vatican II was greatly influential in activating the decrees of the chapter in their own
communities. Given the historical orientation of most religious to
directives from Rome, it could not have been otherwise. In fact, when
asked to cite the five major reasons which they felt led them to make
changes, 41% of the delegates chose the call of the Vatican documents
as their greatest impetus.

    Another kind of support for implementation came from the ex-
istence of new arms of communication created by the chapter delegates. Among these was the committee approach first used on the
federation level for the development of agenda items. As women from
several different communities came together to work on position
papers, the interchange of views and experiences enabled the brave to
assert themselves and the timid to take heart. Their belief in each
other bolstered their faith in the work before them. Consequently,
when they returned to their own priories, they were able to call upon
their own members to organize themselves into similar committees
using their own experience as delegates as a model and reaping the
same benefits. The purpose of the local groups was to facilitate renewal on the priory level, and committees, with their involvement of
more sisters than just the delegates themselves, greatly increased the
dissemination of data necessary to effect the renewal. In essence, a
series of concentric circles took shape with the delegates in the center
reaching out to the local committees who in turn contacted the broad
base of membership. That such a process was effective is attested to
by the 50% of the delegates who believed that the development of
committees to study and call for implementation of chapter decrees
greatly contributed to renewal in their communities. Another 43% felt
it contributed to some degree.

    For the same reasons, the newly-devised self-study method made
by a community in preparation for its official visitation was cited by
58% as greatly contributing to implementation. In a search together
for the answers to questions raised by renewal, community members
defined their own strengths and weaknesses, their goals and limita-
tions and measured them against what had been called for by chapter
decrees. Such attempts at honest assessment served to put a commu-

nity in touch with its real feelings about renewal and pointed out a direction to follow.

A third element which proved helpful in the implementation process was the introduction of organizational changes at both the federation and local levels. In addition to the two cited above, these changes included the pre-chapter sessions, expansion of the federation council, use of consultants and the creation of a conciliation board on the federation level. On the local scene the make-up of the priory council was expanded to include community-elected members; senates, personnel boards and other advisory groups were formed; the term of the prioress was subject to adjustment; branch houses were allowed to elect their own superior/coordinator. The concepts of collegiality and subsidiarity were thus actualized in religious government. Of the respondents, 54% felt that changes such as these greatly affected the implementation of the decrees of the General Chapter.

Experimentation as mandated by the Chapter was another contributing factor to implementation according to another 54% of the delegates. The Chapter had officially sanctioned certain areas of common practice for the local priories to approach in new ways of their own devising: local chapter meetings, local council membership and functions, retreats, the monthly retreat day, election of local officials, funeral masses, penance, postulancy and notiviate, temporary profession and the title given to the prioress. In addition the paper on community life had submitted and the chapter had accepted three proposals of a more general nature:

(1) . . . to experiment with creative patterns of community living within the framework of Benedictine authority and principle . . .
(2) . . . to make needed adaptations in the horarium and enclosure . . .
(3) . . . to direct their experimentation in liturgy toward the achievement of Benedictine eucharistic assembly.

With such broad prescriptions to follow, it was left to the ingenuity of each priory to determine how to concretize them. In so doing sisters were able to experience at first hand distinct changes in their mode of life, changes which for the first time they themselves had helped fashion. They were able to realize renewal as a process which directly involved and affected each individual as she assumed the responsibility for making decisions about her own life style, not merely as a process handled by a structure beyond her reach.

The last of these five organizational supports was the publica-

tion in 1974 of *Call to Life*, a synthesis of all that had evolved since
the 1968 chapter. In very clear terms it spelled out the principles,
policies and organizational structures of the Federation of St. Scholastica. It was a document of very high credibility since it reflected
the lived experience of those who had created it over a period of eight
years. With it in hand, communities were enabled to take stock of
their own positions as these measured up against the ideals expressed
in the document. Although only 51% of the delegates felt that *Call to
Life* contributed to implementation, this comparatively low figure
probably reflects the fact that the document was published only at the
conclusion of the eight-year renewal period when implementation of
earlier decrees of the chapter was already an accomplished fact.

The last group of five factors facilitating renewal on the local
level deals largely with the investment of personal leadership. Two of
these treat of the priory administration, two with the delegates and
one may refer to emerging leadership among the members themselves.

On the administrative level, the leadership consisted of the
prioress and her council. It should be remembered that 20% of those
present at the Chapter were prioresses and another 38% were in an administrative position of some kind or another, either a local superior
or a council member. These sisters had been highly instrumental in
shaping the decrees of the Chapter; it stands to reason, therefore, that
they would strongly identify with them and be equipped in a variety
of ways to make them operational in their priories since they already
occupied positions of leadership there. Sixty-two per cent of the delegates gave assent to this leadership as being highly effective in implementation.

Furthermore, 53% believe that the more frequent involvement of
prioresses at Benedictine and national or diocesan meetings both
within the Federation and external to it was also effective in this
implementation. In the decade before Vatican II, major superiors of
women religious had begun to meet on both local and national levels.
In 1976 the Leadership Conference of Women Religious (LCWR)
was holding regional meetings twice a year in which there is an interchange of views and ideas among all orders of religious women.
During the annual national assembly of LCWR which meets for a
week, a conference of Benedictine prioresses is also held at which the
president of the Federation discusses current ideas and problems of
general concern to American Benedictine women. At the biennial retreat of the prioresses, frequently given by the Abbot Primate in recent years, a world view of the state of Benedictinism is presented as

part of what might be considered the on-going education of the prioresses.[12] Many dioceses have organized their own groups of women religious leaders who meet to discuss issues of common interest. All of these opportunities furnish the prioresses with data and opinions which can serve to broaden their views and thus enhance the service they bring to their sisters. Most of the prioresses of the Federation attempt to attend as many of these national and regional meetings as possible, knowing that from them they can attain a wider perspective of religious life than concentration on merely the local level can achieve.

The two factors which directly involved the delegates were their personal commitment to implementation (54% rated this as greatly contributing to implementation) and their ability to articulate their experiences (52%). It is interesting to note here that the delegates were reporting on their own attitudes and behaviors and did not give themselves very high marks; 44% said their own commitment contributed only somewhat and 42% felt the same way about their ability to articulate their experiences. The task of the delegates on the local level after the Chapter concluded was a large one; they had to serve as reporters, persuaders, teachers and organizers to their sisters in order to effect renewal at the grass roots level, to make real to them what they themselves had experienced at the renewal chapters. Their ability to articulate their experiences depended to some degree on how actively they had participated, how ready their community was to receive chapter proposals. There were delegates who had contributed often to the chapter discussions while others took a more passive stance, listening attentively but not participating in the discussions to any extent. The assessments of commitment and articulation are therefore probably honest.

On the other hand, the delegates were quick to realize that leadership at other than administrative levels operated effectively to implement the decrees of the chapter; 64% felt that leadership among the sisters in general was a great influencing factor in their communities. There were many sisters in the priories eager to hear and to respond to the chapter proceedings. After all, they had been involved in filling out questionnaires sent out by the delegates before the Chapter convened; they had read the Vatican documents and the committee's position papers; they had received bulletins from the Chapter as it progressed. Furthermore, there was a general stirring of interest in renewal in popular religious periodicals as well as discussions with sisters from other congregations who had either already conducted or were planning their own renewal chapters. Consequently, sisters in the local priories were both informed and concerned, so that when the time came for them to be asked to volunteer for committee work to activate renewal in the community, they were quite ready and able to do so. Some communities already had senates whose leadership assumed much of the responsibility for this work. Leadership was also operating on a less formal basis in the priory; the simple interaction of one sister talking to others of her reactions to community affairs was also effective in the communication system. Discussion groups in local branch houses were often of an informal nature but nevertheless made their own impact.

When all of these groups who felt a real sense of involvement for implementing chapter decrees were put together; i.e., prioresses, delegates, and local non-administrative leadership, a truly formidable section of the local community emerged as a body committed to change. The moral suasion of such a presence was bound to contribute to the attitude of the total community regarding change. This was a period which had seen a large number of sisters with great potential leave their communities. The poor effect this had on the morale of the sisters remaining was to some degree counterbalanced by the felt presence of those who were actively committed to implementing decrees intended to produce change. Sixty-three per cent of the delegates believed that this continued presence was a significant factor in implementation.

It should be noted in passing that there were three factors which the delegates felt were of no value whatsoever in bringing about change in their communities: 1) assessment studies of diocesan needs made in conjunction with community planning, 2) support of changes from the diocese and 3) support of changes from the laity. It seems clear that the delegates felt that if the renewal of religious life was to be effected, the sisters themselves were the ones who would have to do the task.

Obstacles to Implementation

The delegates were asked to indicate the degree to which each of 23 factors was an obstacle to instituting change in their communities. Eight proved to be a great obstacle to almost 25% or more of the respondents. When the category "somewhat of an obstacle" is added to these, the percentage ranges from 80-90% in all cases but one.

OBSTACLES TO CHANGE

	Great	Somewhat	Total
1. Fear of change	38%	52%	90%
2. Lack of theological preparation	28%	61%	89%
3. Psychological pressures	23%	66%	89%
4. Confusion over meaning of monastic tradition	28%	61%	89%
5. Confusion between values and behavior	22%	64%	86%
6. Overextension of personnel	36%	47%	83%
7. Changes in form of religious life destructive of essence	35%	45%	80%
8. Lack of value of clarification skills	27%	51%	78%

It is not surprising that fear of change leads the list. The safe, stable, protected environment of convent life prior to Vatican II had hardly prepared its followers for risk of the dimensions called for by chapter decrees. The reliable and unvarying horarium, the permission syndrome and the absolutism of theological understanding during this period had acted together to produce for sisters the static atmosphere of an immutable world. Experimentation called for by chapter resolutions posed a threat to both the security and identity of those who for so long had lived in complete obedience to authority. But it was not only their life style that was changing; the Church itself was undergoing radical adjustment. On an even broader scale, the American culture was in a state of rapid flux: space technology, race riots, campus uprising, the adoption by large numbers of the population of a code of open sexual permissiveness were only a few signs of this flux. The repercussions of these societal and ecclesial changes were bound to impinge in some way upon the heretofore unimpregnable walls that surrounded convent life. To complicate the change process even more, there was no official sanction for the changes made in religious life from the hierarchy or clergy to whom the "good sister" had looked for so long for advice and support.[13] They had to generate self-esteem, a quality in which they were little prepared by their background of conformity, as they finally took on the responsibility for direction of their own lives. The uncertainties and tentativeness of this radical change from the highly predictable existence of the past can surely account for the great fear which had to be overcome before renewal could become effective.

Three of the factors cited: i.e., (1) confusion between a person's values and her behaviors, (2) lack of value clarification skills, and (3) the notion that changes in the forms of religious life were destructive of its essence have a common theme. It is the tension that exists between the ideals of religious life and their actualization in the lived experience. The ideals or values of the life are transcendent to it; the group creates the norms which make these values operative and from these the individual acts out behaviors which she feels are appropriate to the norms. But this personal development cannot be legislated, although the customs books of the past made it appear possible when they detailed religious reasons for many functional actions. For example,

> When walking, each sister crosses her hands under the scapular in honor of our suffering Lord bound with cords. At no time should a sister swing her arms while walking.[14]

Two of the obstacles deal with the spiritual training and background of the American Benedictine sister; i.e., her lack of theological preparation and confusion about the meaning of monastic tradition. The first was due in large part to the pragmatic approach towards education which had been almost universal among female American religious: she was to be a teacher and consequently needed to be prepared professionally, not theologically. Her spiritual reading was more pietistic than truly spiritual and hence not calculated to supply what was lacking in her development. She did not even have a clear idea of the meaning of monasticism in her life for although there was much literature on the subject, a great part of it interpreted the tradition selectively. There was the tension created by the concept of *fuga mundi*, flight from the world, a concept that never became clear in the American Benedictine experience. There was the "angelism" interpretation of what it meant to be a Benedictine, a theory based on the division of all matter into spiritual and carnal and the consequent necessity of the religious always to choose the spiritual element. With these evident gaps and errors in the sisters' preparation, it is no wonder that 89% of the delegates considered these two factors as significant obstacles to the implementation of chapter decrees in their communities.

The seventh of these serious obstacles deals with the psychological pressures created by the adaptations in religious life. It was popular in the 1960's and 70's to talk about the "identity crisis" then operating at all levels of life but perhaps nowhere made more real than among religious. If it was a problem for the young, it became much more so for the older religious who was being asked to consider an almost totally new outlook on her vocation as a consequence of change. The ensuing insecurity and fear of the unknown ran high and was very likely a factor in the decisions of many to leave religious life at this point.

The need for acceptance and approval on the part of those committed to change exerted another real pressure. Some communities experienced polarization over change; friends with differing views found themselves at odds with one another; "liberal" sisters were considered suspect by the more "conservative." They were truly uncomfortable times, for one does not enjoy being labeled, disregarded or ostracized, yet all of these happened. There were wounded sisters in every community; the price of renewal was not cheap.

Another of the psychological pressures was the feeling of anomie, a loss of meaning experienced by some as a consequence of seemingly endless and unanswerable questions on the role and function of contemporary religious life. The human psyche can endure just so much probing before it begins to question whether there is meaning in the very core of its being, in this case the living out of a life-style which ran counter to the prevailing culture. For those who found no meaning to the system under which they had been living, a dispensation seemed the only answer.

The last of these significant obstacles to implementation of change on the local level was the overextension of personnel. A look at the demographic profile of the delegates themselves indicates that 65% of them occupied administrative positions either within or outside of their communities which means that they already occupied positions which demanded much of their time and energies. A prioress, a hospital administrator, a college dean, a high school principal, were involved on a daily basis in endless activities which pulled them in many directions and sapped their psychic energy. To expect them as chapter delegates to assume also the leadership on the local level for setting up the machinery necessary to effect change throughout the community was to push them into further hours of work. Even the 35% who did not occupy any administrative position were full-time teachers, nurses, graduate students, etc., whose schedules already caused them to experience a lack of time to devote to additional concerns. And time was essential to study the issues, to prepare them for presentation to the community, to follow them through to implementation. All sisters, not just the delegates, found themselves with too much coming at them all at once and they were often unable to reach out to all that was expected of them. There was more parish involvement after Vatican II than ever before, more outside projects of social concern to which they were now giving their attention. The multiplication of committees to be chaired, meetings to attend and papers to write were creating new burdens at a time when sisters could ill afford to shoulder them. When the respondents to the Participant Profile were asked how they felt about the pace of their lives, 26% indicated they always felt rushed, 69% sometimes and only 4% never. It is for perhaps these reasons that 50% of the delegates welcomed *Call to Life* as a great help to implementation as it facilitated the approach to this process on the priory level.

A study of these preceding eight factors reveals that what they have in common is their focus on the person and her problems in adapting to renewal. Each of these arose from a personal/psychological base which hindered the ability of sisters to respond with ease to the challenge of chapter proposals. On the other hand, an examination of the seven factors which proved to be no obstacle to change will show that they have for their base the institution rather than the person.

NO OBSTACLE TO CHANGE

1. Overemphasis on autonomy in priories	78%
2. Lack of commitment by delegates	75%
3. Calling for chapter vote on matters that did not require it	65%
4. Existence of large buildings and/or debts	63%
5. Obstruction by clergy	59%
6. Inability of delegates to communicate rationale for change	55%
7. Lack of personal and financial resources to create programs leading to change	51%

The autonomy of each of the twenty-two houses of the Federation has always been a jealously guarded right; the president and her council do not have the power to interfere with the operation of a local priory except in extraordinary circumstances or well-defined areas of canonical jurisdiction. A review of the resolutions of the renewal chapters, unlike the chapters which preceded them, will reveal that they are in general recommendations to these priories to explore new approaches to contemporary religious life, not laws binding on all members. It would have been possible for a priory to use its autonomy as a kind of institutional defense mechanism to avoid being called to implement new concepts. Its members could have developed such internal self-sufficiency that they would declare no need for an external agency such as the federation to provide guidelines for them to follow. But as a matter of fact, this did not happen; 78% of the delegates disclaim that overemphasis on autonomy deterred implementation. The function of the federation to call its own members to agreed-upon goals was still respected.

As has already been shown, the delegates believed in themselves and their work sufficiently to rate high their commitment and ability to effect change. It should be remembered that they are in fact evaluating themselves on these items and the objectivity of their responses may well be questioned. Nevertheless, it is an accurate interpretation of how they viewed themselves and their work.

The chapter of the priory is the legislative body of the community and is composed of all perpetually professed sisters. Certain matters must be decided on in chapter by a majority vote. These matters include admitting members to the novitiate, to temporary and final profession, contracting debts, undertaking new or giving up old institutional commitments and establishing a new priory. There are other matters for which the prioress must ask for a consultative vote only: major policy changes or items of consequence to the entire community. It has happened in the past that the chapter vote has been misused in some communities by requiring it in circumstances which clearly did not call for it, an attempt, perhaps, to overprotect either the prioress or her council from making decisions which were definitely theirs to make. However, the delegates rejected by 65% this overuse of the chapter vote as a factor which hindered renewal in their communities. This indicates a willingness on the part of the priories to arrive at both personal and communal decisions in a responsible manner without undue reliance on formal means intended only for more weighty concerns.

The existence of large buildings and/or debts was no problem to 63% of the delegates, a quite high figure when one considers that buildings and debts loomed large on the agendas of some communities after the exodus of many sisters in the late 60's and early 70's. With the lower number of personnel came decreased income to the motherhouse; novitiates and other buildings used to house young sisters in formation were no longer needed when vocations fell to a new low. The introduction of small group living away from the conventional branch house or motherhouse left these buildings operating at less than full capacity. At the same time, the number of retired sisters was increasing, with the double result of a reduction of income and added costs for their maintenance and medical care. It is a sign of the faith of the delegrates that these real concerns were not seen as deterrents in furthering ongoing renewal.

That obstruction by the clergy was not operating as a barrier to implementation is attested to by 59% of the delegates. Their experience on the chapter floor supported their view, for there had been priests present as consultants at each session who strongly supported the move by the sisters to assume more responsibility for their own lives. This had not always been the case. The history of American women is full of examples of domination by bishops and clergy over the internal details of their lives; Benedictine women were no exception to this pattern. In fact, a kind of dependency grew up in women's communities as a result of this domination which a study of the archives correspondence in almost any house will verify. But by the time of the renewal chapters, sisters had gained sufficient confidence in their abilities to deal with their own problems that they no longer needed nor looked for clerical support. Nor did they permit the remonstrances and disapproval of some of the clergy to block them in their pursuit of renewal goals. There was no change in the courtesy and respect afforded the clergy but the old habits of deferring to their judgment in all cases gave way to the recognition that in the last analysis sisters were the best determiners of how they should live out their commitment to the vowed life.

Finally, the delegates did not feel that personal and financial resources were lacking to create programs leading to change. They had at their disposal not only their own experience and ability to call on but those of the federation council as well, whose members had pledged themselves to serve the autonomous houses by whatever means possible. Workshops on the chapter document *Call to Life* were available; by June of 1976 there had been thirteen of these given in local houses by either the president or members of her council; a larger one in Florida in the summer of 1975 had been attended by seventy-two sisters from eighteen communities of the federation. The money to sponsor or attend these and other workshops was considered money well spent, judging from the number of those who participated.

To review: the factors which were determined to be obstacles to change are all person-oriented, while those factors which were seen to be no obstacles are organization-oriented. The conclusion which can validly be drawn from these data is that the system changed more easily than the person in it. This is not surprising; it is always simpler to change structures than people. Variations in the institution are objective, non-threatening, somewhat removed from the mainstream of daily living. When it is a question, however, of values, of psychological pressures, of personal investment, the problems are much more complex. It then becomes an identity issue, not a systemic one.

DEMOGRAPHIC AND PERSONALITY PROFILES OF THE CHAPTER DELEGATES

Who were these 142 sisters who responded to the Participant Profile and what can be learned about their backgrounds and personality profiles that will shed light on their responses?

Age

In age they ranged from 30 to over 60 with a balance in each of four age groups: 20% between 30-40; 28% between 41-50; 27% between 51-60; and 23% over 60 years of age. They had been members of a Benedictine community from ten to more than fifty years with 45% of them members for 11-25 years and 4% for more than fifty years. There was no one represented who had been a religious for less than ten years; sisters from that age category were somehow not elected as delegates from their communities, a fact that was seen as a possible handicap and which was later addressed on the chapter floor.

Family Background

Their family backgrounds were primarily Catholic; 83% of their fathers and 94% of their mothers were Catholic. They came mostly from larger families; 67% stated that there were more than four children in their family with 16% having eight or more. Six per cent of the delegates were the only child in the family. The position in the family of the others varied from 28% who were the oldest, 21% the youngest and 47% between the oldest and the youngest. Perhaps the fact that animated debate could and did take place on the chapter floor can be related to the number of middle children who by virtue of their position in their families may have become accustomed long before to fending for themselves. The oldest child (28%), the family leader in many cases, would most likely be prepared to maintain a leadership position in religious life.

The occupational status of parents falls in mainly middle class roles: of the fathers, 39% were blue collar workers, 15% white collar clerical, 26% were small business men and 13% were farmers. Only 8% were professional men. Of the mothers, 83% were occupied at home full time, 10% worked outside the home part time and 7% full time. Thus family patterns were fairly traditional.

The educational level of the parents of these sisters shows that their fathers had slightly more education than their mothers.

EDUCATIONAL LEVEL OF PARENTS

	Father	*Mother*
Less than four years' high school	65%	66%
High School graduate	12%	18%
Beyond high school but with no degree	16%	13%
College graduate	6%	3%

Delegates' Education

The sisters' own education level was quite high; 69% had masters degrees, 16% were college graduates, 10% had a doctorate and only 5% held less than a bachelor's degree. Two-thirds of this education was obtained in Catholic schools entirely: 60% had attended Catholic elementary schools, 65% Catholic high schools and 66% Catholic colleges and universities. The percentage of those who never attended Catholic schools was low: 23% had gone entirely to public elementary schools, 16% to public secondary schools and only .7% to only public or private colleges. In view of the fact that most, if not all, of a sister's college education was obtained after her entrance into community, it can be seen that ecclesiastical legislation requiring that religious attend Catholic colleges and universities was operating in communities to a very high degree. Today that trend may be considerably lessened as there is evidence that younger sisters pursuing graduate degrees are enrolling in non-Catholic colleges in greater numbers, both because of their lower cost and the availability of particular programs there.

It is interesting to note that 64% of the delegates had more education than their brothers and 69% more than their sisters. For the most part, this is due to the emphasis the community placed on obtaining professional training for those entering the teaching field.

Priory

The size of the priories from which the delegates came ranged from over 200 (9%) to fewer than fifty members (27%). Most came from communities of between 51-100 members (35%). The greater number of these priories are located in rural (25%), small city/town (29%) or suburban settings (29%). Only 17% of the delegates have a large city as their priory location.

Living Conditions

The respondents themselves live in the priory (54%) or in traditional branch houses (22%). Another 23%, however, have moved out into newly-established community residences of smaller groups, a result of the re-thinking about community living that emerged from chapter discussions. In these groups, 26% of them are composed of from three to nine members, 6% live with one other person and 4% live alone. But two-thirds still live in groups of ten or more and 44% of these are in groups of more than twenty members at which level communal interaction may become more difficult to achieve.

Ministry

As for the ministry of the delegates, 29% held positions internal to community and 19% of these were prioresses. By far the largest portion (64%) were in educational work of some kind. Health (4%) and social work (3%) account for the remainder.

Investment in Renewal

When asked to what degree they had been involved in community affairs prior to the renewal chapters, 58% of the delegates claim to have been very involved, 35% somewhat involved and 7% uninvolved. These percentages changed considerably when it became a question of involvement since the chapters: high involvement rose to 71%, lesser involvement fell to 26% and only 2% felt no involvement at all. These figures correlate well with those cited earlier in this study regarding the personal commitment of the delegates to the implementation of the decrees of the chapters and their own ability to articulate their experience.

PERSONALITY PROFILE

In addition to these sociological factors, delegates were asked to respond to a series of questions of a personal/psychological nature; e.g., how they felt about their past and future religious life. The results are indicative of a healthy outlook despite the trauma of a decade of change.

Twenty-eight per cent believe that their life over the past ten years has been much happier than they expected, 19% somewhat happier and 41% about as happy as anticipated. Only 2% felt less happy. Projections for a happiness level ten years from now continued to be healthy: 10% expect to be much happier than now, 32% somewhat happier and 56% about as happy as they are now. Again, 2% expect to be somewhat less happy than at present. When they compare themselves to most of the sisters in their community, only 1% believe these sisters are much happier than they themselves are, 6% feel their sisters are somewhat happier and 64% about as happy. They believe that 28% of their sisters are somewhat less happy than they.

The confidence level in their guiding values is also encouraging. Forty-five per cent are very confident, 38% considerably confident and 9% somewhat less confident, a total of 92% positive reaction. It is of interest that another 7% indicate that they are questioning their values constantly, a not altogether unexpected response in an era of momentous change.

About their own lives, 29% feel very optimistic, 66% optimistic, 4% pessimistic and .7% very pessimistic. But about the future of their community, although 18% were very optimistic and 63% optimistic (a total of 81%), 16% were pessimistic and 3% very pessimistic, a notable increase in pessimism for the institution as compared to the self.

Eighty-two per cent of those attending the renewal chapters believe that their lives have meaning and direction; 18% disagreed. This correlates closely with the figure above on the future of their community (81% optimistic, 19% pessimistic). The inference is that if someone does not believe her community has a future she is going to be pessimistic about her own.

The delegates were then asked to compare themselves to the average sister in their communities and rated themselves as follows: more confident, 74%; more intelligent, 61%; more assertive, 59%; more likeable, 58%; more conscientious, 53%; less impressionable, 61%; less conforming, 51%. Assuming that members of their community saw them in the same way, it is clear what led to their election as delegates.

The delegates' perception of themselves as compared to the community's perception of them was sought twice in questions that dealt with the labels often attached to community members, at the time of the chapters and after their close. The shifts in perception from progressive, moderate and traditional are interesting.

How did you and your community perceive yourself in relation to the changes in religious life?

AT THE TIME OF CHAPTER (1968-74)

	Progressive	Moderate	Traditional
Self-perception	21%	65%	14%
Community perception	42%	42%	17%

AT TIME OF PARTICIPANT PROFILE (1976)

Self-perception	32%	67%	.7%
Community perception	43%	52%	5%

The delegates saw themselves as being moderate at both the chapter and later, but there is a considerable change in the other two percentages. Ten per cent considered themselves as more progressive after the chapters than they were before, and more than 13% felt they had shifted from the traditional to another point of view. They also felt that the community continued to see the same per cent as progressive but shifted 12% from the traditional to another category.

It can be inferred from these shifts that general chapters caused people to alter their points of view. There is some data available that indicates that this is precisely the case. Those attending more than one renewal chapter were asked if there had been a change in their attitude between the first and last chapters attended. Thirty-nine per cent said there had been a significant change. This group was then asked if the change had been positive or negative; 72% indicated it was positive.

Finally, when asked to characterize their participation in the first renewal chapter attended, 50% or more chose the following adjectives as descriptive of their performance: serious, 98%; open-minded, 96%; sensitive, 89%; affirming, 85%; analytical, 73%; calm, 72%; quiet, 71%; relieved, 60% and timid, 52%.

From the data submitted in this section of the Participant Profile, it is possible to draw a demographic and personality profile of the typical delegate to the renewal chapters of 1968-1974. In 1976 she was between 41-50 years of age and had been in her community from 26-35 years. Her community numbered from 51-100 members and its priory was located in either a rural area or a small town/city. She lived in the priory itself. All of her education, elementary, secondary, and college, was obtained in a Catholic institution. She had a master's degree (and more education than her sisters and brothers) and was engaged in some phase of educational work. She was also an administrator in her community, either a prioress, council member or a local superior/coordinator.

Both of her parents were Catholic and she was between the oldest and the youngest in a family of 4-5 children. Her father was a blue collar worker and her mother worked full time at home. Both had some high school education.

She had been very involved in community affairs both before and since the renewal and had served on at least one federation committee. She was still a member of religious life at the time she responded to the Participant Profile (1976).

The typical delegate was somewhat happier than she had expected to be over the past ten years. She considered most of her sisters about as happy as she and expected to be just as happy ten years from now. She felt considerably confident that her guiding values were right and will last. She was optimistic about both her own life and the future of her community. She strongly agreed that her life had meaning and direction although she sometimes felt that the pace of her life was rushed. She considered herself more intelligent, more likeable, more assertive, more conscientious, more confident, less impressionable and less conforming than the average sister. In the first renewal chapter which she attended her attitude was serious, sensitive, calm, affirming, quiet, timid, open-minded, analytical and relieved. Her perception of herself both before and since the renewal chapters was that of a moderate and her community viewed her in the same way at both periods.

In the language of Aesop's fable she was a grasshopper (56%), living for the moment and trying to make things as bearable or enjoyable as possible, in contrast to 44% who claimed to be ants, working and planning for the future.

Conclusions

From the above data the following conclusions can be validly drawn:
1. The changes in the life style of sisters in the Federation of St.

Scholastica were not made, as some have suggested, solely by a younger element in communities who were dissatisfied with the status quo. The decision-making process for change was shared by sisters in four comprehensive age groups.

2. Strong Catholic family backgrounds fostered vocations in these sisters at an early age.
3. The educational background of the participants was strong, enabling them to make their decisions with competence and confidence.
4. The priories in the Federation are not large, for the most part, thus facilitating communication at a time when it was crucial to the change process.
5. New trends in small group living to foster personal growth and interpersonal relations as encouraged by the chapters are already evident in the Federation.
6. So far, the ministry of the delegates has remained consistent with that of the past; new areas are emerging only slowly.
7. Change has not been experienced as disruptive on either the personal or institutional level; most of the respondents felt secure about their own future and that of their communities.
8. The delegates who attended more than one chapter experienced a positive change in attitude between their first participation and their last, evidence that the chapters were provocative, dynamic and productive.

PART III
American Benedictine Women
in the
Roman Catholic Church

The intent of this section is to situate some of the recent developments in religious life in the United States in the context of developments within the Roman Catholic Church. The pages tell how the sense of the church and religious life as professed publicly by the 2200 Catholic bishops of the world through the key documents of the Second Vatican Council was responded to by another group of 2200, namely American women living according to the Rule of Benedict in a monastic tradition older than any other western religious institution except the Roman Church itself.

The section joins history and theology to account for the common understanding of the nature of the church and Christian vocation which undergirds all current renewal efforts in Roman Catholic institutions. It also uses these same historical and theological resources to reflect on the contributions American Benedictine women have been making toward the renewal process in the first post-conciliar decade. It uses them, finally, to shed light on some developments in Benedictine spirituality which renewal has evoked.

"I FAIL TO SEE THE LOGIC OF THIS APPROACH"

My letter to . . . the Sisters was dictated by a desire to encourage them—and not at all to discourage them—in the prudent and careful implementation of the Council Decree. . . . .

The only proper approach, in my judgment, is an analytical one: to take the Council Decree addressed to Religious as the major; to take the Benedictine traditions and the present Rules and Customs as the minor; and from them to draw the obvious conclusions.

. . . They have started with a "Thesis," and have offered as "Proofs" of that Thesis quotations from various Council documents (some of them addressed to the laity, some addressed to the modern world). I fail to see the logic of this approach, and fear that it will lead to considerable confusion. To become concerned about the implementation of the Decree on the Church in the Modern World will distract the Sisters from their assigned area of concentration: the Council Decree addressed to Religious.

It all seemed so clear and simple, back during the days of the Council. . . . Now, three years later, it is not nearly so simple. . . .

Letter of an American Bishop to the
Federation President, 1968.[1]

The renewal undertaken by the American Benedictine sisters from 1966-74 can be understood only as a response to the Second Vatican Council of 1962-65. That Council in turn must be viewed in historical perspective. Vatican II had a single focus: to clarify the nature of the Roman Catholic Church, its mission, and its structures. All of its sixteen documents spoke to some aspect of ecclesiology. Although the single focus was not surprising to students of church history, more typical Catholic clergy, laity, and religious were unprepared for it. Few among them had any awareness of the need to complete the work begun at a First Vatican Council almost a century earlier.

VATICAN I: THE PAPACY AND CATHOLIC IDENTITY

Pope Pius IX had convened that first Vatican Council in Rome in 1869-70 to talk broadly about a full range of 19th century ecclesiastical concerns. But in the short time the council was in session the church's bishops produced only the brief dogmatic statement *Pastor Aeternus*, a four-chapter document treating first, the institution of the papacy; second, the perpetuity of the Roman pontiff's primacy; next, the power and nature of the Roman pontificate; and finally, papal infallibility.

The emphasis on the papacy was at least partially provoked by internal disputes between those European churchmen who wished to minimize papal claims and those who wished to maximize them.[2] The maximalists gained the day, and in fact the century. As a result, bishops and priests, laity and religious had to wait until the convening of Vatican II to have the topic of their presence in the church explored with full seriousness.

While the necessity of that century-long delay in discussing the fullness of the church can be attributed to the absence of ecclesiastical readiness at any number of levels, the immediate occasion for the delay was the invasion of the city of Rome in the fall of 1870 by Italian armies. The invasion succeeded because the French—who had been defending not only the concept of papal power but also the city of Rome—were forced by political circumstances to withdraw their troops and cede the territory. Thus, only three months after the church in council had solemnly proclaimed a fullness of papal authority, Pius IX was forced to suspend the First Vatican Council indefinitely. The council was never reconvened. In the ensuing century leading to Vatican II, confidence in and loyalty and obedience to an almost absolute and universal papal authority became the hallmark of Roman Catholicism.

AMERICAN BENEDICTINE SISTERS BETWEEN THE COUNCILS

During that century, most of the communities which comprise the Federation of St. Scholastica had been established from the original North American foundation at St. Marys, Pennsylvania, in 1852. These houses of American Benedictine women were part of the western monastic tradition for men and women that was unbroken from its origins with Benedict of Nursia in 6th century Italy. Most immediately, they had their origins from the convent of St. Walburga in Eichstatt, Bavaria, which continues its own ways at the end of the 20th century untouched by the shoot it set out at St. Marys.

Independent foundations by heritage, the American houses had at various times been under the jurisdiction either of a Benedictine abbot or of local bishops.[3] In order to preserve the local autonomy of each convent which is characteristic of the Benedictine tradition and at the same time to gain official ecclesiastical recognition in Rome, a number of the houses had begun as early as 1880 to try to establish a federation of houses directly under papal jurisdiction. That federation was formally effected only in 1922. Nevertheless, during the half-century of organizational preparations, the notion of establishing a direct relation with the Roman See was maintained as a persistent goal for the developing communities.

Juridical Developments

While they suffered delays in establishing themselves as communities under pontifical jurisdiction, the self-understanding of American Benedictine women was being shaped, perhaps irrevocably, by ecclesiastical circumstances on both sides of the Atlantic during the period from 1870-1922. Three formative elements stand out. First among them was the juridical reform that was a consequence of the 1870 council. Its earliest impact on the Benedictine women came through a set of norms promulgated in 1901. Intended originally to standardize groups of religious women founded in the modern period, misapplication of the 1901 norms to Benedictine women in the United States influenced the course of community histories until the post-Vatican II renewal.[4] The reform movement after the First Vatican Council culminated in the 1917 Code of Canon Law. That compilation brought forward into the 20th century the aura of juridicism and legalism which was the inheritance of the 16th century counter-Reformation. That aura had only intensified with the threats to ecclesiastical authority across the European continent throughout the 19th century.

In the 1917 Code all relationships in the church were given juridical definition. When, in 1922, a core group of seven houses of American Benedictine women was finally ready to submit to Rome a constitution in the name of the Congregation of St. Scholastica, they were faced with the need to represent their lives in a way that more clearly fit definitions of Benedictine life under European cultural circumstances reaching back through the modern into the medieval world. When they could not match Roman expectations of how Benedictine nuns should live with the demands of immigrant life, their Benedictine authenticity was questioned.

According to the 1917 Code, monasticism for women demanded

strict papal enclosure, on the authority of juridical definition, if not that of the Rule of Benedict. No place existed in the ecclesiastical consciousness of that time for the concept of development within a living tradition or of cultural adaptation to new circumstances. What adaptations American Benedictine women had made, generally at the direction of abbots and bishops during their first half-century in the United States, constituted grounds in 1922 for their treatment in the hands of Roman authorities as a new institute rather than as a group living according to the ancient Rule of Benedict in new circumstances.[5] Conflicting self-understanding and expectations were thus woven into the fabric of American Benedictine women's history.

Local Church Developments

The second ecclesiastical development of the century which had direct consequences for American Benedictine women was the decision of the American Catholic bishops, at the Third Plenary Council of Baltimore in 1884, to promote as a national goal the opportunity for every child of the burgeoning immigrant population to be educated in a Catholic school. The communities of Benedictine sisters, Bavarian immigrants at their origin, had from the start in 1852 lived among immigrant families and conducted schools as a way to support themselves and to help the immigrant church.[6] In the wake of the 1884 decision they were to become part of that large ecclesiastical labor force of religious women—Benedictines, Franciscans, Dominicans, Sisters of Charity, all transmuted to School Sisters—who were to build a cohesive American Catholic church on the youngest segment of the Catholic immigrant population, school children. All other aspects of the Benedictine way of life were pragmatically subordinated to this overriding goal in the American church, sometimes by the sisters themselves, but often against their wishes at the direction of local churchmen. Thus, Benedictine women in the United States became teachers in parochial or community-owned schools.

The Americanism Controversy

A third circumstance of the century between Vatican I and Vatican II which was less tangible in its impact than either of the preceding two developments still had indirect bearing on the lives of American Benedictine women. That circumstance was the papal reprobation in 1899 of the phantom heresy "Americanism."[7] French defenders of papal authority and prerogatives watched scrupulously for signs of deviation from monarchical thinking about church governance in the years after Vatican I. The environment fostered by democratic systems of government was specially suspect. Thus, the rapidly expanding church in the United States, under the liberal leadership of James Cardinal Gibbons, received special scrutiny.

The teachings of American born Isaac Hecker, founder of the Paulist Fathers, one of the first religious institutes of American origin, were singled out as examples of "Americanism." The pejorative term coined by the French critics was directed against the *"moderne, democratique, individualiste"* quality of Hecker's spiritual writings. Hecker was accused of new ideas: promoting undue devotion to the Holy Spirit, diminishing the importance of external spiritual direction, rejecting the church's teaching about religious vows, and extolling individuality at the expense of religious humility and obedience.

Under the pressure of intense debates in France over the dangers of "Americanism," Pope Leo XIII wrote the letter *Testem Benevolentiae* to James Cardinal Gibbons.[8] He asserted on the one hand that no one was actually being accused of holding heretical positions, yet there were in fact five censurable errors which should be drawn to the attention of the American church as a warning. Leo XIII's list included much the same charges that the French critics had raised against Hecker, despite the protests of the Paulist superior that Hecker's teaching was being deliberately misrepresented. Pope Leo's letter warned against the rejection of external spiritual direction as meaningless; the extolling of natural over supernatural virtues; the preference for active over passive virtues; the rejection of religious vows as not compatible with Christian liberty; and the adoption of a new attitude and method of approach toward non-Catholics.

This late 19th century sparring with a phantom error anticipated by more than 50 years the Vatican II efforts of the Roman Catholic hierarchy to dialogue with the modern world. The unfamiliar spirit, then designated "Americanism" to mark the territory in which it was first clearly identified, was more sympathetically described in the Vatican II pastoral Constitution on the Church in the Modern World as the legitimate concern for the dignity and freedom of the human person rooted in each one's capacity for personal communion with God.[9] But at the turn of the 20th century Leo XIII and James Cardinal Gibbons had stalemated. No one was being accused, but accusation was in the air. No one needed defending, but the American church became defensive. Thus, a sizeable measure of damage was done. No theological reflection was ventured; none was encouraged. The five issues—all of them related to the nature of spiritual authority and the dignity of the person—were suppressed for two generations. Meanwhile, the American church leadership and membership learned to doubt itself in the face of Roman disapproval.

Within a decade after the Americanist controversy, a new pope. Pius X, altered the juridical status of the American church. Until that time, the colonial and immigrant church had been included in the group of mission churches under the supervision of the Congregation for the Propagation of the Faith. In 1908, the church in the United States was given equal standing with the churches of the European nations. The new status did not confer new confidence. Rather, self-doubt about the validity of a distinctive American Catholic experience was internalized by Catholics in the United States.

One American Catholic journalist writing contemporary with the events of the "Americanist" controversy offered the judgment that the underlying issues were ascetical and strategical and not dogmatic.[10] Nevertheless, the European expressions of Catholic Christianity and religious life were to remain normative. Only with the Second Vatican Council did the church begin to explore publicly the fundamental issues of religious authority, religious life, and the human person.

The story of the full impact of the climate of that period on the Federation of St. Scholastica is told in *The Benedictine Congregation of St. Scholastica—Its Foundations and Development: 1880-1930* by Sister Regina Baska, O.S.B. That history recounts the faithful attempt of American Benedictine women to meet both the demands of juridical definitions of monastic life for women and the expectations of the American hierarchy about their place in the American church.[11] It shows little indication that they were ready at that time to invest either credence or confidence in the authority of their own lives and their sense of Benedictine vocation when they were confronted with the irreconcilable tensions of conflicting expectations.

VATICAN II: THE SIXTEEN DOCUMENTS AND CATHOLIC IDENTITY

By the end of the renewal period 1966-74, American Benedictine women who were the delegates to the renewal chapters of the Federation of St. Scholastica had moved to a new level of ecclesial consciousness. They showed a striking sense of personal and corporate autonomy and responsibility which went far beyond legalism and juridicism. Having come to a strong sense of their own Christian adulthood, these American Benedictine sisters in the Federation of St. Scholastica were no longer able to concede to the church's hierarchy universal and absolute authority for interpreting their lives as Benedictines. They had come to recognize that the interpretation and expressions of the Benedictine vocation they had learned were unnecessarily restrictive. Some of the catalysts of this change in attitude can be identified. Present among them was the Council itself.

The Mandate and the Response

The pivotal document of the Second Vatican Council was the dogmatic Constitution on the Church, *Lumen Gentium*. Fifteen additional documents grouped in constellations around this text. One such constellation was comprised of documents dealing with special cases of internal relations within the church: priests, religious, laity, bishops. Another cluster was formed by the documents reflecting on the historical and cultural environment of the church at the end of the 20th century. Those texts dealing with internal relations within the Roman Catholic church continued to reflect the juridicism of earlier centuries. Hierarchical absolutism and the concern for prerogatives of ecclesiastical office persisted in the description of how the church is constituted, even while newer perspectives were being introduced in the discussion of the 20th century social conditions.

Among the documents dealing with intra-church matters was the decree calling for the appropriate renewal of religious life, *Perfectae Caritatis*. It was this decree which prompted prioresses and community elected delegates of the Federation of St. Scholastica, as well as all other religious communities, to assemble in a series of renewal chapters in obedience to the mandate of the hierarchy.

The sense of dependence on the command of authority to initiate action was still high in the mid-1960's. Minutes of a meeting of prioresses of the Federation of St. Scholastica held in August, 1966, indicate that although they discussed the prospect of community renewal and reform in the wake of Vatican II, they were not really ready to initiate serious reform by establishing their own committee to revise their constitutions. The secretary noted:

> The group finally decided that such a committee was not necessary at this time. If the new "Instruction" from the Post-Conciliar Commission advises otherwise, action will be taken later.
> In the meantime, we were advised to make a thorough

study of the Council decrees in each community in preparation for the General Chapter.[12]

The study apparently was done. In response to questions posed in 1976 research, almost two-thirds of the chapter participants acknowledge that the documents of Vatican II generally and the mandate of *Perfectae Caritatis* particularly had a considerable and conscious effect on their voting patterns in the renewal chapters.[13] Three-quarters of the chapter participants say that they were directly influenced in their thinking by the dogmatic Constitution on the Church. Four-fifths of them acknowledge that the companion pastoral Constitution on the Church in the Modern World had a discernible impact. Similarly, three-quarters admit the strong influence of the Constitution on the Sacred Liturgy on their thinking and voting.

The Theological and Procedural Issues

What theological concepts did these focal documents put forward, and what principles for renewal did they present as a challenge? Six theological issues stand out for the obvious bearing they had on the thinking of the renewal chapter participants of the Federation of St. Scholastica. Three were drawn from the dogmatic Constitution on the Church. First, the nature of the church itself was treated primarily as the manifestation of the Trinitarian mystery of unity with diversity. Further, that same document also explored the source and nature of religious authority as well as the nature of religious life, grounding both in the one Holy Spirit of the Risen Christ given to all the baptized. Three other theological issues found in the pastoral Constitution on the Church in the Modern World also called for response: the dignity and freedom of the person, the quest for human community, and the demands of social justice. Each of these six issues and their bearing on renewal in the Federation of St. Scholastica will be considered in turn in a later part of this chapter.

Guiding principles for renewal were drawn from at least two textual sources readily identified by the chapter delegates. In the Constitution on the Sacred Liturgy the note had been sounded that the cultural forms of religious expression were relative, so that distinctions were to be made between changeable and unchangeable elements. That Constitution further proposed as principle the notion that religious expression should reflect different cultural experiences. It stated that new forms were to grow organically from old ones, and that only those innovations were appropriate which promoted the good of the church.[14]

The decree on the appropriate renewal of religious life likewise proposed principles to guide institutional renewal. *Perfectae Caritatis* directed all religious to reflect profoundly once again on the gospel, on the particular spiritual tradition in which they shared, on the present situation of the church and the world in which they participated, and on the quality of their own spirituality and the human needs of their own membership.[15] Here, in the historically critical outlook of these documents, was authorization to deal with the tensions and the conflicting expectations about Benedictine life for American women.

Although the renewal chapter participants began their work with a study of the Council documents, they did not long tie the scope of their task to explicit directives in particular documents. They indicate in retrospect that they were responding to the whole constellation of perspectives that had been opened up during the council era. In fact, four-fifths of them say that it was the total impact of new theological insights which led them to different understandings of the gospel, and of the nature of the church and religious life. A legitimate question must then be raised: were these women competent to deal with the emerging theological perspectives of the conciliar period?

Theological Readiness for Renewal

It is a fact of western religious history, already evident in the pre-Christian rabbinic prohibitions against teaching Torah to women and still present in 20th century restrictions against women enrolling in Catholic schools of theology, that women have consistently been excluded from the formal study of their religious and theological traditions. The officially approved Declarations on the Rule of Benedict for the Congregation of St. Scholastica still required, in 1953, only a minimum of religious knowledge and understanding of Catholic thought prior to a sister's religious profession. They stated:

> During the time of postulancy and of the Novitiate the young aspirants are to review and to acquire a more thorough knowledge of Christian doctrine so that every Sister has not only memorized, but is also able to explain the same correctly. A Sister is not to be admitted to vows who has not given proof in an examination of sufficient knowledge of her religion. . . .[16]

"Sufficient" had generally received a minimalist interpretation.

The fact is that what formal secular or religious education Benedictine communities of women had been able to provide for their members over the years had been highly pragmatic. Education was aimed primarily to equip sisters to teach the catechism and to meet the minimum qualifications for state certification as elementary and secondary school teachers and for school administration. Occasionally some received advanced education in order to prepare for college teaching. The educational pragamatism had its origins partially in social and religious expectations about women's roles, partially in the pressure coming from pastors and bishops to provide ever-increasing numbers of sisters to fill the classrooms of the burgeoning Catholic school system, and partially as a result of the limited financial resources of communities which had never received more than subsistence wages for work in the schools. The situation began to change in the 1950's.

One of the first official signs of a departure from this minimalist approach to education for religious women came when Pope Pius XII and the Sacred Congregation for Religious promoted the establishment in Rome of Regina Mundi, a special house of theological studies for sisters. This movement for special theological programs for women had been anticipated in the United States by St. Mary's College at Notre Dame, Indiana. Already in the 1940's, under the leadership of Sister Madeleva Wolff, C.S.C., St. Mary's had initiated a program for lay and religious women to study the sacred sciences. In the 1950's St. Mary's was conferring the doctoral degree in sacred studies on women, the only institution in the United States to do so. But no Benedictine sisters from the Federation of St. Scholastica were recipients of that degree.

In 1950, American Benedictine women were typical of religious women generally. They suffered from a dearth of opportunity for in-depth theological education and a lack of awareness of their deprivation. Sister Mary Anthony Wagner of St. Benedict's Convent in St. Joseph, Minnesota, one of the few theologically educated Benedictine women of this era, recounted the situation in a paper, "Theology As An Influence in Convent Life," delivered before the American Benedictine Academy in August, 1950. That paper prompted the Academy to establish a committee of monks to consider ways to provide special programs for sisters. Meanwhile, the four prioress-presidents of the congregations of American Benedictine sisters had also begun to explore the prospect of their own sponsorship of an institute for Benedictine theology and spirituality for religious women. They were pressured not only by the dawning awareness of need in their own houses, but also by the papal action and the recurring invitations to send their sisters to Regina Mundi, the papal institute in Rome, to St. Mary's in Indiana, or to Catholic University in Washington, D.C. where sisters might take courses but not yet qualify for a degree.[17] The national Sister Formation Movement of that era likewise was challenging all religious communities of women to provide appropriate professional education for all their members, including theological education.

Thus, in October, 1957, thirty-seven Benedictine prioresses from the four congregations of American Benedictine sisters, among them seventeen prioresses of the Congregation of St. Scholastica, approved and signed a resolution establishing the Benedictine Institute of Sacred Theology, a program that they believed would best suit the needs of their own communities. They located the institute at St. Benedict's Convent in St. Joseph, Minnesota, because of its proximity to St. John's Abbey, and asked the local Benedictine abbot to designate one of his monks as director.[18]

The program began in the summer of 1958 from the same operating premise that Regina Mundi reflected, namely that formal theological education for sisters should still be separate and special education. The sisters were not convened at a major Catholic academic or theological center, despite invitations to develop the program in that setting. Neither was recognized academic credit or an academic degree initially considered essential to the credibility or academic seriousness of the undertaking. But it was not long before Paschal Botz, O.S.B., the director of BIST, and Sister Mary Anthony Wagner, then assistant director of the program, began to deal with the rising expectation among the faculty and students alike that the program could and should have academic depth and lead to the MA. The BIST program quickly received accreditation through St. John's University at Collegeville, and by the mid-60's had evolved into a graduate theological program admitting not only Benedictine sisters, but any qualified religious women and men, Catholic laity, or seminarians and clergy who sought the degree.

Meanwhile, however, the Benedictine women enrolling in the early summers of the five-year, six-week special program had the opportunity to study not only with American but also with European teachers conversant with the best Catholic scholarship of that era, scriptural, doctrinal, and liturgical studies, moral theology, and Benedictine history and spirituality. During the years of the Vatican Council, they were kept informed by an international faculty about many of the theological issues the bishops were in the process of debating in Rome.

Twenty-one women who were participants in the renewal

chapters, 15% of the chapter delegates, were enrolled in the BIST-St. John's University program prior to or during the renewal period. These sisters, from thirteen of the twenty member houses of the federation, were known to one another through successive summers and constituted a core group of theologically educated delegates. Their number was augmented by another 10% of the delegates whose backgrounds included formal theological study at both the MA and PhD levels in other Catholic universities in the United States. In all, one quarter of the chapter delegates involved in the renewal effort between 1966-74 had earned advanced degrees in theology.

Not only for these women, but for all religious women, educational opportunities had opened up significantly in the 1950's and 1960's. Under the influence of the Sister Formation Movement and the pressure of state certification requirements, communities regularly provided baccalaureate programs and encouraged advanced studies to meet the professional standards for the fields in which the sisters were already working. Communities also provided for intensive short courses, summer schools, and comparable opportunities for all sisters to be introduced to contemporary approaches to scripture, theology, liturgy, and Christian morality. It is not surprising then that, whatever their professional specializations, almost half the delegates indicate they have devoted more time to current theological reading since the start of the renewal period. Two-thirds of them indicate that they read and reflect more on scripture than they did prior to Vatican II and the challenge of renewal. Thus, while the renewal chapters from 1966-74 worked with theological consultants who provided a touchstone for testing new understandings and formulations of the Benedictine vision of gospel life, the group developed no overdependence on its outside consultants. In fact, almost three-quarters of the delegates express a high degree of confidence that there was theological and scriptural competence within the group of elected chapter delegates who had undertaken the work of renewal.

Permanent Changes

At one level, nothing had changed, and at another level nothing would ever be quite the same in the lives of American Benedictine sisters after the post-conciliar renewal period. Nothing had changed: the sisters still found their basic identity in relation to the universal church focused in Rome, and so they undertook renewal in response to the direct mandate of the Roman church. Yet nothing would ever be quite the same: having been told by the church in council to assume authority for interpreting their own lives within their distinctive tradition and in accordance with the needs of their own members, the sisters would no longer take official ecclesiastical definitions and the expectations of churchmen as the only norm for development in Benedictine community life.

Benedictine women in the United States have entered decisively into the culture of modernity. A basic intuition of this culture is an awareness of the historicity of nature, of humanity, and of human institutions.[19] Among its characteristics is the prominence given to critical reflection on the past and present as the means to personal and corporate freedom. The Roman Catholic church publicly incorporated this culture of modernity into its self-understanding during the Second Vatican Council. It took less than a decade for Benedictine Sisters in the Federation of St. Scholastica to reorient their own lives publicly in this culture. They did not simply adopt whatever the modern world had to offer, a response that would be highly uncritical. Rather, they began their own work of critical reflection to explore the forms Benedictine life for women might have to take to retain the vision of the gospel, the wisdom of the Rule of Benedict, and their own distinct heritage, while acknowledging also that these were to be expressed in a world which was indeed American—*"moderne, individualiste, democratique"* in the words of the 19th century critics of emerging American Catholicism.

What the chapter delegates did with these cultural tendencies is significant. In their adaptation of Benedictine life for the educated American women they had become, they reaffirmed distinctive values of the Catholic and monastic heritage in decidedly new ways. The larger Roman Catholic theological and institutional developments which made these adaptations possible and even necessary are the subject of the remainder of this chapter.

The rapidly emerging American character of the communities of the Federation of St. Scholastica is undoubtedly traceable to the circumstances of their century-long role in Catholic schools more than to any other factor. Had American Benedictine women not been numbered among the school sisters on whom new professional demands were placed by the American church in the American society in the third quarter of the 20th century, they might not have been so ready academically for critical exploration of their lives as they were. But, because of their responsiveness to the local church's educational needs for more than a century they were themselves educated, confident, reflective and questioning, and capable of organizing and effecting a corporate undertaking.[20] Twenty years of strong emphasis on professional and theological education for sisters has only begun to have its impact on religious life for American Benedictine women who are part of the Catholic church in the modern world.

THEOLOGICAL ISSUES IN RENEWAL: 1966-1974

It was noted earlier that six central theological themes recurred during the course of the renewal chapters of the Federation of St. Scholastica, namely, the nature of the church, religious authority, religious life, the person, community, and eschatology. Each of these themes had figured in the theological foundations of the Vatican Council itself, and so each was an inevitable topic for consideration by a renewal chapter. Thus, despite the fact that communities of religious were directed to give their attention specifically to chapters five and six of *Lumen Gentium*, the dogmatic constitution of the church as the theological basis for their renewal efforts, critical reading showed that those two chapters of a single document could not stand by themselves.[21] In the successive treatment of the topics of the universal call to holiness and the theology of religious life, *Lumen Gentium* had juxtaposed traditional teachings with contemporary theological developments, and these were in tension at times.

This key section of *Lumen Gentium* and its implications could be understood only by enlarging the base of inquiry. What was said about holiness and religious life had to be understood as part of the dogmatic constitution on the church itself. And that dogmatic constitution had to be read in relation to the pastoral constitution on the church in the modern world. Many new questions were raised through these companion texts. At some points the documents apparently confirmed the life experiences of the delegates. At other points, the perspectives set forward for religious life were out of touch with that experience, so the subsequent cause of developments seemed to indicate. It is appropriate to consider, then, how the chapter delegates took up and responded to the themes and the theses of the conciliar texts about the place of religious within the church. What is at issue is the understanding of church which prevailed in the deliberations and in the results of the renewal chapters of the Federation of St. Scholastica.

Ecclesiology—The Nature of the Church

The dogmatic constitution *Lumen Gentium* explored two basic ecclesiological issues. First, it identified what unites all those who belong to the church of Jesus Christ, prior to any distinctions among them. Secondly, it considered what distinctions must be valued, sanctioned, and protected because they are believed to be gifts of the Holy Spirit necessary for the life of the church.

The first concern was that of unity. The oneness of the church was said to be a reflection of the trinitarian mystery at the heart of the church's life. This mystery points to a unity among the baptized which, paradoxically, demands diversity in order to reflect the relation of the Creator and Word united in and through the Holy Spirit. In the words of the document, citing age-old tradition, "the universal church is seen to be a people brought into unity from the unity of the Father, the Son, and the Holy Spirit."[22] Theologians were exploring this aspect of the church's nature by speaking of the-church-as-communion.

The second concern was that of distinctions among the baptized. These were said to be of two kinds, each of them to be affirmed and maintained. On the one hand, the Spirit, the bond of unity, was said to give some of the baptized special gifts for mediating Word and Sacrament in the service of the community. These gifts produced the structures or hierarchical aspects of church life. On the other hand, that same Spirit also pours out additional gifts to give vitality and spontaneity, creating the dynamic or charismatic dimension of church life. This church is thus constituted as ordered, yet dynamic.

The affirmation and exploration of both of these dimensions of the church signaled a distinct advance in thinking about the church, for the church was long accustomed to thinking only about structure. The reintroduction of theological consideration of the dynamic element in the church restored a balance.[23] The development was especially important for clarifying the meaning of religious life, which has never been understood as one of the essential structures of the church but always as one of the manifestations of the dynamic gifts of the Spirit.

According to the dogmatic constitution *Lumen Gentium*, each believer is understood to participate in both the structured and the charismatic dimensions of church life in some way, according to the measure of the spiritual gifts given. For instance, the whole community of those baptized into the Spirit was to be distinguished structurally into hierarchy and laity. The hierarchy were essentially and officially the mediators of the Word and the Sacrament. As mediators, they had themselves experienced the direct mediation of the church in the conferring of their office by the laying on of hands.

Historical and theological commentaries of the post-conciliar renewal period were asserting that the hierarchy's place as mediators in the church was not essentially a position of superiority. Some noted that the Greek word *hierarchē* spoke of holy origin, not of superior status, when used in a Christian context. It was a fact, nevertheless, that the coincidental similarity of sound of the English word *higher* had long reinforced the notion reflected in different behavioral expectations, that greater dignity, holiness, and personal worth resided in the mediating ministers. In popular idiom, some laity had coined the term "lower-archy" as a self-designation to reflect lesser importance and lower status in the church which characterized the laity. From within the perspective of historical scholarship at least, it was widely acknowledged that the long-standing notion of superior social status for church leaders reflected not the gospel but the influence of medieval social structures on the church, and that the notion remained as a vestige of the meeting of church and culture in an earlier era.[24] That realization had a discernible impact on the renewal process.

The American Benedictine women participating in the renewal chapter of the 1966-74 period did not claim it as their official role in the church to be mediators of the Word and Sacrament. No women held office by the custom of centuries. The appropriateness of that arrangement was not a renewal chapter issue. In accordance with the structured scheme of things, they recognized and affirmed their place among the laity as the gift of the Spirit given to them. They were called to holiness from a starting point as *laos*, the people.

Nevertheless, the dogmatic constitution specified more for their self-understanding. Not only were the baptized to be distinguished as hierarchy and laity. They were all, hierarchy and laity alike, further differentiated by the distinctive gifts of the Spirit each one received. Admittedly, it was easier to distinguish hierarchy from laity than it is to delineate the full range and the relationships of the distinctive personal gifts of the Spirit which appear in the church at any given time. Yet the Benedictine monastic charism had been recognized for more than 1400 years as a dynamic element within the church. It was this gift that the renewal chapter delegates believed they shared in common with their sisters and all other Benedictines, however diverse the past and present expressions of that charism. Yet if their own monastic charism was being expressed authentically, they knew it must be able to stand being tested against the criteria Paul had offered the Corinthians as the way of testing all spiritual gifts: there are in the end three things that last forever, faith, hope, and love, and the greatest of these is love. The question was rather: how would they express the mystery of the church—a communion, ordered and dynamic?

The renewal chapter participants began immediately to recognize and live with some of the implications of their insights, even those which were never enunciated as renewal principles in their documents. Thus, the deference to clerics formerly so characteristic of religious women was consciously set aside during the period. Only 5% of the chapter participants during 1966-74 subsequently placed high value on treating the clergy with greater respect than is generally shown to others. "Higher" and "lower" gave way to the notion of communion as the starting point for renewal thinking about the church.

More importantly, the chapter participants set aside their own claims to special privilege due to office within the community or status within the church. Before Vatican II, the custom delineated in the Rule of Benedict of observing rank according to the order of profession had deteriorated into a privilege system for older members and for local superiors and administrators, as well as for prioresses and council members. Although two-thirds of the chapter delegates held some administrative position which in the past had brought special status or the privileges of rank, only 4% of them indicated in 1976 that they still valued and would choose to maintain rank in community. The presence of distinctive gifts of mind and spirit among the sisters was being increasingly valued. But such gifts no longer seemed to warrant the designation of special status in the group. Furthermore, many of these same sisters also divested themselves of distinctive religious garb as a way of dealing with the compromising influence of special privileges and status accorded sisters many places in both church and society.

Having come to recognize the meaning of the profound unity of the church membership and their own distinctive place among the baptized laity, the sisters nevertheless had to clarify this very issue of their distinctiveness. What did it mean to be laity who were also called to be bearers of the Benedictine monastic charism in the church? Thus the chapter delegates made a commitment to undertake a critical study of their own Benedictine lives and heritage. The results of that six-year inquiry into the Benedictine charism are the subject of the fourth section of this work, "This Is the Crux of the Problem."

Religious Authority

The second profound gain in self-understanding which came directly from studying the theological perspectives of *Lumen Gentium* related to the nature of religious authority. The new understanding of religious authority which grew up in the Federation of St. Scholastica built upon the deepened awareness of the church as a communion. It was strengthened by the recognition that each sister herself and all the sisters together in community had distinctive spiritual gifts vital to the life of the church. Suppression of these from any quarter would constitute radical unfaithfulness to the Holy Spirit. Not only was such suppression not the post-conciliar church's intent, but religious were now being asked to recover and augment the dynamic and vital aspects of their Christian and Benedictine callings.[25]

Still the rediscovery of the source of religious authority in the diverse gift of the Spirit posed a set of questions: what kind of authority resided in religious communities? what structures of community government were called for to express this authority? how would these structures relate to the authority and structures of government within the ecclesiastical institution?

The language of the 1965 dogmatic constitution retained heavy overtones of the legalism and juridicism which had absolutized hierarchical authority. By contrast, the implications of the communion theme were underdeveloped. For example, in chapter three of *Lumen Gentium* the bishops' spiritual gift of leadership and mediation of Word and Sacrament was described in terms of monarchical authority and sacred power, in virtue of which bishops have "a sacred right and duty before the Lord of legislating for and passing judgment on their subjects. . . ."[26]

Taken in isolation this language seemed to leave little place for any spiritual authority outside the hierarchy, let alone for participatory structures of government at any level in the church. Yet in the chapter on religious life, a better balance appeared. The text affirmed the necessity of hierarchical wisdom and of docility to the Holy Spirit when responding to religious institutes. But at the same time the document still seemed to presume that in every case the hierarchy could and must improve upon the way of life proposed by the founders and leaders of religious communities. It stated:

> . . . in docile response to the promptings of the Holy Spirit the hierarchy accepts rules of religious life which are presented for its approval by outstanding men and women, improves them further, and then officially authorizes them.[27]

The renewal chapter participants clearly had no authority to deal directly with the juridicism and authoritarianism retained in *Lumen Gentium*. However, they had been authorized to undertake their own renewal. They could reflect upon the implications of maintaining authoritarian and juridical approaches to government in their own communities and in their federation. They could explore the more fundamental mystery of communion.

Not surprisingly, in the years between Vatican I and Vatican II those same qualities of juridicism, authoritarianism, and absolutism had generally pervaded the understanding and exercise of authority within the houses of Benedictine women: someone designated superior was understood to have a God-given right and duty to legislate for and to judge subjects. By the end of the renewal period, the understanding of authority within communities and in the federation had been modified significantly through reintegration of the doctrine of the Holy Spirit as the foundation for all structures of community government and all exercise of authority.

Thus, the theological statement on authority in the 1974 federation constitution *Call to Life* declared:

> The source and foundation of authority in a Benedictine community is the Spirit . . . . the authority of a Benedictine community is present in the community itself, but expressed and exercised principally through the prioress.[28]

The text further designated the complementary roles of the prioress and the community members in the exercise of authority. The prioress was not to be considered superior to the members. She was rather a focus of unity within a community of more or less spiritually gifted Christian women:

> The most important and fundamental service of the prioress to her community is to unite them through Christ in His Spirit. . . .[29]

All the members, for their part, were seen to have a proper share in the authority of the community. Without their participation it was believed that the authority of the Benedictine community is diminished:

> . . . authority is actualized to its fullest potential when each sister assumes her responsibility to be attentive to the Spirit and share with the prioress and community the insight she has discerned as they deliberate together concerning matters of importance to the community.[30]

In summary, the text acknowledged that structures of government which reflected this spiritual authority hardly were devised for the sake of efficiency. The purpose of new governance structures was "to give recognition to the ecclesial nature of the community where all the sisters are united in Christ around the prioress and are free to bear witness of the gifts of His Spirit through the monastic charism."[31]

In the years leading to the writing of the new constitution of the Federation of St. Scholastica, the exercise of new forms of shared authority based on the doctrine of the church as a communion in the Word and the Holy Spirit was actively cultivated by the chapter participants and the member communities of the federation. The impact of this development was beginning to be evident at the close of a decade. For example, as awareness of spiritual authority within the community increased, community life gained a depth dimension. Thus, in 1976 four-fifths of those who were chapter delegates indicated that they make continued effort to elicit the insights of their sisters in matters concerning community life. Two-thirds of them looked to their sisters for possible wisdom concerning forms of service in church and society, and two-thirds also found more occasion to share their own spiritual insights with others informally. Nevertheless, almost half of these same women identified as one of their own continuing or growing concerns the persistence of the older environment which the superior-subject relationship had fostered. Clearly, a lifetime of functioning within monarchical structures of government was not to be overcome quickly, either by those who were expected to govern or those who were expected to obey. Yet the new experiences growing from a renewed theology of religious authority may prove to be the environmental watershed for spiritual adulthood for Benedictine women's communities.

The decade of experience with the cultivation of new patterns of authority had external as well as internal consequences for expectations about governance. Having explored and affirmed the authenticity of shared authority and spiritual discernment in their Benedictine communities, the group subsequently manifested a conviction that this mode of authority and governance should also extend to their ties with the ecclesiastical institution. These formal relationships are two: through the Federation of St. Scholastica and with the Sacred Congregation for Religious.

The delegates were clear about their desire for participatory structures of authority in their own federation. Maintaining the internal autonomy of member houses of the federation was repeatedly affirmed as a desired norm. In fact, four-fifths of the chapter participants concurred that this corporate autonomy has been a vital issue for them, for their communities, and for the chapter itself during the renewal period. In their new constitution they unanimously assented to the description of the federation as "a union of autonomous priories which are related essentially to the universal church, but juridically and practically to the Federation." They went on to say with complete unanimity, that in areas beyond those which must be determined juridically, "the authority of the Federation" in local priories "is that of moral suasion."[32]

Furthermore, even as they were preparing to submit their 1974 federation constitutions for approval to the Roman Sacred Congregation for Religious, less than a third of the renewal chapter participants were willing to endorse without some further qualification the notion that the Holy See alone has the right, through that Roman Congregation, to interpret the norms of religious life for the universal church and within each diocese. In the renewal process sisters had learned to be interpreters of their own law and tradition. They had seen and lived with the consequences of the 1922 decisions in which they had not shared. As a result, confidence had grown dramatically, not only in the authority of their own experience, but also in their sense of obligation to participate in shaping the church's understanding of religious life. The confidence and sense of obligation was not abstract and general. It related to specific issues concerning the Benedictine way as a distinctive form of religious life. The sisters of the Federation of St. Scholastica had discovered that they had something to say as well as to learn in the process of church renewal. In 1976 at the end of the first renewal decade, almost nine out of ten expressed strong conviction that as chapter delegates they were competent to take positions and make decisions affecting their own lives in the church.

In the course of the renewal process it had become increasingly clear that government at any level in the church which was based on a simple dynamic of coercion by leadership and submission by membership was to be rejected as incompatible with the authority of the Spirit. Genuine religious authority was shared by all who were empowered by the Spirit. Adequate community, federation, and ecclesiastical structures would need to provide ways to gather, discriminate, order, and unify whatever wisdom was in the ecclesial community. Although the decree *Perfectae Caritatis* had continued to restate a traditional ecclesiastical superior-subject model for governance in religious communities, the search for a renewed understanding and exercise of religious authority went well beyond that model in the Federation of St. Scholastica, to a search for communion.

Religious Life

The development of more adequate modes of religious government based on a more profound understanding of the doctrines of the living Word and the Holy Spirit was a major gain for American Benedictine women in the renewal period. Yet as they came to a fuller understanding of the nature of the religious authority in which they shared, they also had to find or to formulate for themselves theological language adequate to their experience of Benedictine life as gospel life. The official ecclesiastical language describing religious life found in the dogmatic constitution on the church and *Perfectae Caritatis* was the starting point for inquiry. Yet the repetition there of quite conventional declarations on the nature of religious life and on monasticism generated sufficient dissatisfaction to cause the chapter participants to inquire further. If new theological understandings of religious authority and government were potentially so important to the renewal of Catholic Christianity generally, could the conventional definitions of religious life and monasticism just stand without any investigation?

For example, the section on monastic life in *Perfectae Caritatis* had opened with a statement which reflected juridical definitions of monasticism, but which in fact impoverished, diminished, and distorted the historical reality of Benedictine life. The document declared:

> The principal duty of monks is to present to the divine majesty a service at once humble and noble within the walls of the monastery. This is true whether they dedicate themselves entirely to divine worship in the contemplative life, or have legitimately undertaken some apostolic or charitable activity.[33]

In this description, the distinctive monastic reality would seem to be walls, since the range of monastic service was left quite open. American Benedictine women were admittedly experiencing great confusion about their distinctive identity at the start of the renewal period. Yet that statement equating the monastic life with an external environmental circumstance or its metaphorical equivalent was clearly inadequate to their experience of Benedictine vocation, regardless of its authoritative ring. They had never lived "behind the walls" in the technical juridical sense of that phrase; yet they had lived Benedictine life for more than a century.[34]

The official statement on the essential nature of religious life was also less than wholly adequate to experience. *Perfectae Caritatis* characterized all religious life as "the pursuit of perfect charity" by means of the evangelical counsels "and the profession of chastity, poverty, and obedience," restating the teaching derived from Thomas Aquinas.[35]

On a first reading, this seemed to pose no problems. Apparently it had posed none for the council fathers. The statement simply made the ordinary vows of religious life, based on the so-called evangelical counsels, the heart of the religious life. Yet it overlooked the fact that religious life had existed in the church for centuries before the appearace in the 12th century of the first formulas of religious profession according to that particular triad: poverty, chastity, and obedience. The 6th century Rule of Benedict had presented the monastic life as the commitment to "seek God," a commitment which was to be sealed by a public promise in the community oratory of stability in the community, reformation of life according to the monastic observance, and obedience.[36] These orientations were unconsciously presumed to be identical. But were they?

The question was not merely theoretical. The archives of houses of American Benedictine women show that the sisters had been professing five vows for parts of their history, four vows at other times, and three vows in some eras. Was a formula of Benedictine profession in fact arbitrary? The vows formulas had generally contained the three promises specified in the Rule, with or without the two explicitly stipulated by church law since the later medieval period.[37] The text of the 1922 Declarations and Constitutions of the Congregation of St. Scholastica attributed to the authority of Pope Gregory IX (1227-1241) the requirement that the Benedictine profession formula be amplified by the teaching of the early scholastics about the essential nature of religious life.[38] In fact, that account oversimplifies eight centuries of history. Benedictine monks and nuns of the 13th century were not required to adopt the later vow formulas of the newer orders. Then and in subsequent centuries they were allowed to honor their own tradition concerning the vows pronounced in their act of religious commitment. Only in the late 19th and early 20th centuries did these new developments occur for Benedictines. Furthermore, among American Benedictines, women alone were singled out as obligated by new legislation.

The actual Gregorian reform had occurred in the context of the decline in monastic observance in the late medieval church because of social and political circumstances. The period of monastic decline had coincided with the rapid rise of the new orders, particularly the Dominicans and Franciscans. Widespread in the reform orientation of the 12th and 13th century church was the expectation that any new religious, unlike the many decadent monks who had preceded them, should clearly have nothing of their own, should be celibate, and should be under ecclesiastical authority. To this end, all religious institutes newly approved by the church were to make explicit public vows of poverty, chastity, and obedience as the expression of commitment to evangelical perfection in this life.

At least implicitly at issue in the 12th and 13th century reforms was the question whether the means proposed by the Rule of Benedict and the traditional Benedictine ways were any longer sufficient of themselves to support evangelical living or whether they needed to be supplemented or supplanted. Was there sufficient direction for gospel life available to someone, man or woman, who promised to seek God in a stable community whose members were committed to "loving one another with a chaste love," to regularity in the celebration of the church's liturgy, to serving each other according to the needs of each, to the study of Scripture and the wisdom of the Fathers? Was there sufficient discipline available to women and men through the practice of a spiritual craft which combined works of mercy and moderate ascetical practices and which insisted upon the daily labor of those who must support themselves as a community by their own work? Could this be accomplished under the guidance of someone elected from among them to whom they owed obedience and from whom they could expect mercy and judgment, discretion and moderation? This was the wisdom and discipline of the Rule.

Although monastic observance had unquestionably weakened, the medieval reform of Benedictine monasticism acknowledged the fundamental integrity of the tradition, reaffirmed it as an authentic form of religious life, and mandated a system of visitation within the order to insure discipline. Some monastic groups withdrew from the pressures of the society and the compromising obligations of ancient abbeys to begin again. Other groups remained where they were and set out to reform themselves from within. Enclosure legislation was a recurrent ecclesiastical means for reform and control. Only in the case of women's houses was cloister strictly enforced; only there was it maintained long after the historical circumstances which gave rise to it had passed.[39]

The medieval church then went on to develop a newer theology of religious life to articulate the self-understanding of the new religious professionals who were not monastic—canons regular and clerics regular, military orders and mendicants. The theologians of the medieval schools developed a new theology of religious life around the controlling concept of perfection. Their theological method brought together a notion about holiness or perfection in this life and a rational demonstration that the commitment to poverty, chastity, and obedience would effect that perfection.

The 12th and 13th century schoolmen drew upon the ascetical tradition which had identified as the obstacles to human perfection a triple concupiscence, namely, "the concupiscence of the flesh, the concupiscence of the eyes, and the pride of life." In the words of the greatest of the schoolmen, Thomas Aquinas, who cited the authority of 1 John 2:16, "All worldly objects may be reduced to three types, honours, riches, and sensual pleasures." But "religious bind themselves by vow to abstain from worldly things which they could lawfully use, in order to dedicate themselves more freely to God, and this constitutes perfection in the present life."[40]

According to the schoolmen, such perfection called for two levels of renunciation: 1) negating everything incompatible with the love of God, that is, renouncing all sin; and in addition, 2) rejecting whatever would prevent the soul from being directed totally to God—namely, honors, possessions, and pleasure. In their analysis, there was no practical need to demonstrate that in every case these goods were impeding the search for God. What was more fundamental was the rational demonstration that human esteem, ties of human intimacy, and possessions were the prospective obstacles. This being the case, a commitment to holiness in this life would logically demand the triple renunciation and also a detailed program of asceticism to counter any natural attraction to these goods.[41] With the pursuit of a rigorous kind of logic, in later centuries, it became possible to reduce religious life to a series of negations, and so to overlook in the pursuit of perfect charity narrowly defined the simpler truth of the New Testament that the one who claims to love God and does not love his neighbor is a liar.[42]

As Thomas' stature grew after his death, this teaching about religious life as the pursuit of perfect charity through a triple renunciation became at first common teaching and then the normative tradition, dominating all church thought and discipline. Yet a brief comparison of the earlier Benedictine monastic tradition with the scholastic theology of religious life is instructive, for there are distinctive orientations within each.

In the monastic tradition, having nothing of one's own and holding all things in common was an outcome of the desire to imitate the apostolic community which the Acts of the Apostles (2:44-45) characterized by the words: "Those who believed held all things in common; they would sell their property and goods, dividing everything on the basis of each one's needs." Having no property of one's own was implied in the cenobitic monastic commitment, because the monk had become a member of a community. But poverty itself was not the direct object of a vow as a means of perfection in this life. Corporate stewardship of goods was the challenge to Benedictines, rather than an individualist asceticism of divestment and dependence characteristic of scholastic thought.

Likewise, in the earliest tradition, the commitment to celibate life was not understood to originate from an abstract desire for perfection in this life. In fact, the Rule of Benedict does not call for a vow of celibacy at all, but a promise to be faithful to the monastic profession. That profession grew from the Pauline notions of single-mindedness and availability for the Lord.[43] For Paul, celibacy was not an ascetic means to perfection in this life, but an eschatological gift of the Spirit calling some Christians to live solely in view of the Lord's coming kingdom.

Benedict's reform of monasticism "for beginners" set this celibate monastic life in the context of a community which would provide human structures of support. The cenobitic celibate, one who lived an ordered life of prayer and work and service in a stable community, would in the long run be "the strongest kind of monk." Community life would direct its members to a balance of mundane and transcendent concerns, "doing now what will profit for eternity," while avoiding overwhelming loneliness and overwhelming busyness.[44] Monastic celibacy was a gift and an invitation, not the object of a vow. It was, nevertheless, intrinsic to a vocation to seek God according to the monastic profession.

In monastic spirituality, poverty and chastity were not themselves objects of choice, but consequences of the central cenobitic promises: obedience, stability, and conversion of life. The oldest monastic tradition had founded religious obedience in lifelong listening to the call of God in the living Word. Benedictine monasticism incorporated some rudders into this tradition of listening to the living Word. First among these was the mediating influence of the Rule itself. Next, the spiritual wisdom of the past and the present was held up, as this wisdom was available through the church fathers, the community members, and the abbot. The last, focuser of the Word, was said to hold the place of Christ, the living Word, in the community.[45] Obedience was the object of a public promise in the monastic tradition, not as an absolute commitment to an ecclesiastical institution, but as an expression of the monastic way of seeking God, by listening and responding. This vocation the church had approved as good.

Stability, "persevering in the monastery until death," was made the object of a promise to assume the long-term discipline of the monastic quest in the company of similarly committed persons. The promise of conversion to the monastic way of life served to confirm the intention and strengthen the dedication of the monk to use the means for growth in Christ available within the tradition. Thus, the distinctive emphases in Benedictine monasticism—obedience, stability, conversion—fall not upon the pursuit of personal perfection in this life through an asceticism which renounces. The means it provides for religious transformation center rather on listening to the living Word supported by the discipline of a stable community, a Rule, and an abbot.

It is a matter of record in the story of the Federation of St. Scholastica that American Benedictine women's monastic identity and vitality had been eroded by rigid interpretation of law and inappropriate extension of scholastic teaching. The preliminary approval of the first constitution of the body was delayed from 1909 to 1922 in a dispute over secondary issues of category and definition based on legal distinctions.[46] These issues were clear enough. Monastic groups, monks and nuns, were defined in terms of the companion juridical elements of papal enclosure and solemn vows in the 1917 codification of church law. Exceptions to the observance of enclosure could be made in the case of male monasteries; no such exceptions were accorded monasteries of women, even at the turn of the 20th century.

Because of the logic of the law, which treated women as special cases, American Benedictine women faced an institutional impasse. Unless they were enclosed and under total ecclesiastical supervision in their lives and so qualified technically as nuns, they were not authorized to make solemn vows.[47] On the contrary because of the cultural inability to meet this requirement of enclosure, they were forced to greater autonomy, despite their desire to be nuns. Yet the consequences of the situation were not totally advantageous. For unless they were authorized to make solemn vows, they could not, by juridical stipulation, make the triple promise of obedience, stability, and conversion of life within the monastic community which is the distinctive Benedictine way. Unenclosed American Benedictine women making simple vows by Roman mandate since 1859 were technically "sisters," and so could only profess the vows of poverty, chastity, and obedience authorized for sisters according to the 1901 norms and the 1917 code of canon law. By the force of definitions imposed on them, yet alien to their experience, they were in danger of forfeiting their Benedictine identity.

The communities were rescued from this early entanglement in a web of juridical stipulations and secondary distinctions by the concern of a cardinal protector, Adrian Gasquet, O.S.B., who intervened to see that they were approved as unique monasteries of women, Benedictines who were not nuns but sisters. As sisters they would profess poverty, chastity, and obedience according to the law. As Benedictines they would vow obedience, stability, and conversion of life according to their heritage.[48] Two traditions and two spiritualities were thus joined to maintain the distinctions of the law. As the fourth major section of this study shows, that action was the greatest source of confused identity with which the renewal chapter delegates had to struggle.

Another act of negotiation and juridical compromise effected during these first efforts to federate also added to the confused sense of Benedictine identity. Roman authorities had asked these unique monasteries of women to designate which specific apostolic works they would undertake, after the juridical requirements for active orders of sisters. To honor this requirement, Benedictine sisters of the Congregation of St. Scholastica officially became teachers for Catholic schools, not because of any inner necessity of the Benedictine vocation nor because of any identification and continuity with the reputed greatness of medieval Benedictine scholarship or education. They designated themselves teachers because the circumstances of their first 50 years in the immigrant American church had directed them to this work.[49]

It should be no surprise, given the legalistic accretions of centuries and the immediate past history of negotiation and compromise that confused identity regarding Benedictine monasticism was a major problem at the beginning of the renewal period. Nevertheless, the wisdom that directed institutes to assume the main responsibility for their own renewal and adaptation yielded results in a short time.[50] In the self-sorting process undertaken by the Benedictine sisters of the Federation of St. Scholastica, two movements are evident. The first was a movement toward clearer affirmation of the core elements of the Rule of Benedict, the living Word, and the community as the means to seeking God. The second was a movement away from an understanding that they were essentially sisters who had a specific apostolic work of school education entrusted to them by the church and to be performed in its name.

The results of the first movement toward identifying the living Word and the community as the core elements of monasticism can be seen in the subsequent thinking of chapter delegates about the essential nature of religious life. In 1976, two-thirds of them rejected outright the perfectionist understanding of religious life as a call to special holiness expressed through special vows of religion. Correspondingly, three-fifths of them found fully adequate the judgment that religious life is simply one form of gospel life.

Nevertheless, three-fourths of them also said that their religious life was a way distinguished from other forms of Christian life. Specifically, they lived in community, and as a community they owed obedience to their elected superior. Further, as a community, they celebrated a regular program of liturgical prayer. More than nine out of ten concurred that the Benedictine community would be celibate and that its members will be dedicated to the service of God's people. The resurgence of the elements of Benedictine monastic identity was clear. Just as clear was the persistent commitment to the ministerial dimension of Christian life which has characterized American Benedictinism.

The sisters engaged in renewal work did not presume to write a comprehensive theology of religious life which recognized different emphases in monastic and active orientations. No one has yet undertaken that contemporary work. It may in fact be premature for anyone to try it. Theology arises from critical reflection on the lived faith of the church. In this first decade after Vatican II, the many corporate stories which will give rise to a new theology of religious life are only slowly unfolding. However, through the effort expended in the renewal period to get their own story straight, twenty-two houses of American Benedictine women have begun to rediscover and to adapt "their ancient beneficent traditions" to present day needs so that their communities might "carry in themselves the seeds of the growth of the Christian people. . . ."[51]

Three such seeds from the monastic heritage which beg to be broadcast in contemporary society were uncovered in the harrowing and winnowing of the decade. These seeds for future growth correspond to major areas of concern set out in *Gaudium et Spes*, the pastoral constitution on the church in the modern world: the meaning and dignity of the person, the meaning of community, and the meaning of mundane existence in the world.[52]

Person

The meaning and dignity of the person was a central renewal issue in houses of American Benedictine women. The notion that "persons are to be preferred over institutions" was raised to the level of principal in much renewal discussion. The recurrence of the theme signaled distress within Benedictine community life as it was being lived before the onset of the renewal period. Many members of American Benedictine communities were themselves numbered among the moderns who even as religious prized freedom as a sign of God's life in them and who wished to come to a fuller understanding of the mystery of that freedom in Christ.[53]

Neither before nor after the Second Vatican Council had the vowed life existed solely to provide an ecclesiastical labor force. The various forms of vowed life existed, were affirmed by the members of religious communities themselves, and were approved by the church because each was a recognized means to the valued goal of personal holiness. For the Christian, that holiness meant transformation to the likeness of Christ.

The 1922 Declarations on the Rule of St. Benedict, according to which all the 1966-74 chapter delegates had made religious profession, had specified the goal of holiness in its opening sentence:

> The Sisters of the Congregation of St. Scholastica have as their object, first, their personal sanctification, by means of the observance of the vows, according to the Rule of St. Benedict. . . .[54]

Renewal was possible as it became clearer that the concept of personal sanctification does not have a timeless, self-evident meaning, even among Catholic Christians.

Meanings do not persist simply through the repetition of familiar language. Some particular understanding of Christ and some particular theology of person and personal relatedness to God is always operating behind the talk of personal sanctification through Christ likeness. It is important, therefore, to look at the Christological imagery and the theological understanding of person and personal sanctification which were put forward in the pre-conciliar era of American Benedictine life for women, to see what changes these concepts underwent during the renewal period, and to note the forces that contributed to the change. Eras of spirituality are always marked by a selectivity of emphasis which is powerful because of what is affirmed, but liable to criticism in a later age for what is omitted or left unexamined in the selection.

The prominence of persons within the Benedictine community has always been affirmed historically. The suitable selection and formation of members has always been central to community life. In the words of the 1922 Declarations:

> Let it not be forgotten that the success or ruin of a religious institute depends to a great extent upon the manner in which its Novices are chosen, instructed, and trained. . . .[55]

One of the purposes of the novitiate year was to test the character of the woman and the strength of her resolution to live religious life through a program of curbing passions and acquiring virtue.[56] What passions were to be controlled and what virtues were to be acquired can be determined from what is praised and what is repudiated in the full text of the Declarations.

Two images of Christ were offered to the sisters in the 1922 Declarations. One was the suffering Christ of Calvary. The second was the "most loveable Spouse of the Eucharist."[57] Both images were part of a venerable tradition of Christian spirituality. In the particular form in which they occur in this document, they reflect a narrowness characteristic of nineteenth century middle class domestic sensibility and domestic piety. Personal affirmation of women was not prized as part of the program of formation. Yet such an omission was quite in harmony with the general cultural and religious attitudes of the era.

On the one hand, faithful imitation by religious women of the suffering Christ was said to call for the cultivation of the most passive manifestations of humility, docility, and obedience. On the other hand, personal communion with the risen Christ set out in the spouse image was to show itself in cultivation of domestic virtues by the sisters. The well-formed Benedictine women presented in the 1922 Declarations was dependent, grave, sober, frugal, urbane, and reserved. All of these are quite obviously the marks of a model wife by some cultural standards. It is not so clear that they are the expression of holiness gained through profound mystical communion with the risen and glorified Lord.

Many young women coming to novitiates before the renewal era had reason to question this spirituality. To offset doubts about the ultimate validity of this as the way to transformation in Christ, the religious woman was advised by the 1922 Declarations to show to the religious superior the reverence, loyalty, affection, simplicity, and candor of a child toward her mother. The religious superior in turn was instructed about her role:

> Like a mother in a household, she will vigilantly and with maternal solicitude provide for the Sisters' wants, both temporal and spiritual. . . .[58]

The fostering of the appropriate religious spirit in young women regularly began with the development of this dependency relationship.

The passions to be curbed on the way to acquiring religious perfection were the inverse of these recommended virtues. Self-expression was not a suitable characteristic of the woman who was faithfully imitating the suffering Christ or who was beloved by him. According to the 1922 Declarations, a sister was considered to be growing toward perfection to the degree that she was able to restrain her speech, so that in speaking she was never "ill-tempered or bitter," never "forward," and never "personal." Her thinking was to be restrained; she was to learn to be submissive and even to repudiate her own judgments. Her feelings, like her ideas, were to be controlled. The religious woman acquiring perfection was to move away from everything sensual, learning to live even without friendship. In all of this, endurance was called for in imitation of Christ who was faithful to the end.[59]

What is notable in the document is the way the gospel calls to risk faith, hope, and love in the spirit of Christ Jesus had been seriously diminished and the strength of the Benedictine way of life weakened. The monastic quest to seek God and so to come to a true understanding of oneself had been replaced by ecclesiastical standardization of appropriate religious behavior for women.

Two cultural factors which contributed to this deterioration of Benedictine spirituality can be identified. The first is the philosophical dualism that has permeated western religious thought and so also Catholic spirituality almost from its beginnings and which has at times worked havoc with them. A dualistic spirituality clearly dictated the understanding of human perfection and the means to it which controlled the 1922 Declarations. The second factor, derived from the first, is the understanding of woman's place in this dualistic scheme of things.

Classical western dualism not only recognized the presence of spiritual and material elements in the world of experience. It made value judgments about them, in most forms equating things spiritual and impermeable with the good and alternately calling matter and changeability evil. In this tradition, the personal religious quest was regularly depicted as an individualistic combat between the spiritual and carnal elements of the human person. Theoretically, religious perfection was achieved when the spiritual element of personality equated solely with rationality finally dominated, and the carnal element equated with emotion and sensation had been subdued.

If women were to undertake the quest for perfection, a handicap factor had to be introduced, for a series of mental transpositions and equations in philosophical dualism had generated a bias giving the male the advantage in the spiritual life. This advantage was presumed to exist because dualism said that natural dominance of rationality in the male was one of the structures of reality. By contrast, the female was fundamentally disadvantaged for the pursuit of perfection because sensation and emotion were of the essence of woman's nature. These could only be subdued by rigorous discipline, if at all. Hence, there was stricter regulation and closer supervision by churchmen of the lives of women who presumed to undertake the pursuit of perfection.

Other serious consequences for women religious flowed from this kind of dualistic male/female worldview. For example, the assumption prevailed that even those women with the best of intentions, women who had made religious vows with the church's approval, were ill-equipped by nature for the spiritual quest and the spiritual combat. Because of this assumption religious women's spirituality was subject to mediation, interpretation, and judgment by ordained men who were thought to be specially endowed both by nature and grace for leadership in the spiritual life.

The assumption had further consequences. The system of ecclesiastical education denied presumably ill-equipped women access to advanced study of either theology or church law. So it was inevitable that women were unable to reflect in a disciplined way on their own spiritual experience. The ecclesiastically supervised cloister and the ensuing cloister mentality of religious women was the certain outcome of this orientation to personal perfection, to the nature of the human person, and to the persons of women.

The attitudes toward women generated patterns of church life which were guaranteed to make the assumptions self-fulfilling prophecies. The doctrines that male and female were created alike in the image of God and that all Christians had been baptized into the one same Spirit were effectively eclipsed for centuries by the cultural prejudice of male superiority.[60]

The Vatican II Council mandate to religious women to renew themselves undermined the passive spiritual posture that churchmen had so long inculcated in women's communities and that religious women themselves had cultivated. The sisters of the Federation of St. Scholastica were American women educated in American schools and working within American educational institutions. Even if many of them were initially reluctant to take responsibility directly for religious renewal, they were already predisposed culturally to organize themselves for group reflection and problem-solving. In order to undertake the work of renewal within the church, the passivity, dependence, and childlike manner idealized in the past had to be set aside. The community-elected leadership proved itself capable of doing this quite promptly. In the process, it put into question much of the centuries-old orientation to Christian spirituality for women and women religious.

Despite their formation to be restrained in what they felt, what they thought, and what they expressed, the renewal chapter participants experienced their own competence to evaluate ideas, feelings, and institutional forms and to articulate their emerging vision. At the close of the first decade of council-mandated institutional and spiritual renewal, the women who were often reluctant initial participants were ready to assert that they had competence to make decisions regarding their own lives. Furthermore, two-thirds of them were ready to agree in 1976 that one of the consequences of the renewal process was their own increased desire for the greater autonomy of women in the church.

In the light of the other express commitments of the group to life in the church, it is clear that what is at issue for these women is not a desire to dominate or repudiate all existing authority, but to participate in its exercise. Some clearly do intend to affirm their own capacity for participating in the leadership functions of the church. Even more fundamentally, they are asserting their right to adult personhood as Christian women.

The chapter delegates had a decade of personal experience as responsible deliberators and corporate decision-makers; they had a laboratory setting to overcome personal and spiritual formation that failed to prepare them for that work. Not surprisingly, these women were almost unanimous at the end of the decade in their judgment that the matter of the personal formation of present and future community members is an important issue. Evidently new ways must yet be found to prepare women to live contemporary religious life. Time-honored notions about what constitutes holiness and about women's spiritual capacity have no hold on the future.

As the chapter delegates accepted the task of bringing themselves and their communities to greater self-awareness, to increased autonomy, and to personal responsibility within the church, they saw the need for firmer biblical and theological bases for their lives. They took up the task of reestablishing foundations with full confidence that faithfulness to the gospel and the call of the Spirit renewing the church demanded it. A new set of Christological images became part of that foundation.

The identity of the Benedictine woman had been focused through the pair of Christ-images presented in the 1922 Declarations, namely the suffering Christ of Calvary and the beloved spouse of the Eucharist. The 1974 constitution *Call to Life* which was the outcome of the renewal chapters similarly offered an understanding of Benedictine religious life as a participation in the Christ life.[61] The Christ-image set forth as a model for renewed Benedictine spirituality was consciously selective:

> In the living body which is the Church, no one person or group of persons can reflect all the richness of Jesus's personality; each one lives out one or another of his characteristics.

The text then designated the Christ-model for those American women who live today according to the Rule of Benedict. Two complementary images appear. The first specifies the God-centeredness of the person Jesus:

> Outstanding in the life of Jesus is his passion for the Father.
> . . . As with Jesus, too, our life is an ever increasing passion for the Father.

The second image sets in relief the human relatedness characteristic of Jesus:

> . . . we are . . . as was Jesus to enter compassionately into the struggles, pain, and suffering of our fellow men and women.

It is the Christ who joins rather than separates passion for God with compassion for humanity that the contemporary American Benedictine woman proposes to emulate.

Whether consciously or unconsciously, that pair of images recaptured as a starting point the directive of the fourth chapter of the Rule of Benedict. There the listing of the tools of the spiritual craft begins with the gospel call: "In the first place, to love the Lord God, with the whole heart, the whole soul, the whole strength. Then, one's neighbor as oneself."

Both the desire for communion with God and the capacity for human compassion are represented in *Call to Life* as religious attitudes which grow in the person in the measure that she is spiritually open and responsive. In the seeking of God, the follower of Jesus believes the Spirit of Jesus works in her to lead her "to become ever more detached and simple." In the ascetical process of approaching simplicity, the touch of the Holy Spirit is said to be purifying. It is the same Spirit who brings the contemporary Benedictine woman to Christ-like compassion, freeing her from her own bondage and empowering her to be concerned about the dignity and destiny of others.

The Christ-centered spirituality of the pre-conciliar and the post-conciliar versions of the declarations and constitutions of the Federation of St. Scholastica have two obvious things in common. First, both share an enduring orientation toward union with God. Second, each endorses a continuing commitment to self-surrender as a way to God. But in the post-Vatican II document there are some notable differences from the spirituality of the past. For example, in the 1974 document, the tending toward God does not have an exclusive focus in communion with the eucharistic Body of Christ. The text states:

> We know the Father's continual choice of us, especially through the Eucharist. . . . Our extended response is . . . in the *opus dei*, in *lectio divina*, and personal prayer . . . . through stewardship and hospitality.

Spiritual mediation is available in the sacrament. But the living Lord's presence is asserted also in the Word, in moments of personal interiority, in the good things of the earth, and in other persons. This dilation of spiritual focus reflects both the true breadth of the Benedictine heritage and also the general broadening of contemporary Catholic spirituality.[62]

Furthermore, in the 1974 document, suffering is not seen as a religious experience having its own inner coherence and absolute value. Rather suffering in the name of Jesus is set out in terms of compassion, that is, readiness to enter redemptively into the suffering of others in order to "assist in creating a just and compassionate society where persons can experience human dignity and be encouraged to work out their own destiny."

Other developments in the self-understanding of American Benedictine women during the renewal period are reflected in their general approach to religious life for women. First, femaleness is nowhere construed to make them a special class of Christians characterized by passivity within the church and in the society. They matter-of-factly reestablished the groundwork for personal spirituality directly on the gospel and the Rule of Benedict with the full strength of its demands. Second, although the chapter delegates would reaffirm the tradition of celibate community, they responded with total silence to the elaborate ecclesiastical tradition that made virginity the heart of identity for the woman religious—though not for the male—and the foundation for her spiritual capacity for communion with God.[63] The significance of this omission should not be underestimated in the light of the centuries' long tradition in the church. Apparently the received tradition did not have power to express the self-understanding of the group of women who produced the renewal documents. Neither did they have any sense of urgency or concern to explore the traditions as central to the renewal of Benedictine life for women.

COMMUNITY

Clearly, a distinct spiritual vision was being described in the renewal document *Call to Life*. This spirituality affirmed access to the grace of Christ in ways not limited by the structural elements of the ecclesiastical institution. A central element in this new vision of American Benedictine women was a deepened understanding of the meaning of the religious community itself. For if Benedictine community was not one of the structurally necessary aspects of the church, it was nevertheless seen to be a dynamic sign of God's saving grace. Religious community was, and was to become, a promise in microcosm of a future which went beyond the possibilities of social and political history. Perhaps it was called to go beyond the historical possibilities of the ecclesiastical institution itself. In any case, community renewal was undertaken with the hope that it might manifest in miniature the mystery of God's saving activity in the world.

The vision of community set out in the renewal document *Call to Life* was a vision of cenobitic community, not of a functional collectivity which can produce enormous amounts of work with great efficiency. Those gathered in Benedictine community were understood to share a common monastic vocation. Each had publicly committed herself to pursue for a lifetime the search for a clearer vision of God and the truth about her own human identity. Those gathered had committed themselves to Christ as the way to singlemindedness and undivided hearts. Yet they recognized that while solitude and prayer were basic components of the monastic quest, community was also essential for the Benedictine.

The premise of the cenobitic life was that the gathering of baptized adults who opened themselves daily to the living Word was already a revelatory and redemptive reality. Life within a stable community was reaffirmed as an intrinsic aspect of Benedictine vocation, for "this allows community members to know one another more intimately and enables them to enter into a dialogue of salvation in the healing ministry of reconciliation."[64]

Theological development alone did not produce this new valuation of community life among American Benedictine women. Another factor was the contemporary cultural experience. Many had learned for themselves outside community the value of interpersonal communication for growth in openness and readiness for a change of heart. Yet as earlier discussion indicated, personal freedom and a personal search for communion with God had been underdeveloped in pre-Vatican II religious life for women in favor of institutionalized responses and dependence on a superior's judgment. The development of distinctive personality and the capacity for personal relatedness had been encouraged to atrophy in the name of total religious commitment to the suffering Christ, the divine spouse of the eucharist. A critical tension had to be resolved.

Those sisters in American Benedictine communities delegated to undertake renewal, had been trained in a spiritual tradition that placed only negative religious value on personal development and interpersonal relationships. But they were also women of their own age and culture. They were no longer able to be persuaded, as 1976 research shows, that the call to Benedictine monastic life demanded total isolation and withdrawal from human contacts and personal friendships, whether inside the community or outside of it.[65] They proposed a new synthesis.

Women of their age, they were also women of faith, committed to the gospel and the Benedictine way of life. They not only saw no fundamental incompatibility between the human aspiration for personal intimacy and the call to holiness in cenobitic community; they recognized the religious meaning of both celibacy and the lifelong search for personal wholeness through interpersonal communion. Thus, they proposed to build up community life as a network of interpersonal relations, replacing an earlier form of common life dependent on uniform behaviors.

The role of the other community members and the role of the prioress were declared to be complementary in the life of the woman committed to the Benedictine monastic way. Neither could be dispensed with. Neither was absolutized. The assertion of the formative role of the religious superior is quite characteristic of all traditional theologies of religious life and certainly of the Rule of Benedict. However, the new valuation of the importance of community members for one another was a distinctive development. While the Rule of Benedict does make provision for the constructive interaction of community memberships with one another, the role of the abbot is clearly dominant. The renewal document *Call to Life* presented the prioress and the community in correlative roles, because all share the one same Spirit, each in distinctive ways. In this respect *Call to Life* both mirrored and heightened the explicit complementarity of structured office and unstructured dynamism attributed to the church in *Lumen Gentium*.

The renewal chapter participants judged community interaction to be necessary for the vitality of Benedictine monastic life:

> It is through living this stable life in community that the American Benedictine woman receives many opportunities to confront the basic question of life: "Who am I? Where am I? Whence have I come? Where am I going?"[66]

Daily life was understood to have a transforming power for those who are present and open to one another.

Call to Life also asserted the prioress' necessary role in the life of the individual sister. It did so through a description of the sister's relationship to the prioress:

> Because the members of the community are still pilgrims on their way to the Father, there exists in them a tension between what they are and what they are called to be. Hence they will always look for indications of the way to travel and will sometimes find them in the healing and reconciling ministry of the prioress.[67]

The apparent diminishment of the superior's spiritual authority—("always look . . . sometimes find")—needs to be viewed in the context of the recent history of women's religious communities. Apparently at issue, at least in part, was a rejection of the dependent spirituality of the past which too easily allowed religious to transfer responsibility for their action to another person holding office. Also at issue was a rejection of the excessively institutionalized practices of obedience in communities of religious women which at times presumed to coerce both human spirits and even the Holy Spirit. The double rejection was simultaneously an affirmation of the mystery of grace within the Christian community.

While personal conscience and responsibility were given new prominence, they were not set in opposition to religious obedience in community. The reverse was the case. *Call to Life* proposed that when each member was participating actively in the exercise of cenobitic authority and obedience, firm direction would be available to all. *Call to Life* set out a clear expectation that when a decision had been reached each sister would accept it "with a sincere effort to be open to its truth and value." The prioress, in turn, was said to lead her sisters in faithful obedience "by being a sacrament of unity in the community."[68]

Still, the 1974 renewal document *Call to Life* spoke clearly of personal responsibility for gaining maturity in Christ. It described the contemporary Benedictine woman as one who "freely chooses to participate in a conversion which is a gradual passing over from death to life." Because of the personal nature of her vocation, "she does not expect the community to assure the transformation, but only to provide the opportunities for dialogue and conversion which will prepare her for the timeless moments of encounter with the Lord."[69]

While calling for interpersonal community life, the renewal chapter participants also reaffirmed the religious power of the celibate vocation to bear witness to the resurrection, hope and promise of the coming reign of God. They injected words of realism in their directives for the formation of new members within a celibate community that affirmed the importance of personal development and interpersonal relationships.[70] Speaking of the developmental tasks of the initiate, the renewal chapter decree on formation focused first on the sister as an individual:

> She must discover whether her personal goals and gifts are consonant with those of the community. Likewise the community has to judge whether her charism is suited to life in the community and whether she has matured sufficiently to give free expression of her gifts in the service of others. . . .

The document next directed the prospective member to consider her capacity for interpersonal relationships:

> She must discover her need for intimacy and determine whether or not it is compatible with celibate life. At the same time, she must consider whether or not she is capable of expressing the degree of love and friendship that is essential to personal growth as well as to community life.

Finally, it asked her to consider the life orientation toward personal communion with God which this kind of Benedictine commitment presupposed. It acknowledged that the positive values of community life would never displace the solitary dimension of the monastic vocation:

> She must have realistic expectations of celibate community life and be able to face the fact that chaste love and faithful attention to the Lord in Scripture and prayer will at times seem to demand more of her than they immediately give back in satisfaction and assurance.

The document concluded with the observation that if the initiated reached these levels of self-understanding she would have "sufficiently internalized the values of monastic life and grown to a personal interior freedom" so that she might make and be faithful to her "permanent covenant relationship with God and with the members of her monastic community."

The impact of this orientation toward person and interpersonal relationships in renewed cenobitic community is evident in the judgments of the chapter participants about their Benedictine life since Vatican II. Almost all (97%) agree that the life is now developmental, 94% call it affirming, and 89% call it loving, while 90% continue to call it sanctifying.[71]

The renewal of community through the development of persons also resulted almost immediately in pluralism at all levels of community life. Nearly half the delegates (47%) agreed that the experience of pluralism in the United States contributed to the acceptability of diverse modes of behavior within a single community which shared common values. Yet the renewal documents these delegates produced also indicate that for them the changed orientation toward persons had its theological foundation in the mystery of the human person as the image of God. Since the central mystery of faith, the mystery of the divine trinity of persons, affirmed distinction and oneness at the heart of creation and redemption, they could risk no less.[72] Pluralistic community life ordered to the mystery of persons was not primarily a concession to the individualism of the times. It was a commitment and a risk taken in faith.

That risk has already had discernible results, according to the renewal chapter participants. Almost three-fourths of them (74%) concurred that greater respect for individuals in community has been a marked consequence of the renewal period. But 78% of them are unwilling to agree that there had been any serious disintegration of community cohesion, although for a time that may have seemed to have been the case. Apparently, beneath the divergence in behaviors within the renewing communities, the chapter delegates are aware of a fundamental and persistent commitment to the values of Benedictine life.

Pluralistic Benedictine community which shares common values and goals but honors a range of behaviors as appropriate expressions of these values is the ideal set out in *Call to Life*. Whether it can be sustained in reality over a period longer than a decade has yet to be tested. Nevertheless, the renewal document *Call to Life* proposed that the living sign of such community is an essential Christian service in a world racked by division and conflict. Therefore, it asserted as a principle of renewal that "whatever the work of ministry of its members, each priory must be aware of the fact that the central ministry of the Benedictine woman is community."[73] Living human community is a sacrament, a pledge and a foreshadowing of the reign of God. In the renewal vision of the Federation of St. Scholastica, the Benedictine charism in the church is to live out this hope.[74]

Eschatology: Ultimate Truth Foreshadowed

The prologue to the Rule of Benedict states that the cenobitic life is directed toward the reign of God. Benedictines are counseled to walk in the Lord's path by the guidance of the gospel so that they may be prepared to see him who has called them to the kingdom. They are identified as those who wish to dwell in the tent of the kingdom; and to achieve their heart's desire they are encouraged to do now what will profit them for eternity. Through perseverance in the monastery according to the Lord's teaching throughout a lifetime, they are assured that they will share in Christ's kingdom, having already shared in his suffering.

The language of the prologue is biblical. The kingdom, the tent of the kingdom, and eternal life are all symbols for human destiny in God. The biblical symbols convey a rich tradition of multiple meanings which begin in the scripture itself and extend through the whole Christian theological tradition to the documents of Vatican II. At times, for example, when the church was under the influence of Platonism or other forms of dualism, the hope for God's salvation has been confined to hope for the kingdom outside the course of human history. At other times, the hope for achieving God's redemptive purpose within history has predominated. In the American theological tradition, the social gospel movement at the beginning of the 20th century epitomized that second understanding of the kingdom as a design for the social order. Martin Luther King set the civil rights movement of the 1960's within a third horizon. In that perspective, Christians worked in history for greater justice in society, confident of God's ultimate redeeming purpose which would come as gift.

The theological issue is an ancient one. Is the kingdom not yet available, and so only a future reality for those who hope? Or is it already available and a present reality for those who believe? Or is God's reign in some way already present and yet not fully established? At the time of the origins of western monasticism, the first formulation had the greatest influence. In the theological milieu of the Second Vatican Council, the third formulation has gained in cogency. The earliest official document promulgated by the Council described the church in the language of paradox:

> . . . essentially both human and divine,
> visible but endowed with invisible realities,
> zealous in action and dedicated to contemplation,
> present in the world, but as a pilgrim,
> so constituted that in her the human is
> directed toward and subordinated to the divine,
> the visible to the invisible,
> action to contemplation,
> and the present world to that city yet to come,
> the object of our quest.[75]

The church understood itself to reveal in and through its humanity the ultimate mystery of God's presence and God's promised future.

The sense of ultimacy in religious life will predictably reflect the sense of ultimacy that prevails in the church. If the mundane world is set in radical opposition to the future kingdom, religious life's justification will be found in the desire to withdraw from the world in order to prepare more adequately for the life to come. If the awareness of the redeeming presence of God in the world gains strength, religious life invites understanding as a form of participation in that saving activity. In either case, religious life has eschatological character, since it hopes to express in this world the ultimate mystery of redemption. Renewal in the Federation of St. Scholastica had to come to terms with this issue, too, in order to "adapt its beneficient tradition" to present day needs.[76]

Cenobitic community based on the gospel and the Rule of Benedict is the oldest continuous form of religiously inspired monastic community life in western culture. Benedictine community's capacity for survival through fourteen centuries is related to two factors in its own inner logic. One is its organizational principle of autonomy for each community. The other is the injunction of the Rule to attend daily to the call of the living God: "Today, if you hear his voice, harden not your hearts."

The principle of local autonomy, when it is not interfered with, not only encourages but even forces adaptation of community life to the circumstances of its membership, its place and time. The principle of attentive listening to the living Word guarantees that every generation of Benedictines caught in an era of rapid cultural transition will have to decide how to live out the Christian mystery of which Jesus spoke. How are they to be in the world without belonging to the world? How are they to live now within the mystery of eternal life and the new creation?[77]

Religious life is by its very inspiration a commitment to a degree of social marginality because of its commitment to ultimate realities. Monasticism in its earliest forms contained a commitment to marginality in the church as well as in the society.[78] All forms of religious life past and present have publicly affirmed some values that do not prevail in other existing institutions. In essence, Christian religious communities say to their contemporaries, "The ultimate truth about human dignity and human destiny is more than you believe in and hope for." To make their point, each then lives out particular gospel values in high relief to give evidence of alternate possibilities. Religious may choose values which are world-denying and become a testimony to God's ultimate truth through a life of renunciation. They may choose to affirm and give greater depth to selected cultural values or aspirations as testimony to the belief and hope that God's future is already dawning. In every case, the selection of gospel values and the way they will be lived out is necessarily related both positively and negatively to the culture from which the community's members are drawn.

The renewal documents of the Federation of St. Scholastica designated community life itself as the central eschatological truth which Benedictines can offer to the contemporary church and society. Cenobitic community rooted in the living Word was set forth as pledge and promise that God's ultimate purpose is saving communion.

In this regard, their renewal vision offered a positive response to the cultural analysis set out in the Vatican II pastoral constitution on the church in the modern world. That pastoral statement noted that "one of the most striking features of today's world is the intense development of interpersonal relationships due in no small measure to modern technical advances." However, the text went on to say that any genuine depth to these relationships must come from respect for the full spiritual dignity of each person.[79]

Clearly not every set of communal living arrangements was adequate to the task of bearing the truth about salvation. Benedictine community could not speak hopefully about the coming reign of God if it simply mirrored the depersonalization of mass society or imitated the impersonal efficiency of mass production or minimized the spiritual capacity of women. It could be pledge and promise of God's salvation only if it could be a gathering of persons who were visibly participating together in the mystery of the world's redemption.

As a self-description, the chapter delegates wrote at the end of the renewal period:

Becoming freer ourselves through the Spirit's action, we are

thus empowered as was Jesus to enter compassionately into
the struggle of our fellow men and women.[80]

Neither the scholastic notion of religious life as a state of perfection in this life nor a 19th century understanding of it as a collectivity
whose members lived a uniform existence was adequate to speak to
the 20th century aspiration for human community. Both of these
ideas gave way during the renewal process to an understanding of
religious community as a gathering of those open to God's transforming power working in and through them for a lifetime.

The renewed vision of community itself as the saving mystery
was challenging. Intensification of each sister's personal search for
God was an immediate renewal priority if American Benedictine
women were to be communities evidently open to God's transforming
power in them individually and corporately. Evaluation of community works was a second renewal priority, apparently more susceptible
to direct decision and action—but only apparently so.

The delegates were pulled in two directions. There was need to
develop the contemplative dimension of Benedictine community life,
in order to be a group rooted in and transformed by the living Word.
There was need to be present to the struggle for peace and justice
which was so intense in American society in the renewal period from
1966-74 in order to acknowledge God's judgment of human dignity
for all.

The resolution of the tension finally came through synthesis. The
delegates proposed that Benedictine communities in the Federation of
St. Scholastica must be worshipping communities whose prayer over-
flowed into service for the creation of a more just and compassionate
society. The first manifestation of God's saving power would be their
own presence as a communion of distinct persons in a world racked
by division and conflict.[81]

Furthermore they proposed that contemplative Benedictine communion need not lead community members away from human concerns and into physical separation from society. But contemplation of
the Christian mystery could lead them to greater freedom from the
negative values of that society and readiness to bring the gospel hope
to it. They could and must be in the world but not of it.

The presumed tension between Benedictine contemplative life
and involvement in the demands of justice was finally judged to be a
false issue. Admittedly, some Benedictine communities in the past
had at times lived quite literally behind walls. But even the walls had
their own history. What was just as true was the fact that whenever
Benedictine life had thrived it had had some form of impact on the

people of the place. The problem for American Benedictine women was to determine how they might now be present to their world yet not of it. Before every other consideration, Benedictine life was rooted in the gospel of the incarnation of God in human history as a sign of hope.[82]

Formulating this renewed spiritual vision of Benedictine life as eschatological community being formed and becoming active in history was one aspect of renewal. Internalizing it and living with the implications of the vision was another. The two did not occur sequentially but concurrently during the renewal period. At the end of that decade the question remained: Could the new perspective become normative or would it exist only as an abstraction, an exercise in composition by committee?

All renewal chapter participants were asked, in 1976, to indicate whether and to what degree they had modified their own religious practices and attitudes since the beginning of the renewal period in 1966. The inquiry was directed to the matters of spiritual reading, liturgical prayer and other prayer, interaction in community, ascetical practices, and understanding of ministry.

The most obvious development in spiritual practice among the delegates is their reported new commitment to scripture as a basis for sustaining Benedictine life. More than two-thirds of the renewal chapter delegates from 1966-74 acknowledge that they have increasingly taken up scripture study and meditation. Only a quarter say their attention to scripture has not changed significantly.

The absence of a profound scriptural foundation in the lives of American Benedictine sisters up to the recent past can legitimately be inferred from the testimony of this leadership group. The impetus to return to the scripture as the source of all Christian life came most immediately from the renewal mandate of *Perfectae Caritatis*. Only subsequently did the delegates begin to speak of the centrality of biblical *lectio divina* as the heart of Benedictine life. The strong monastic tradition of *lectio divina* had been displaced by moralistic and pietistic matter written specially for sisters as a circumstance of the 19th century origins of the communities. That scriptural void in American Benedictine life reflected in a particular way the consequences of the post-Reformation prohibition of popular reading of the scripture.

The recovery of the monastic tradition of *lectio divina* during the renewal decade in the houses of American Benedictine sisters had been prepared for by the general restoration of scripture to its rightful place in Catholic Christianity by the action of Pope Pius XII as early as the 1940's and by the subsequent biblical movement within the church. An improved level of scriptural education among sisters in the 1960's contributed further to the readiness for biblical *lectio divina. Call to Life* testified to the final reintegration of this tradition into American Benedictine life for women. In the section on the formation of new members the link was reestablished between the monastic vocation, the gift of celibacy, and the readiness to be attentive to the Lord through devotion to the scripture.

A change in prayer patterns is equally significant. Four out of ten chapter participants reported that they spend more time than they had previously in personal prayer. Only 15% said they pray less than they did before the onset of renewal. Four out of ten chapter participants also reported increased participation in shared prayer groups or devotional prayer gatherings. Part of the impetus for this development of personal prayerfulness was undoubtedly the recommitment to scriptural reading and reflection. But another factor was also operating.

The daily liturgical observance for American Benedictine women had been so extensively developed in the years before Vatican II and the demands of the educational works of the communities so weighty that little time or encouragement was given to the cultivation of personal prayerfulness. It is hardly surprising then that one fifth of the sisters noted that they attend Mass less often than they did earlier. What may be more surprising in the light of the liturgical and pastoral developments of the past decade is that almost three-fourths said they attend Mass as much as before. For one thing, it was once common that teaching sisters attended both a community Mass and a school Mass daily. That was uncommon in 1976. In many places, schools and parishes no longer scheduled daily Mass. Moreover, only a few Benedictine households apart from a priory have regular chaplains assigned to celebrate Mass daily. In such cases, circumstances outside the sisters' control have contributed to changed patterns of Mass attendance. But these changed circumstances may not be the total explanation for the decline in Mass attendance among 20% of the chapter participants.

The extended theological and pastoral discussions of the 1960's on the frequency of eucharistic celebration may also have had some impact. Daily Mass attendance was no longer absolutized in the way it had been in the past for sisters. The understanding of the eucharistic orientation of Christian life has developed, so that it is no longer equated with a piety of quantitative acts. Both the quality of liturgical celebration available and the personal readiness for eucharistic worship had become determining factors for some religious women as they had for many others in the church.[83] Nevertheless, neither the theological discussion nor the pastoral developments of the decade seemed to have eroded eucharistic piety. A full 96% affirmed the choice of attending Mass when they were able; for two-thirds this choice extended to daily Mass.

The celebration of the liturgy of the hours constitutes the second aspect of the Benedictine community's daily corporate worship. Almost four-fifths of the federation chapter delegates indicated that they still participated as much as before in this corporate prayer. Since there has been an actual decrease in the number and length of scheduled liturgical assemblies daily throughout the Federation of St. Scholastica, that self-estimate invites the judgment that the participants were not calculating clock hours or numerical recurrences in making their response. It apparently refers rather to the delegates' participating in all the regularly scheduled assemblies of the community now as in the past. So only a fifth perceived themselves as attending the hours less.

A distinctive prayer pattern emerges when a composite is drawn from these data. Delegates testified to a slight but discernible decline in the frequency and duration of daily liturgical prayer within their Benedictine communities. Simultaneously, they report sizeable growth in the devotion to scripture and to personal and shared prayer. The balance emerging is undoubtedly one foundation for the judgment of a full half of the chapter delegates that they are integrating prayer into their lives more than they had previously. Only 2% express the judgment that their prayer is less integrated now.

Another foundation for the experience of greater integration of prayer and life may be the development of new ways to bring the fruits of prayer to bear on community life and ministry. Interaction in community was the third area in which questions were posed to determine how the formulation of the new spiritual vision had actually influenced the delegates' lives and how their lives had helped shape the new vision. Much had been said during the renewal about the authority of the Holy Spirit present within the community itself. Yet personal interaction among community members at all levels had clearly been minimized in pre-Vatican II religious life.

Chapter delegates were asked whether they personally had changed their approach to community interaction since the beginning of renewal. Specifically, they were asked whether they spend time getting to know the other sisters, whether they are responsive to the circumstances of other sisters' lives, whether they talk at a level of seriousness about matters of community concern, and whether they seek out the insights of other sisters concerning the community's ministry to others.

More than four-fifths indicated a noticeable growth in their readiness to hear others out on community matters. Two-thirds claimed actively to seek the counsel of community membership more than they did previously in matters related to community service to the church or the society. Seven out of ten reported that they not only spent more time in conversation with other sisters on topics related to community life, but also found themselves to be more responsive to the women with whom they lived.

The delegates also testified to another related development in their lives that warrants attention in any effort to understand the present spiritual climate in houses of American Benedictine women. American Benedictine convents have had almost no tradition for encouraging individual members to emerge as spiritual directors or counselors. Although the duties of the prioress, as these are derived from the Rule of Benedict, clearly include providing spiritual direction for the community, and although the Rule also includes provision for members with some measure of wisdom to offer spiritual counsel within the community, neither custom nor training actually encouraged the pursuit of these activities within houses of Benedictine sisters in the United States. Yet within this group of elected delegates two-thirds say that they now regularly find informal ways to share their personal spiritual insights into the Christian life. One third of the group do this spiritual sharing formally by giving retreats, conferences, and homilies.

These new levels of personal interaction within communities are in accord with the increased valuation by the sisters of themselves as bearers of the Holy Spirit. That valuation is in turn supported by the testimony of renewed commitment to liturgical prayer, personal prayer, and devotion to the scripture. Their listening to the Word of life daily and of venturing at times to speak that living Word in community seems to constitute the basic spiritual discipline of the renewing communities who hope to be evidence of God's transforming power in history. Moreover, commitment to the living Word also gave authority to other forms of asceticism.

Ascetical practice was the fourth aspect of post-conciliar spirituality among American Benedictine women for which data were sought. Two areas were singled out for inquiry: fasting and the work of reconciliation. The practice of voluntary fasting as a form of spiritual discipline has approximately the same level of endorsement in post-Vatican II life as it had in the pre-renewal period. About a quarter of the delegates say they fast more now and another quarter fast less. Two-fifths continued their earlier practice, and the remaining 10% said they have never undertaken voluntary fasting. In summary, two-thirds are positive about voluntary fasting now as before and one-third are not committed to it.

This is not completely unexpected for those in the Benedictine tradition which has always emphasized moderation in private ascetical practice. While the Rule of Benedict in one place enjoins monks to "love fasting," elsewhere special abstinence from food and drink is recommended primarily as a Lenten practice, and even this is to be done only with the approval of the abbot in order to control extremist tendencies.[84]

On the other hand, given the American cultural disposition toward overconsumption in all areas of goods, alternate explanations derived from the cultural rather than the religious heritage might well be proposed to explain the limited affirmation of fasting. To discriminate further on this point, delegates were asked to indicate to what degree fasting voluntarily "as a form of personal discipline or recollecting oneself" was essential to the religious life according to the Rule of Benedict. Almost half expressed the judgment that it had a great deal to do with Benedictine life; nearly another 40% saw it as somewhat central. But the remaining 15% said that voluntary fasting had very little or nothing at all to do with Benedictine life as gospel life.

When the matter of voluntary fasting was posed on more contemporary terms, similar perceptions were recorded. Slightly more than half concurred that "modifying eating habits in response to world hunger needs" was essential to Benedictine life. Another third saw it as somewhat related, while the remaining 12% disclaimed any essential connection.

The consistent difference of opinion is notable. It seems that neither religious renewal nor cultural critiques of American consumerism have significantly altered perceptions of and approaches to the place of fasting in Christian life for this group of Benedictine women. Fasting was affirmed—with moderation.

The Rule of Benedict also proposes forms of mortification other than prayer and fasting among the tools of the spiritual craft. The directive to make peace with one's adversary before the sun sets has always provided a basis for the spiritual discipline of reconciliation. The Rule further directs that the morning and evening offices are to close with the communal recitation of the Lord's prayer so that those who hear themselves will remember and be renewed in the covenant: Forgive as we forgive.[85]

Chapter delegates reported that they have given themselves to this discipline more actively since the onset of renewal. Two-thirds of them said that they are seeking ways "to bring about reconciliation in community affairs and in their work relationships." A comparison of the responses in these two areas shows a clear preference for the active spiritual discipline of reconciliation as an essential element of the Christian life.

The fifth and final area probed for insight into the effects of the renewal vision concerned Benedictine ministry in church and society. At the end of the renewal period, the chapter delegates had taken some clear positions about the present and future forms of their Benedictine ministry in American society. In *Call to Life* they declared:

> Whatever the work or ministry of its members, each priory must be aware of the fact that the central ministry of the Benedictine woman is community. . . .[86]

In itself, vital Christian community was prophetic of God's future and already redemptive in the present. So Benedictine community was to be so organized that its members might achieve a balance in their lives among prayer, work, ministry, and leisure.

That ministry which is an extension of the Benedictine community toward the church or larger society was also to be reconsidered. In 1976 four out of five chapter delegates said in retrospect that they had been aware throughout the decade that changing needs in contemporary society called for a reevaluation of community modes of service. They had been primarily school educators for more than a century. The continuation of that service in that form was not judged to be inevitable throughout a second century. In fact, four out of five expressed the judgment that service outside existing community or ecclesiastical institutions might provide the most dynamic way to respond to needs in a time of social and ecclesiastical transition. If few existing ecclesiastical and community institutions seemed to be reaching the victims of contemporary social neglect or to be dealing with the post-conciliar spiritual needs of the Catholic community, perhaps it was because they had been designed to counteract the neglect and to meet the spiritual conditions of previous eras. In all, 93% of the renewal chapter delegates registered their rejection of the idea that a corporate institutional apostolate under the direction of the hierarchy was the best work they might do as a community at this time.

This particular posture was an obvious expression of the recovery of their Benedictine identity. Benedictines did not exist in the church to do any specific task. They could be open to the full range of Christian ministries. The Rule of Benedict had listed among the tools of the spiritual craft the basic commitments of every Christian life: to relieve the poor, the clothe the naked, to visit the sick, to bury the dead, to help in trouble, to console the sorrowing. Undergirding all the works of mercy was the injunction "to become a stranger to the world's ways."[87] The world's ways were clear. American Benedictine women lived in a technological culture marked by profound injustice, indifference, violence, and complicity with the exploitation of the poor and the socially marginal. The call to a measure of involvement and even leadership in local efforts for human dignity could not be ignored. If they had affirmed the cultural aspiration for community, they would have to negate openly the cultural affronts to human personhood. Simultaneously, the post-conciliar effort to renew the church had created pastoral situations which called for new forms of dedication to which they must make some response.

The specific demands this emerging understanding of ministry in a new situation would make on each of the twenty-two communities and their members was not too quickly pronounced. The renewal document *Call to Life* proposed a course of action which made it both possible and necessary for the ministry to reflect the identity of the local community:

> Each priory should periodically evaluate its existing ministries to determine if they are responsible to the contemporary needs of the people of God and give adequate expression to the unique gifts of its members.[88]

No adequate evaluation and decision could be made without the participation of those who were the local Benedictines searching for God in a praying community. At the end of the decade, three out of five delegates were themselves working in self-chosen ministries, and two out of five were working outside the institutional ministries of the community, extending the impact of Benedictine life in new ways.

CONCLUSIONS

Some summary observations are in order concerning the spiritual horizon within which the renewal in the Federation of St. Scholastica is occurring.

First, central values and practices of the Benedictine tradition have been retained and even augmented: cenobitic community and authority; liturgical celebration, personal prayer, scriptural *lectio divina*; moderation in bodily asceticism and eagerness for the work of reconciliation; daily work to support themselves; service to one another and extension of the community in the service of others.

Second, the affirmation of the Holy Spirit's presence to the world through the Benedictine community and in each of its members reflects the rediscovered theology of the-church-as-communion enunciated at the Second Vatican Council.[89]

Third, the manner in which the renewing community is being ordered and authority exercised reflects the American experience of participation in group interaction. Accordingly the delegates themselves advised their communities that the structure of authority in Benedictine life is cenobitic rather than autocratic or democratic.

Fourth, the understanding of cenobitic monastic life as a saving communion which foreshadows God's plan for the world's salvation through divine communion constitutes a distinctive theological development in American Benedictine women's communities. With this development in self-understanding, American Benedictine women may have found a way to overcome the false analyses imposed on them in the past which led them to think of themselves as would-be contemplatives who had been circumstantially deprived of a cloister and so of monastic identity.

Fifth, the orientation toward Benedictine life as pledge and promise of saving communion was accompanied by preference for constructive asceticism like works of reconciliation and personal openness to others in community rather than for more passive forms of self-denial.

Sixth, those ministries of American Benedictine women beyond the ministry of community life itself were understood to draw their inspiration from the prayer of the community, from the gifts of the members, and the needs of the place, and so would predictably be diverse rather than uniform in the future.

The Federation of St. Scholastica has ventured a distinctive identity within the Benedictine tradition based on the premise that the capacity of the Benedictine institution to persist over centuries has been the vitality of its membership, "because a living institution influences and is influenced by its contemporaries."[90] One sixth of the women who helped shape these developments said that the effect of this more intense and more expansive form of Benedictine life has been unsettling for them, so that they think more often about leaving. Only 3% of the delegates have done so during the decade. Another sixth said the greater demands have had the opposite effect, so that they think less about leaving. The remaining two-thirds noted no measurable impact on their fundamental commitment to Benedictine life. These American Benedictine women who are least self-conscious about the significance of the situation they have shaped may be the best testimony to its timeliness and its adequacy, and the best indicators of its durability.

PART IV
The Development
of a
Theology of Monasticism

This essay is an historical-conceptual treatment of the development of a theology of monasticism by the Federation of St. Scholastica from 1966 to 1974. It is divided into two parts. The first deals with the theological climate in the Federation as revealed at the beginning of renewal through the 1966 General Chapter, the pre-Chapters of 1967-68, and the Opinionnaire on Benedictinism. The second is an explanation of the theology of Benedictinism developed during the Renewal Chapters of 1968-74.

The material presented in this essay is important to the understanding of renewal in the Federation because it discloses the problems and tensions in American Benedictine communities prior to renewal and explains how the Federation, in attempting to resolve them, reached a new self-understanding consonant with the Theology of Vatican II. Granted that the language used in this essay is peculiar to the monastic tradition, it would seem that the concepts underlying the explanation of the constitutive elements of monastic life explain in large part the same changes which have also occurred in other congregations.

"THIS IS THE CRUX OF THE PROBLEM"

How can we define Benedictinism in a monastic sense to include Regina Laudis, groups like ourselves here, communities like Clyde, and the two-Sister mission? This is the crux of the problem, isn't it, Mother?

I would like to suggest that perhaps an answer to this problem is as essential and fundamental to our lives as the updating of the Declarations and Constitutions. May I propose, then, the formation of a committee within the Congregation . . . which would be assigned the important task of the research and study necessary for the correct and full consideration of something so vital to our part in the life of the Church.

. . . Mother, I submit this idea to you for what it is worth. I presume to do this only because it seems to me that it is of such vital concern to our continued life in the Church that we come to know what we really are and that we have the courage to translate this knowledge into daily living.

Letter of a Delegate to the President, 1966

CLIMATE FOR RENEWAL
IN THE CONGREGATION, 1966-68

RENEWAL CHAPTERS, 1966-68

The development of a theology of Benedictine monasticism in keeping with the concepts of Vatican II began formally with the Renewal Chapter of 1968-69; however, it had originated in the General Chapter Extraordinary of 1966. The task of that Chapter was the revision of the *Declarations and Constitutions of the Congregation* which had remained essentially the same with only minor changes since their approval forty-four years earlier in 1922.

In a letter to the delegates of the General Chapter Extraordinary, Mother Mary Susan Sevier, O.S.B., the president of the Congregation of St. Scholastica, informed them that the purpose of the revision of the constitutions was to adapt the Rule of Benedict to changing times through a responsible interpretation which recognized the aims of Vatican II. She urged them to be broad and mature in their revision and to leave room for the "living voice." She then reminded them of the centrality of the Eucharist in their lives and of the need for a new concept of Benedictine liturgical contemplation.[1] At the end of the General Chapter, the delegates went home mandated to ponder with their communities the question, "What is monasticism?"

The response was immediate. Ten days later in a letter to Mother Mary Susan a delegate asked that a Committee on Benedictinism be formed within the Congregation to study how American Benedictine women can "define monasticism to include the diverse traditions" which were already a part of the experience of American Benedictine women. The delegate explained that she was making this request because she felt that this was "the crux of the problem" in the renewal of the communities in the Congregation.[2]

That request was not granted, however, because it was thought that the members of the Congregation in 1966 did not possess the theological expertise to undertake such a work.[3] Nevertheless, a seed had been planted. Eight months later in preparation for the Renewal Chapter of 1968, Mother Mary Susan suggested that each community elect as delegate "one who understands the need to reanimate the traditions of St. Benedict which are directly rooted in his Rule or have been legitimate developments" of it.[4]

As part of the preparation for the Renewal Chapter of 1968-69, the Congregation Council organized the delegates into six committees to examine the constitutive elements of Benedictine life but overlooked the formation of a committee to study the monastic tradition and the theology and spirituality of the Rule of Benedict. Realizing the need for this, several delegates asked that a Committee on Benedictinism be formed. This time the request was granted.

The task of these seven committees was to develop position papers that would reflect a renewed theology and spirituality of Benedictine life based on the Scriptures, the Rule and the documents of Vatican II. The juridical norms governing the lives of the members of the Congregation would then flow from the theological principles enunciated in these position papers.

To develop this renewed theology of monastic life, it was necessary that the members of the Federation engage in reflection on the Word of God in Scripture, the Rule, and the experience of their lives. Furthermore, it was essential that the delegates bring to the Renewal Chapter the results of that self-reflection. In order to effect this, Mother Mary Susan proposed

   . . . that the delegates bring any suggestions they may have
   from community members . . . any suggestions that are

submitted will be discussed and commissions according to the various categories will be formed to handle them and all future suggestions. Participants in the meeting will be free to propose any organizational forms, consultative procedures, and/or any workable method designed to involve all the members of the Congregation in preparation for the General Chapter.[5]

This kind of consultation and reflection was a feature of the entire renewal process. It enabled the communities of the Congregation to participate in that self-reflection necessary to develop a theology of monastic life which corresponded to the church's new self-understanding.

When the 1967 pre-Chapter began the task of redefining Benedictine monasticism, it was a critical time to do so. In the minds of many religious both in and outside monastic communities, monastic life had become the cause of all the trouble religious were facing.[6] Besides being influenced by this kind of thinking, the chapter delegates had themselves found it difficult to reconcile their experience of monastic life with the prevailing interpretation of it. The Rule and the tradition as explained to them said one thing; the life they lived demanded other things of them.[7] A substantial number of the delegates were so frustrated by their experience of conflict between monastic practice and monastic interpretation that they were opposed to a special treatment of the theology of Benedictinism by a chapter committee. Some believed that the concepts would evolve from a study of the specific elements of monastic life; others thought that it was not worth the trouble to clarify a specific monastic identity and that it might even be bordering on the triumphalistic to do so; another group felt that American Benedictine communities were what they were and that nothing could be done about it; still others maintained that they knew quite clearly what monasticism was all about and that a study was not needed. Immediately following the discussion, the Committee on Benedictinism met and decided to prepare for circulation among all the members of the Congregation an Opinionnaire on Benedictinism which they hoped might break down the resistance of the chapter members to the study of Benedictinism.[8]

The purpose of the Opinionnaire was to ascertain the general thinking of the sisters in the Congregation concerning Benedictinism in the modern world. Eighteen out of twenty communities and 1539 members out of approximately 2200 in the Congregation responded. The committee analyzed the information gathered from the opinionnaire to determine how much consensus about monasticism existed in the Congregation and what the problem areas were. The results proved to be an invaluable guide to the Committee on Benedictinism in directing its study and a strong argument in convincing the Chapter of the urgency of such a study. The Committee synthesized the results and presented them to the pre-Chapter of January, 1968. The report included an analysis of the responses of the total population, a comparison of the data from each of the eighteen communities and a summary of the comments made by the sisters in answering the opinionnaire.

AN ANALYSIS OF THE OPINIONNAIRE ON BENEDICTINISM

In the first question of the opinionnaire, the committee listed ten elements which standard commentaries on the Rule of Benedict judged essential to Benedictine life.[9] In the response of the sisters, they received widely varying degrees of acceptance as absolutely essential elements of Benedictinism:

TABLE I: TEN ESSENTIAL ELEMENTS

Elements:	*% of total population responding "yes":*
Liturgical prayer	91%
Common life	85%
Work	79%
Lectio divina	78%
Solitude and leisure	72%
Scriptural orientation	59%
Choral office	57%
Contemplative orientation	30%
Ascesis	22%
Enclosure	20%

The response to this question revealed some degree of consensus concerning the essentials of Benedictine life: over two-thirds of the sisters accepted five elements—liturgical prayer, common life, work, lectio divina, solitude and leisure—and rejected three—contemplative orientation, ascesis, and enclosure. The results also seemed to indicate, however, weak conviction concerning the importance of scriptural orientation and choral office, since they were endorsed by less than two-thirds of the sisters. This conclusion is confirmed as valid when it is also examined against the background of the additional information provided in the opinionnaire.

Liturgical Prayer and the Common Life

The sisters were asked not only to choose the elements they judged essential but also to comment on them. Concerning liturgical prayer, they remarked that it is the "essential apostolate" and the "first responsibility" of Benedictine life. They stressed throughout the opinionnaire that it takes precedence over service in the apostolate.

In their observations about the common life, the respondents pointed out that the ideal of Benedictine life is to be a community "united in Christ." "If this is achieved," they remarked, "the other elements would be taken care of." The sisters did, however, take issue with the practices of the common life saying that "many permissions, penances, chapter of faults, etc., destroy the individual and the community" and that the common life does not necessarily produce community when it is like living in a "common herd" and being formed in a "common mold."

Liturgical prayer and the common life received such a high degree of acceptance as essential elements most probably because of two influences which had a considerable effect on the lives of American Benedictine women during the three decades prior to the renewal of Vatican II. One was monastic, the Beuronese-Solesmes revival of the monastic life in Europe during the nineteenth century; the other was ecclesial, the liturgical renewal in the United States.

In the Beuronese-Solesmes revival, liturgy and the common life were the central foci of Benedictine life. This interpretation was gradually brought to the monasteries in this country by those American monks who had gone to Europe to study at the monasteries of Beuron and Solesmes. Between 1930 and 1960 the communities of American Benedictine women were being strongly affected by the Beuronese-Solesmes tradition through the retreats and guidance being given them by the monks. As a result, the priories in the Congregation placed much emphasis on the liturgy and the common life and spent much time in preparing elaborate liturgical ceremonies and in performing the Divine Office with great care and solemnity.

The second influence which gave the liturgy such prominence in the lives of the sisters was their experience of the liturgical movement in the American Catholic Church. They participated in this movement with pride and enthusiasm as liturgy was so integral to their Benedictine heritage. In the Participant Profile of 1976, 95% of the delegates affirmed that the liturgical movement was a catalyst of change in the post-Vatican II renewal period.

Choral Office

The statistics concerning choral office were confusing: most of the respondents had endorsed liturgical prayer but slightly less than three-fifths had accepted choral office as essential which, along with the celebration of the Eucharist, makes up the community's liturgical prayer. Furthermore, the comments about choral office were both positive and negative. Those affirming the importance of choral office said that it was the "most necessary element, one of the sources of contemplation . . . and should not be omitted." On the other hand, those denying its value maintained that it needed to be said in the motherhouse only and that those who desired to say it privately should have the option to do so.

Since the results were so contradictory about an element so central to the lives of the sisters, the committee sought to determine the cause of the conflict. Other data from the opinionnaire pointed to several factors which seemed to shed light on the rejection of choral office and the dissatisfaction with it. The sisters observed with concern and anxiety throughout the opinionnaire that they were "overburdened" and that "their lives were not a balance of prayer, lectio, and work."

These comments reflected the fact that prior to Vatican II the eight units of the choral office were combined to "fit in" the liturgical prayers between long hours of apostolic activity. This resulted in an arrangement of the times for prayer that was not in harmony with the rhythm of the day. Furthermore, the choral office had become so encrusted with intricate details of content and rubric that the sisters needed a handbook called the "Ordo" to guide them through the complex details of the office for the day. The Ordo itself was so complicated that one needed instruction to learn to read it correctly. Finally, the office was said in Latin thus making it unintelligible for all except the few Latin scholars.

All of these circumstances precluded the possibility of praying so that the mind could be in harmony with the voice. Choral office was for many no longer praying but "getting in" long hours of formalized prayers. It is for this reason that the sisters rejected it as essential to Benedictine life.

Solitude and Leisure

In their comments concerning solitude and leisure, the sisters again emphasized that they did not have sufficient time in their lives for prayer and human development. They characterized solitude and leisure as desirable elements, but noted that "putting them on paper would not make them a reality" in the "present highly pressured apostolate." More than two-thirds of the respondents endorsed these elements as essential.

Contemplative Orientation

Although nearly two-thirds of the sisters rejected contemplative orientation as essential, the minority affirming it described it as the element integrating the active and contemplative poles of Benedictine life. Since solitude and leisure had received a firm endorsement, the committee was puzzled by this rejection of contemplative orientation. In the context of Benedictine life, the desire for leisure and solitude ought to reflect a desire for contemplation in one's life. After discussion, the committee concluded that the lack of correlation of these elements might possibly be due to the fact that some had interpreted the term to mean the life led by Trappists and Cistercians, or more importantly, that the sisters had found it impossible to orient their lives to contemplation because of the constant pressures of formalized liturgical prayer and apostolic service.

Work

The sisters explained in their comments that the pressures caused by too much work were creating anxiety in their lives. They observed that work is stressed as the "most important thing" and is "all out of proportion to the time and leisure demanded for prayer life."

From the very beginning of the American experience, Benedictine women had taken a more active, missionary orientation than their nineteenth century predecessors. Since that time they have continued to be involved in apostolic work not only because they desired to serve others but also out of the practical necessity of surviving economically.

Although the overemphasis on work was rejected, the concept of work as essential received the endorsement of almost four-fifths of the respondents. In making this judgment the sisters may have been affected by 1) the nineteenth century monastic emphasis on prayer and work as the poles of activity in the life of the Benedictine sister; 2) the work ethic of Puritan society reinforced by the Industrial Revolution and still operative in twentieth-century American society; 3) the need to provide for themselves.

Lectio Divina and Scriptural Orientation

Seventy-eight per cent of the sisters accepted lectio divina as essential but only 59% endorsed scriptural orientation. In making these choices, the respondents were most probably influenced by the fact that "lectio divina" is a traditional monastic term and specifically prescribed by the Rule of Benedict. In addition, they may have perceived it as the practice of spiritual reading. On the other hand, the term "scriptural orientation" may have presented an ambiguous meaning especially to those not familiar with the new trend in the church of giving scripture a greater emphasis.

Ascesis

The strong rejection of ascesis (i.e., the practice of self-denial) by 78% of the sisters may simply have been an expression of their dissatisfaction with the modality of asceticism in their lives. It was not a self-denial integrated into the whole purpose of monastic life but a superficial doing "penance," a puritanical repression of the affective life and of legitimate forms of self-expression. Some examples of these kinds of mortification were the severe restriction of communication and personal friendships, maintaining custody of the eyes, keeping one's hands under the scapular, begging penance for breaking a dish or spilling food, and not being allowed to sit in the same seat of the car with one's father.

Enclosure

Judging from the data and the comments of the opinionnaire, the need to redefine enclosure seemed to have been one of the highest priorities of the sisters in 1967. To understand why this was so, it is necessary to know the history of enclosure, its evolution in American Benedictinism, and the understanding of enclosure in the Rule of Benedict.

Enclosure can be spoken of in two ways: monastic enclosure and papal enclosure. Monastic enclosure has existed since the beginning of the cenobitic life. It means the private monastic domain, a monastery where the community lives as opposed to the hermitage where the hermit lives.[10] In Latin it is called the "clausura" from which our word ·"enclosure" comes.

The kind of enclosure to which the opinionnaire referred, however, is papal enclosure by which nuns could not leave the cloister or others enter it except for grave reasons. Those who violated papal enclosure were excommunicated. Its purpose is ". . . to guard both chastity and silence so that the world cannot disturb or contaminate the monastery."[11] Boniface VIII imposed it in the thirteenth century on all nuns, i.e., members of strictly contemplative orders which was the only form of religious life for women until the sixteenth century.

A new development in the observance of papal enclosure occurred in the sixteenth and seventeenth centuries when congregations of women who professed contemplative life and kept the papal cloister substituted foi the Divine Office apostolic and charitable works. As a result of this, some of the older monastic orders later adapted to new needs by taking up apostolic works compatible with enclosure. Such was the case in 1836 with the nuns of St. Walburg's in Eichstatt, Bavaria, from which the original foundation for American Benedictine women came in 1852.[12] Others, however, retained strict contemplative life with strict papal enclosure. In time a distinction came to be made in canon law between "major" and "minor" enclosure. Minor enclosure was a modification of major enclosure to allow the nuns greater freedom in leaving the cloister for the sake of apostolic works. If they did so without permission, they were liable to punishment by the superior or local ordinary.

In American Benedictine women's communities, major enclosure ceased to exist since 1859 unless imposed in certain cases by the local bishop. Prescriptions for minor papal enclosure were given in the 1922 Constitutions of the Congregation. They direct that no one except the prioress and the convent officials may enter the parlors without special permission and without a companion. The sisters were permitted, however, to visit their parents and blood relations in the parlor without this latter precaution. Furthermore, they could not conduct parish choirs which were not composed entirely of girls. At the conclusion of this list of regulations for observing enclosure, the sisters are cautioned "not to be too trustful of themselves but diligently to observe these clausura rules."[13]

In 1966 Vatican II suppressed minor enclosure[14] but redefined monastic life as an enclosed state and directed that monks and nuns prescribe enclosure in their constitutions.[15] That regulation was mitigated for American Benedictine monks so that they may now regard themselves as monastic even though they are not obliged to observe enclosure. This is not so for American Benedictine women who must continue to observe enclosure if they wish to be considered monastic.

This is of real concern to them because they perceive themselves as monastic and cherish their Benedictine heritage.

The irony of the entire situation is that enclosure as defined by the Church is not endemic to the Rule of Benedict.[16] Nevertheless, some of the sisters commented that one must be "cautious" in interpreting St. Benedict's rules for enclosure since he lived in a different culture. Their confusion was a result of the canonical imposition of the regulation of enclosure through the Constitutions and Declarations of the Congregation which are intended to be an interpretation of the Rule of Benedict.

In spite of this long history of enclosure and the Church's recent reaffirmation of it, four-fifths of the sisters rejected enclosure as an essential element. This was the strongest rejection of any of the ten elements and corresponds with the results of another question which asked the sisters if enclosure needed redefining. Seventy per cent of the respondents agreed that it did and most of the comments also affirmed the need. They characterized enclosure as "obsolete," "a misfit and medieval" in the twentieth century and as motivated by "Manichean and Jansenistic" visions of reality.

In general, the comments revealed the influence of an incarnational theology which considers the world as inherently good and open to the sacred and gave evidence of the sisters' own experience of the world as more sacred than profane. They pointed out the teaching of the church that the things of this world are "essentially good" and have a "true value" and observed that the "age-old" detachment from the "evil world" is no longer valid. Finally, they specified that enclosure should be more "personal, interior and integrated" and provide a "certain amount of privacy so as to have time to devote to God in prayer." The sisters indicated that the redefining of enclosure in this way would have a humanizing influence in their own lives as well as in the lives of those whom they serve.

Considering the traditional obedience of the Congregation members to the church expressed most recently by their serious response to the call of Vatican II, one would have expected their compliance likewise to the practice of enclosure "within the walls of the monastery." Their firm rejection of it flowed from their reflection on their own experience in the light of Scripture, the Rule of Benedict and the Church's new self-understanding generated by Vatican II. This discernment is an example of life coming before theology and theology springing from life. It indicates that a community of faith, realizing that they are a church, can speak in obedience to the church a view opposing its own. Furthermore, it demonstrates that communities of American Benedictine women have, in fact, evolved out of their medieval European model and moved more closely back to the concept of enclosure present in the Rule of Benedict.

Balance Between Prayer and Work

Only slightly more than half of the respondents felt that a balance of prayer, lectio divina and work existed in the life of the American Benedictine sister. This question received the largest number of comments. Most of them emphasized that the lack of balance caused the sisters to be so "overpowered with work" that they were in a "constant state of tension" and living in a "perpetual emergency." They explained how the imbalance and over-commitment made the sisters "physically and emotionally" unable to do their work. Some observed that this imbalance caused the community to develop an attitude of "fitting prayers in" around the work when they were often "too fatigued" and not even "capable of praying." The observations generally registered much dissatisfaction with the unwholesome environment created by the lack of balance. The sisters seemed to indicate that this problem was the most serious in their lives at the beginning of the renewal period.

Difference Between Benedictine and
Non-Monastic Orders

The next topic dealt with in the opinionnaire was the difference between the orientation of the monastic orders and the active orders. Almost three-fourths of the respondents felt that Benedictine communities are distinct from other religious institutes. Their comments indicated that they perceived the difference to reside in contemplative orientation, the primacy of choral office, the family spirit of Benedictine community and the Benedictine vows.[17]

Apostolate Suitable to Benedictine Life

Two questions dealt with some aspect of the apostolate and will therefore be treated together. When asked if they felt that any apostolate is commensurate with a Benedictine orientation, over two-thirds agreed provided it did not conflict with the witness of community, the primary apostolate of monastic life. In a second question, the sisters were asked to suggest areas of apostolic involvement consonant with the monastic ideal for which they should be planning if Catholic education were phased out as many writers were suggesting during this period. Twelve specific apostolates were suggested. The following table lists the grouping of them into five major categories:

TABLE II: SUITABLE APOSTOLATES

Apostolate	*% Endorsement*
Education*	59
Social Work	18
Nursing	12
Pastoral Ministry	7
Counseling	4

*(Includes Religious Education—30%)

According to this grouping, a majority of the sisters believed that educational work which has a pastoral orientation or pastoral work which employs educational skills would be suitable for American Benedictine women if Catholic schools were to close. It is evident that they contemplated no radical departure from their former apostolic involvement. Their choices may well have been influenced by several factors: their training and skills as educators; the opening up of pastoral ministry to sisters; the Benedictine tradition of serving the immediate needs of the local church which would have led them to recognize the necessity of involvement in pastoral ministry to extend their effect in the community; and, finally, the communal-contemplative orientation of Benedictine life which may have motivated them to want to share with others the gospel message and their experience of prayer and Christian community.

Of the four other areas chosen, social work was most frequently mentioned. This is not surprising when one considers the consciousness-raising that resulted from the race riots, problems of the inner city, civil rights movement and so forth. The societal turmoil of the 1960's made the sisters aware of the need for religious women to be involved in social work.

Characteristics of Benedictine Community

Some of the characteristics of Benedictine community were treated in a set of questions. One of them asked if St. Benedict's concept of the monastic community as a family has value today. Eighty-five per cent of the respondents affirmed that it did in spite of the contemporary trend to look upon the familial concept of monastic community as productive of overly-dependent and immature relationships among adults. The comments following this question urged adaptation of life style in community and spoke of the needs for small-group living, mature loving relationships and longer periods of residency on local missions. Sixty per cent of the sisters again indicated a trend toward small-group living when, in answering another question, they said that the Benedictine familial ideal is not possible in large communities.

Two of the questions concerning Benedictine community addressed the possibility of Benedictines fulfilling the vow of stability even though many of the community do not work or live at the motherhouse but in the community's mission houses. Over two-thirds of the respondents affirmed that the sisters did not have to live at the motherhouse to maintain stability and that American Benedictine women who resided in the local mission houses were fulfilling their vow of stability. This is another example of the evolution of American Benedictine women's communities out of the model of medieval monasticism.

Relevance of Benedictine Life to the Twentieth Century

The remaining three questions referred to the problem of the authenticity of Benedictine life and the relevance of the Rule of Benedict to the twentieth century. Most of the sisters affirmed that Benedictine life is a meaningful Christian witness to contemporary society and stated that the Rule of Benedict in its overall vision is relevant to the twentieth century. Approximately three-fourths of the sisters thought, however, that certain areas of the Rule were irrelevant. This confirmed the other data of the opinionnaire which suggested that the Rule of Benedict is very meaningful in its essential vision but that its cultural expression needed re-evaluation and reinterpretation.

Differences of Opinion among the Communities and Their Members

Before concluding this analysis, it is important to point out that the data revealed differences of opinion among the communities and their members. The Committee on Benedictinism not only studied the responses of the total population, but also analyzed them community by community. The results revealed significant differences of opinion among the eighteen communities:

TABLE III: RANGE OF OPINION
AMONG THE 18 COMMUNITIES

Element	*Range* *% Responding "Yes"*
Enclosure	2%-80%
Contemplative orientation	12%-80%
Scriptural orientation	25%-80%
Choral office	18%-70%
Balance exists	27%-75%

Of the total population responding, 43% were 30+ years in community and 12% were 0-5 years in community. An analysis of these two groups disclosed differences of opinion between them:

TABLE IV: DIFFERENCES OF OPINION
BETWEEN YOUNGER/OLDER MEMBERS

Element	*Young*	*Old*
	% Responding "Yes"	
Balance exists	33%	65%
Enclosure needs redefining	90%	59%
Any apostolate compatible	75%	45%
Rule of Benedict: certain		
irrelevancies	80%	52%
Scriptural orientation	75%	49%
Contemplative orientation	70%	51%

These differences of opinion among the communities and their members uncovered the seeds of polarization which engendered conflict and tension throughout the renewal process.

Conclusions

The following tensions and problems in the communities of the Congregation emerged from the data:

1. The concept of community received a high degree of acceptance as essential, but the sisters stated that the common life did not necessarily form community. Existing practices and

structures had become destructive of community and the individual.

2. The members of the Congregation maintained almost thematically throughout the opinionnaire that prayer and community are primary in Benedictine life and that any apostolate is compatible with the Benedictine orientation provided it does not conflict with these. They also indicated that apostolates should be determined according to the needs of the local church.

3. The sisters placed a high value on liturgical prayer but gave a considerably weaker endorsement of choral office. In their observations, however, they explained that they rejected choral office because its form, content and rubrics had made praying difficult.

4. The respondents endorsed the concept of work but stressed that the exaggerated emphasis placed on it did not permit a life balanced by prayer, work and lectio divina.

5. The sisters affirmed lectio divina, scriptural orientation, solitude and leisure as essential to Benedictine life. They maintained that contemplative orientation is the integrating factor of their lives but difficult to achieve because of the pressures of the apostolate and liturgical prayer.

6. The confusion expressed between concepts that are essential to the Rule and practices that are the cultural expression of it seemed to reveal that the sisters had sometimes not been formed in traditional monastic theology and spirituality. Some of the causes of this were: 1) the long-standing exclusion of women from the study of theology; 2) the imposition of repressive canonical regulations, structures, and customs which were aberrations of the Rule of Benedict; 3) the formation of members in culture-bound customs of a preceding age which were a selective expression of the Benedictine ideal.[18]

7. The sisters firmly rejected both the modality of a formalized, non-integrated asceticism and the practice of enclosure imposed on them.

8. The respondents maintained that stability was being observed by those sisters who were not living at the motherhouse but in mission houses located near their apostolates.

9. Significant differences of opinion existed among the eighteen communities and between the younger and older members of the Congregation. This data raised the question of how much pluralism could exist without causing discontinuity with the tradition.

10. Although the sisters almost unanimously affirmed the relevance of the Rule of Fenedict to contemporary society, they also stated that certain areas of the Rule are irrelevant.

A careful analysis of these conclusions indicates that the sisters failed to affirm some of the essential elements in the initial question of the opinionnaire not because they disagreed with the concepts but because they felt a dissatisfaction with the existing cultural expression of them. In such a situation it was necessary to turn back not to the partial tradition of the immediate past but to the entire history of Benedictine monasticism. Only in this way could the Congregation evaluate the existing expression of monastic life in light of its original vision and discover those essential elements which had been obscured throughout the centuries. Once this was done, the Congregation could attempt to give expression to the Rule in a cultural form that met the needs of its members and more clearly articulated the vision of Benedict to contemporary society. The purpose of the renewal chapters was to provide the process and the resources to accomplish this critical re-evaluation.

THEOLOGICAL CONCEPTS DEVELOPED, 1968-74

The church in the document on the renewal of religious life, *Perfectae Caritatis*, had clearly defined the task of the renewal chapters as ". . . a constant return to the primitive inspiration of institutes, and their adaptation to the changed conditions of our time." The Gospel was to be the norm of religious life and given an expression consonant with the charism of each founder. Using this approach, the members of the Federation examined the following theological concepts needing critical re-evaluation which had surfaced in the opinionnaire and become evident during the Renewal Chapters from 1968-74:

1. The meaning of monastic community
2. The American Benedictine community in the modern world
3. Monastic community as prophetic
4. The elements of American Benedictine life

Through discussion and reflection, three successive Renewal Chapters (1968-69, 1971, 1974) developed these concepts in the light of both past tradition and present experience.

THE MEANING OF MONASTIC COMMUNITY

The Committee on Benedictinism presented to the Renewal Chapter of the Federation a position paper on American Benedictine life which, in its approved form, became the document entitled "Benedictine Community: Eucharistic Ecclesiola."[19] The purpose of this paper was to provide the theological principles which would be the basis for experimentation and adaptation in American Benedictine life.

In studying the meaning of the monastic community, the committee reaffirmed that Benedictinism was indeed rooted in the Scriptures and in the pre-Benedictine period of Pachomius, Basil and Augustine, monastic leaders of the fourth and fifth centuries. Through these sources they verified that the most ancient texts view the monastery as a church in miniature. Having established this as the controlling idea of the monastic vision, the committee examined the ecclesiology of Vatican II.

In the *Dogmatic Constitution on the Church*, Vatican II describes the church as mystery, sign, and sacrament making known to man God's love by being a community of love. The committee concluded that the American Benedictine community, as a church in miniature, is a sign and sacrament revealing Christ to twentieth-century America.

Drawing upon Chapter II of the *Dogmatic Constitution on the Church*, the committee further explained the meaning of monastic community by clarifying the analogy between the church as People of God and the monastic community. The Council had described the People of God as called to bring about the Kingdom, as structured and organized on a sacramental basis, as a sacrament of unity with the people gathered around the bishop in a communion in the Trinity; as renewed and built up by the charismatic gifts of the Spirit; and as a community of worship. The Scriptures, ancient monastic sources, the Rule of Benedict as well as twentieth-century scholarship on monastic life all pointed to the characterization of Benedictine community as a worshipping community animated and bonded by Christ's presence, living under the spirit of the Rule of Benedict and belonging to the People of God, constituted by the sacraments and responsive to the guidance of the Spirit.

The committee then emphasized, however, that the relationship of the monastic community to the People of God is primarily charismatic rather than institutional, and that the peculiar charism of the Benedictine community is expressed in its service of prayer and work. They maintained that according to the eucharistic structure of the Rule of Benedict, primacy is given to liturgical prayer, and that, as in the church, it is the heart of the community's life, and the "summit toward which all the activity is directed and the fountain from which all its power flows . . ."[20] They also pointed out that the Benedictine does not see in this dedication to liturgy an obstacle to involvement in the needs of mankind because she too is called to build up the kingdom, to be active in the mission of the Church which has been traditionally for Benedictines the prayer and work of the church.

This study reconfirmed that the historic commitment of American Benedictine women to both prayer and ministry was not only acceptable but also integral to Christian monasticism. It had become clear that the tensions expressed in the Opinionnaire on Benedictinism would not be resolved by eliminating either element. Neither the monastic vision nor history precluded the presence of both elements simultaneously. What had apparently created the problem was the inability of the sisters to resolve these with balance in their lives.

THE AMERICAN BENEDICTINE COMMUNITY
IN THE MODERN WORLD

Having clarified that the monastic community is a church in miniature participating in the mission of the church, the committee recognized that in order to understand the mission of the monastic community in the world it is necessary to consider the role of the church in the world. In the *Pastoral Constitution on the Church in the Modern World*, the Church had rejected the escapist tendency to see the world as something to be fled from, the domain of evil worthy only of contempt; it had likewise condemned the modern world view that persons are masters of their own lives without reference to the transcendent. Against these opposite views, it had posed its own world vision that only in "the mystery of the incarnate Word does the mystery of man take on light" because Christ has restored all to "divine likeness."[21] Like Christ, persons must therefore relate all things to "the Lord and Creator of all." By doing this, they will contribute through "their personal industry to the realization in history of the divine plan" and assist in building up the human family and the Kingdom of God.

In this same document, the church had encouraged persons to become deeply involved in the world rather than to flee from it since the growth of human society advances the growth of the Kingdom through union with Christ who has already returned all things to the Father. The church, through her new self-understanding, had fused the incarnational and eschatological approaches to reality, formerly thought irreconcilable, and had exhorted Christians "as citizens of two cities" to discharge their earthly duties "conscientiously and in response to the gospel spirit."

They are mistaken who, knowing that we have here no abiding city but seek one which is to come, think that they may therefore shirk their earthly responsibilities. . . . Nor, on the contrary, are they any less wide of the mark who think that religion consists in acts of worship alone and in the discharge of certain moral obligations. . . . This split between the faith which many profess in their daily lives deserves to be counted among the more serious errors of our age. . . . The Christian who neglects his temporal duties neglects his duties toward his neighbor and even God, and jeopardizes his eternal salvation.[22]

It became evident to the committee that the church had come to realize that "the earthly and heavenly cities do penetrate one another" and had inserted itself in the modern world as "the universal sacrament of salvation."

Confronted with the synthesizing principles of Vatican II which integrated human efforts in the two cities, the committee perceived that they must develop a renewed theology of the mission of monastic life which paralleled the up-dated theology of the church. Research revealed to them that the history of monastic spirituality had always been one of movement between the eschatalogical and incarnational poles. At times, it had come to rest in a fusion of the two as the Rule of Benedict attests. At other times, that integrated vision of Benedict had been blurred reducing the monk's efforts in his life on earth to a sort of "basket-weaving" to pass time between now and eternal life, since, as it was thought, labor to improve the conditions of this world did not build up the Kingdom. In American Benedictine women's communities, this dualistic view had been expressed in the practice of enclosure which separated the "good sister" from the evil world.

The committee began to see that the clue to a renewed understanding of the mission of monastic life in the world was the concept of metanoia and the eucharistic orientation of the Rule. They examined St. Benedict's essential idea of conversion and concluded that the preservation of metanoia is essential, but its particular form will have cultural variations. The ancient Egyptian monks of the desert had accomplished conversion or metanoia by fuga mundi, i.e., flight from the world; for Benedict this idea of residence in the desert, of total separation from the world, was never essential to conversion. According to the Rule, the monks were to seek conversion by a life that was basically paschal in nature. The monk passed constantly from the old life to the new life of union with the Father in Christ through the service of prayer and work in the apostolate of the church.

In the monastic vocation, eucharistic orientation is the link between prayer and ministry. Like the service of prayer, apostolic involvement is motivated by the eucharistic orientation of the Rule. "Flight from the world" can then be reconciled with "presence in the world" because this eucharistic orientation engenders a sacramental vision of reality. Through this vision redemptive involvement in the world is experienced as an extension of worship by which creation is offered back to the Father through Christ.

These insights clarified for the committee the fact that redemptive involvement in the world is an essential element of Benedictine life, made integral to it by the concept of metanoia and the eucharistic dimension of Benedictine community. They therefore concluded that American Benedictine communities, like the church, reveal Christ to twentieth-century America because they participate in its mission as sign and sacrament. The challenge would be to have the courage to accept the American Benedictine way as a valid expression of the Benedictine vocation.

MONASTIC COMMUNITY AS PROPHETIC

The Benedictinism paper of 1968 had given American Benedictine women the basic theological principles for redemptive presence in the world for the sake of the Kingdom. In 1971 the Renewal Chapter was confronted with the task of giving expression to that redemptive presence in a manner that articulated the Benedictine vision and responded to the needs of its members and the signs of the times.

The delegates came to the 1971 pre-Chapter acutely aware of those signs. During the preceding five years, they had become conscious of the grave social problems facing America and the world. Some had witnessed and some had indeed experienced the demonstrations and riots in several major cities of the United States caused by the oppression of discrimination and the futility of the Vietnam war. Sensitized by these experiences, they sought to enflesh their vision of Benedictine presence in the world in a life style that truly effected redemptive involvement in the urgent needs of mankind. It therefore became the task of the Committee on Benedictinism to study the monastic tradition in order to provide the theological principles for such a life style. They presented the results of their research to the 1971 Renewal Chapter in the position paper "Christian Fellowship in a Prophetic Faith Community."[23]

In the course of their study, the committee turned to the Scriptures, the primitive inspiration of monastic life, the Rule of Benedict,

Benedictine history, and the documents of Vatican II. Their research into the Scriptures revealed to them the correspondences existing between their own historical period and that of the prophets of the Old Testament. They became convinced that this period in history called for a prophetic monasticism in a prophetic church.

Through their reading of the Old Testament prophetic writings, the committee understood that the prophet's principal role was to interpret the signs of the times in the light of the living God and bear witness to Yahweh's message. In the New Testament Jesus is presented as the fulfillment of all prophecy. It became evident to them that many parallels exist between the prophetic ministry of Jesus and the life of the early Christian community: the Church of Jerusalem gave prophetic witness by sharing prayer and material goods; by living in poverty and simplicity of life; and by witnessing to the resurrection even though they were rejected for doing so. It was also clear to the committee that this prophetic witness continued in the pre-Benedictine period through the writings and lives of the Fathers and through the primitive monks of the East who by their asceticism in the desert lived a style of life distinct from the life of ordinary Christians.

The committee members found in Benedictine history the prophetic witness that Benedict's monks had given in the western world. Benedictines had been prophetic to Roman society by stressing the worth of the individual and by testifying to the fact that persons from all different levels of society could live together in Christian fellowship. They had rejected the false values of power, prestige, and wealth by posing instead the values of simplicity, brotherliness, and humility. As centuries passed, however, monasticism had tended, as did the Church, to lose the tension between itself and society by accepting the wealth, prestige, and values of society, thus becoming a culture-bound institution.

The committee realized that Vatican II had explained the Church's prophetic role in much the same way as it had been understood in the beginning of Christianity. The Church, seeing itself as marginal in its influence in the contemporary world, once again was able to define itself as a prophetic people sharing in the prophetic function of Christ. The committee concluded that monasticism, as a church in miniature, must show faithfulness to the Church by itself being prophetic. In the light of the theology of the Church, it is not sufficient for the monastic community to fulfill its prophetic role by proclaiming the message of Jesus through its worship and work. The committee maintained that it had also to demonstrate its opposition to the materialism and alienation existing in the church and society through the simplicity of its life and the practice of Christian fellowship. In addition to this, it had to facilitate the work of the Spirit in the lives of its own members and those of the larger community around it through a mutual sharing of the Word of God.

Through the formulation of these principles, the committee established the conceptual basis for a monastic life style which would be a sensitive response to the "cry of the poor."[24] The women who accepted these concepts were automatically opening themselves up to new ministries. These, in turn, would affect or change life styles organized around past services. Things as simple as the daily schedule would be affected by the fact that all the members of the community were no longer going to or returning from the same work at the same time.

ELEMENTS OF AMERICAN BENEDICTINE LIFE

The document entitled *Call to Life* was approved unanimously by the 1974 Renewal Chapter as the new Constitutions of the Federation of St. Scholastica. It systematically treats in nine chapters the following elements of monastic life: community, authority, vows, prayer, formation, ministry, and temporalities.[25]

THE THEOLOGICAL PRINCIPLES OF COMMUNITY

In one chapter of the Constitutions, the Juridic Commission summarized the theological principles which place the Benedictine community in its proper ecclesiological context and in radical continuity with the monastic tradition.[26] They maintained that the Benedictine community exists to be a sacrament of Christ's healing presence and effects this sign by creating an environment in which its members may live their vowed lives more fully and give priority to prayer, which is the very center of their lives and the source of their rootedness in the Word of God. They explained that by living in a community of faith and love with one another, American Benedictine women can experience and respond to the transforming power of the Spirit released in them and gradually move toward a total conversion to the Father in Christ.

Metanoia

Drawing upon Scripture and the Rule of Benedict, the committee perceived that the element most basic to monasticism is "metanoia," that conversion to Christ so central to the New Testament ideal and to the "monastic pursuit of virtue."[27] The chief characteristic of the Benedictine community is that its members accept the message of Jesus and the demands it makes on their existence, for only by obedience to the word of God would they be able to give prophetic witness to Jesus.

In the past this word of God had been equated with the directions of the superior controlling the most minute details of life and accounted for the complexities of the system of obtaining permissions. Attention to the word of God at the present time focuses on the understanding of adult Christian responsibilities in the context of community.

Fuga Mundi and Asceticism

In keeping with ancient monastic tradition, the Committee on Benedictinism also affirmed in its 1971 document that metanoia is effected by the monk through "fuga mundi," or flight from the world. They asserted that in the context of the prophetic function of Benedictine life, the monk's flight from the world is not a physical withdrawal from an evil world as had been expressed in the practice of enclosure, but rather an ascetical refusal to be conformed to those present values and structures which counter the shaping of a community of love. By witnessing to the necessity of informing the social structure with Christian values, the Benedictine community attempts to affect the future of human community and thereby places itself out on the cutting edge of history. The committee maintained that the asceticism of the monastic community lies precisely in this, for to be out on the point of history is to risk the suffering and solitariness of having no certainty in the present and to order and discipline one's life according to the demands of the Gospel. With these concepts in mind, contemporary Benedictine women accept political involvement, public advocacy for the disadvantaged, and participation in what in an earlier period would have been called secular activities for the sake of influencing them.

Prayer

Reflection on the Acts of the Apostles and the Rule supported the committee's conviction that prayer is as necessary to the Benedictine community as it had been to the Community of Jerusalem.[28] Benedict devotes thirteen chapters to the arrangement and importance of communal prayer. The committee members therefore emphasized that prayer is central to Benedictine cenobitic community and that its members should have opportunities not only for liturgical prayer but also for reflective reading, private prayer and sharing their understanding and experience of the Word of God in Scripture. According to the Rule of Benedict, it is the prioress who, like the apostles, should lead the community in seeking the Word of God by sharing with them her own understanding and experience of the Word in Scripture and by listening as they do likewise. Through these varied experiences of prayer flowing from and rooted in Scripture, the community should gradually become more sensitive to God's presence in his Word. Where devotion to prayer had once been gauged by the amount of time given to it and the solemnity of its structures, new emphasis is now being given to private and shared prayer, to balance and meaning.

Simplicity of Life

In their description of Benedictine community, the committee stressed the importance of simplicity because this characterized the life of the Community of Jerusalem and is demanded by the Rule of Benedict.[29] The early Christians lived simply in their daily sharing of prayer, meals, and the breaking of the bread. They also sold their property to distribute it to the poor and provided for each one's needs by the labor of their hands and the common sharing of goods. This same simplicity of life is envisioned in the Rule of Benedict: the monks are also to live by the labor of their hands, to hold all things in common, to dress simply, to surrender their will, to practice a simple interior asceticism, and, most importantly, to seek God according to the guidance of the Gospel. The committee therefore asserted that the monastic community should give a visibly authentic witness to the simplicity of life envisaged in the Scriptures and the Rule of Benedict. They further proposed that this could be done by adapting St. Benedict's vision to modern society so that the monastic community living among the poor could become a center for sharing prayer, the Scriptures, and joint action with the larger community of Christians around it in an effort to alleviate human deprivation in its many forms.

For the American sister in a culture of affluence the notion of simplicity is a particularly difficult one. Not only is it true that American religious own more than their forebears, it is also true that it would be impossible for them to function professionally without the equipment of a technological society. The xerox machines, tape recorders, automobiles, radios, and telephones that are still luxuries in other parts of the world are essential to the daily functioning of an American professional. What remains essential, however, to the Benedictine concept of simplicity of life in this culture is that personal property be kept to the necessary minimum and that the goods, both of the individual and the community, be cared for reverently and shared responsibly.

The Sign of Sisterly Love

The faith and love of the Community of Jerusalem were certainly evident within that community and to the larger community around it. Likewise, according to the Rule of Benedict the monks are to exercise their zeal with love, to restrain self for the good of the community, and to show reverence for one another.[30] The central purpose of Benedictine life is that its members, bound together by their covenant with one another, grow in love through the presence of the Spirit made visible in their lives. The committee affirmed that this kind of personal and communal development is fostered by sisterly love and shared experiences of faith which make Christ visible within the community.

The notion of community in the past had largely been the notion of the common life. Intent on union with God through the practice of recollection, Benedictine women had emphasized silence and separation and minimized interaction among themselves. Though people learned to live side by side, little emphasis was given to the human dimensions of living together. The contemporary Benedictine woman who comes from a society of multiple opportunities for interaction and intimacy expects to be enriched by the sisters with whom she intends to share the rest of her life. What is more, she sees that Christian community has prophetic vaues in a mobile and fragmented culture.

The members of the Committee on Benedictinism further stated in their 1971 document, that the Benedictine community must likewise transmit the Christian message to the larger community around them. They also maintained that to accomplish this it is not sufficient for the monastic community to be visible only as a task-oriented institution doing some "apostolic" work for the Church. They must also communicate their inner experience of faith as community and as individuals by sharing prayer, discussions, and the concerns of the Church with the community around them. This kind of visible Christian presence, the committee observed, would enable the community to witness dynamically to ultimate values.

THE THEOLOGICAL PRINCIPLES OF AUTHORITY

Using the theological principles of authority present in the Scriptures and further clarified by the documents of Vatican II, the Jurdic Commission affirmed in the fourth chapter of *Call to Life* that the source and foundation of authority is the Spirit who resides in all. They also asserted that authority as Benedict envisioned it for monastic life is neither autocratic nor democratic, but cenobitic; although expressed and exercised principally through the prioress, authority is present as well in the members of the community.[31] They have a responsibility to share in the ministry of authority in the community. The basic reason for acknowledging and actualizing the authority present in the community, the commission explained, is to give recognition to the ecclesial nature of Benedictine community by which the sisters are united in Christ around the prioress and are free to bear witness to the gifts of his Spirit through the monastic charism.

Having established the cenobitic character of authority in a Benedictine community, the commission described the manner in which the prioress exercises her ministry of authority. They maintained that the most important service of the prioress is to unite the community through Christ in His Spirit by dialogue, collegiality, subsidiarity, and the two-fold manner of teaching by word and deed. According to the principle of co-responsibility in the Rule of Benedict, the prioress consults the sisters and, having received their counsel, discerns what the Spirit is saying to the community.

The commission emphasized that each sister, by reason of the Spirit's gift of the monastic charism which she received and accepted in her commitment to monastic life, is called to assume her responsibility in the exercise of cenobitic authority. She actualizes this authority when she contributes to the formation of decisions in community deliberations by sharing the insights which she has received through attentive listening to the Spirit, when she uses her talent in the service of the community, and when she performs administrative tasks delegated to her by the prioress.

Through this renewed understanding of the principle of cenobitic authority in the Rule of Benedict, the commission interpreted the prioress' primary role as that of a mediator of Christ's presence uniting the community in his Spirit and gave secondary emphasis to her administrative function. By rooting the understanding of the prioress' authority in the most scriptural, ecclesiological, and monastic concepts, the commission made her role more authentic and freed her from those formalized, superficial expressions of authority existing prior to Vatican II. Finally, they affirmed that the members also have a responsibility to share in the ministry of authority in the community and delineated the ways in which they fulfill that function. Out of these understandings have come policies like the discernment of ministries and the elimination of the formalized permission system.

THE THEOLOGICAL PRINCIPLES OF THE VOWS

In their research concerning the vows, the Juridic Commission perceived that American Benedictine women, having already committed themselves to Christ in Baptism, further strengthen this commitment by their profession of vows. They maintained that the purpose of Benedictine life is truly to seek God in a community of persons who vow poverty, chastity, obedience, stability, and conversion of life. These vows not only bring into existence a cenobitic form of life which enables the members to listen and respond individually and communally to the Word of God, but are in themselves a prophetic sign of the Spirit's presence communicating to others the meaning of the Gospel in a radical way. Having clarified these general principles concerning the vows, the commission then treated each vow individually.

Stability

Through a careful study of the Rule of Benedict and the existing literature on the vow of stability, the members of the commission concluded that this vow is a commitment of loving fidelity to a particular cenobitic community. This commitment enables the community to know one another more intimately over long periods of time and thus makes possible a continuing dialogue of salvation among the members. Through this stable life in a cenobitic community, American Benedictine women can continually offer support to one another in their mutual search for the Word of God as they strive to confront the basic questions of life together. The commission understood that by this life-long commitment to one another in loving fidelity, American Benedictine women can witness to the union of all persons in Christ and to the Father's love which makes such living possible.

It is an historical truth that American Benedictine women have always accepted the notion that stability in community does not preclude the establishment of smaller dependent groups (branch houses) among members of the same community. In this context, stability is not primarily a matter of geography but a relationship among persons who commit themselves to share together the common search for God.

Conversion of Life

The relationship between the vow of stability and conversion of life was immediately evident to the commission. Through reflection on the spirituality of the Rule, it was clear to them that Benedict chose the cenobitic life rather than the eremitic life as a more viable way for his monks to seek God in their conversion to Christ and the monastic pursuit of virtue.[32] He believed that in a stable community of persons living a disciplined life under a rule and an abbot all could receive the necessary support of love, prayer, and healing to enable them to continue their life-long search for the Word.

The commission maintained that in this context of a cenobitic community, the American Benedictine woman who commits herself to conversion of life rejects a static concept of perfection and replaces it with a dedication to a continuing rebirth and growth toward final maturity in her journey to the Father through Christ. They stated further that this dynamic approach to conversion of life will become a reality in her life only if she commits herself to a continual listening and responding to God's word as it is spoken to her in the daily events of her life in community and in the unfolding of the history of salvation.

Obedience

Cenobitic life is structured by Benedict so as to heighten the person's ability to listen attentively to God's word and to sharpen her response to it so that she may, like Christ, return to the Father by this "labour of obedience."[33] Aware of this central focus of the Rule of Benedict, the commission affirmed that the American Benedictine woman best expresses her obedience by an attentive listening and responding to the Father's revelation of himself to her in the Eucharist, the opus dei, lectio divina, and the daily events of her life. She also expresses her obedience by participating in community and by exercising her cenobitic authority as she joins her community and prioress in prayerful reflection and decision-making. When a community decision has been reached and a policy established, the American Benedictine woman further actualizes her obedience by accepting it with a sincere openness to its truth and value. In other matters she does not shirk the responsibility for personal decision-making but discerns the actions of her life in the context of community.

Poverty

Prior to Vatican II the vow of poverty had been most often understood in the narrow canonical sense of renunciation of material goods. Attuned to the overall vision of the Rule of Benedict and aware of the broader contemporary interpretation of the vow of poverty, the commission maintained that this vow is more than a renunciation of the accumulation and possession of material goods. They asserted that it also requires that the American Benedictine woman turn away from self-centeredness and live in simplicity of life; that she be detached in her use of things and reverent toward all of creation; that she assist in the alleviation of oppression it its many forms by sharing both spiritual and material goods with her own sisters and others in need.[34]

The members of the commissions believed that by manifesting their poverty in these ways, American Benedictine communities would articulate through their lifestyle the principle of Christian stewardship that the possession of property is not an absolute human right and that amassing wealth by depriving others of the basic necessities of life is both inhuman and unchristian. They contended also that this kind of witness would be a sign that abundance of life comes through the building of the kingdom of God on earth and the anticipation of its fulfillment when Christ comes in glory.

Celibacy

In their treatment of this vow, the Juridic Commission distinguished between the gift of celibacy and the vow of chastity. They discerned in their study that celibacy is that gift from God by which his love descends into the very center of woman's being where dialogue is rooted in the body. If the American Benedictine woman responds to that gift by her own all-embracing gift of herself in celibate love, she can bear witness to the reality that God's love can evoke from her the total gift of herself to him and to others and enable her to enter into a dialogue that transcends her natural possibilities. The commission then explained that in professing the vow of chastity the American Benedictine woman accepts the Spirit's gift of celibacy and promises to remain faithful to it through union with Christ in prayer and to give expression to it through loving relationships with others.

This rethinking of the vow of celibacy enables the contemporary woman religious to move beyond the earlier restriction of human relationships. Rather than an obstacle to love of God, the love of other persons is seen as essential to its recognition and expression. As a consequence, contemporary religious now move more freely among people.

The commission also perceived the correlation of stability and conversion of life to chastity. They understood that these two vows sustain the cenobite in her commitment to celibate love because they provide the opportunities for her to experience supportive relationships over a long period of time with those covenanted with her to seek God in a monastic way of life.

By explaining the vows in the context of the spirituality of the Rule and the theology of Vatican II, the Juridic Commission raised their meaning above the level of a purely canonical interpretation. Furthermore, they provided an understanding of them that is uniquely scriptural and Benedictine by emphasizing their importance in making possible a continuing dialogue of salvation throughout the life of the American Benedictine woman.

THE THEOLOGICAL PRINCIPLES OF PRAYER

The chapter on prayer in *Call to Life* begins by delineating the ecclesial nature of monastic life. The Juridic Commission maintained that the monastic community is a worshipping community, a sacrament of unity gathered together in a communion of life in the Trinity, experiencing God's presence in a special way through the celebration of the Eucharist and prayer. They pointed out that in the Rule Benedict organizes the cenobitic community so that the central focus of its life is the celebration of the Eucharist and the opus dei.

In the mind of Benedict, the life of the monk is a constant listening and responding to the Word of God. It is clear in his Rule that he perceived community prayer not only as the prayer of Christ praising the Father but also as the context in which the monk could hear the Word proclaimed, listen to it, and receive it into his being. The Juridic Commission therefore affirmed that the opus dei with the Eucharist is integral to the community's worship and necessary to the development of an attentive listening to the Word by which contemplation gradually permeates the whole life of the American Benedictine woman.

Mindful of St. Benedict's words concerning the quality and quantity of prayer, the Juridic Commission affirmed that intensity or purity of prayer depends neither upon frequency nor duration.[35] They proposed that a Benedictine community which is concerned about its members will care for the opus dei and pray together as often as the needs of its members and the possibility of doing so are present. Furthermore, they explained that Benedict structured the opus dei to point to the paschal mystery as the climax of salvation history and that he arranged it so that the hours of prayer were in harmony with nature. The Juridic Commission stated therefore that the times of community prayer should be integrated into the rhythm of the day so as to allow the members as active and conscious a participation as possible.

The commission then proceeded to clarify the relationship between asceticism, lectio, and prayer. Through the teaching of the Rule, they understood that the Benedictine woman prepares herself for community prayer by practicing asceticism with moderation, by receiving the Word of God in lectio divina, and by pondering it unceasingly in her heart. This experience of lectio is scripturally oriented but not scripturally limited because the Word is revealed also in the events of history and through all of creation. It was evident to the commission members that this ancient concept of lectio should receive renewed emphasis in the life of the American Benedictine woman. To enable her to experience the Word of God through lectio, they proposed that American Benedictine communities create a contemplative milieu.

The Juridic Commission affirmed that the experience of the Eucharist, opus dei, and lectio divina should enable the American Benedictine woman to integrate her ministry and her prayer because it gives her life a contemplative dimension by which her ministry flows naturally from her prayer and leads back to it. In this way the service she renders is an expression of who she is and manifests to society the fact that life becomes whole only through the contemplative experience.

By this theology of prayer, the Juridic Commission placed the prayer of the Benedictine community in an ecclesial context and established its centrality in the life of the cenobitic community. They carefully emphasized that quality rather than quantity is the distinguishing characteristic of monastic prayer, that lectio divina is absolutely essential to it, and that the life of the American Benedictine woman achieves integrity through the experience of contemplation. Through these concepts, the Juridic Commission provided a theological basis for the renewal of the prayer life of American Benedictine communities.

In the period before renewal, communities prayed together six times for almost five hours daily. The federation study of the principles of liturgical prayer led the chapter to arrange prayer life so that its times were in tune with the major poles of the day and its length was in balance with the sisters' ministries and their need for lectio, reflective leisure and interaction with the community.

THE THEOLOGICAL PRINCIPLES OF FORMATION

Although Benedict speaks directly of the training of new members in one chapter only, it is quite clear that he intends the whole experience of the monastic life, from entrance to death, to be a process of formation for transformation.[36] The spirituality of the Rule has as its core the principle of metanoia whereby the monk, having heard the Word of God, freely chooses to participate in a conversion which is a gradual "passing over" from death to life in union with the Father through Christ. In this initial turning to the Lord, the dialogue of salvation is begun and continues constantly as the American Benedictine woman enters more deeply into the paschal mystery by sharing patiently in the sufferings of Christ in the monastery until death. The Juridic Commission therefore affirmed Benedict's principle that formation is a process not completed simply by permanent commitment to a life of stability in the community but that it extends in a continuous dialogue of salvation throughout the life of the American Benedictine woman.

Because Benedict perceives that this life-long conversion is affected by perseverance in the monastery until death, the Juridic Commission emphasized that the community is the chief agent of formation. Both initial and on-going formation, they explained, must take place in the very center of the community's life.

This broadened concept of formation and the pressures of the renewal period have caused communities to initiate regular programs of
on-going education in religious life and personal development for the
professed as well as the non-professed members of the community.
The purpose of these continuing education programs in all areas of
experience is to keep the community continually updated so that the
need for radical renewal can be averted in the future.

The Juridic Commission was careful to clarify that although formation in a Benedictine community is for transformation, the community cannot assure that this transformation will take place but only
provide the opportunities for dialogue and conversion which will prepare the American Benedictine woman for those timeless moments of
encounter with the Lord. To achieve this, the members of the monastic community must continually call forth faith and love in one another and personally participate in those community experiences
which can lead to transformation.

By careful reflection on the spirituality of the Rule of Benedict,
the members of the Juridic Commission concluded that Benedict's
few explicit directives for the formation of new members implicitly
require that personal growth in the initiate which is necessary for permanent commitment. This growth includes the development and ap-
preciation of the initiate's personal gifts and a sufficient resolution of
any conflict which might obstruct the covenant relationship of the
American Benedictine woman to Christ and to her community. Before making a commitment to life in community, the initiate must
also have determined if her personal goals and gifts correspond to the
community's charism. Furthermore, she must have discovered her
need for intimacy, discerned if this need is compatible with celibate
life, and achieved realistic expectations of celibate life.

The Juridic Commission also pointed out that the community itself has a responsibility to discern the suitability of the initiate for
commitment to monastic life. It must judge whether she has sufficiently internalized the values of monastic life and grown to a personal interior freedom that will enable her to be faithful to a permanent covenant relationship with the members of her monastic
community.

This revitalized theology of formation roots the process in traditional monastic spirituality by defining it as a life-long task. It elimi-
nates the rigid pre-Vatican separation of initiates from professed
members by stating that the community is the chief agent of formation. Furthermore, it acknowledges the function of socialization in
the formation process and provides flexibility in determining the
readiness for commitment. Finally, it applies the canonical regula-

tions regarding formation in such a way that they cohere to the monastic tradition of formation as conversion of life.

THEOLOGICAL PRINCIPLES OF MINISTRY

Through their study of ministry, the Juridic Commission recognized an important distinction between apostolate and ministry in the Christian context. The apostolate of the Church is the building up of the kingdom; ministry, on the other hand, is the mode in which the apostolate is performed. By reason of their baptism, all Christians are responsible for the growth of the kingdom but each fulfills her responsibility according to her individual gifts. Ministry in this context is a service by which one "lays down one's life for one's friends." It is therefore characterized by transcendence as well as by professional competence.

The Juridic Commission affirmed that just as each person discerns her ministry according to her personal gifts so too each community discerns its participation in the mission of the church according to its charism and its historical identity. From this it flows that the ministries of American Benedictine communities must be consistent with Benedictine spirituality and the witness of cenobitic community. They must seek to achieve a life style that gives priority to community while maintaining a balance between prayer, work, and leisure. The Juridic Commission insisted that whatever the cultural situation, the American Benedictine woman remains faithful to her communal tradition which enables her to witness in a unique way through both life style and ministry.

Because one's ministry must correspond with one's gifts, the identification of a community with a single corporate ministry which may demand the repression of individual charisms is no longer a self-evident concept in religious life. Corporate ministry is an expectation of some and a source of tension to others.

THEOLOGICAL PRINCIPLES OF TEMPORALITIES

The Juridic Commission perceived that the theology of temporalities is rooted in the traditional monastic attitude that all blessings, temporal as well as spiritual, are gifts from God to be held in wise stewardship. Benedictine communities therefore receive these gifts with gratitude, use them with care, and share them with those in need.

Because the community's goods are owned corporately, the Juridic Commission maintained that the members of the community as well as its administrators are accountable for their prudent use. They explained that in order for Benedictine communities to meet their responsibilities in this regard, they must not only acquire and augment them with wise judgment but also administer them with justice and detachment. This will enable them to witness to the poverty which they have promised, to free themselves from the oppression of acquiring goods beyond their real need, and to hear more clearly the "cry of the poor" in their times.

In this renewal decade, sisters, who receive average salaries ranging from $2000 to $3500, are for the first time allowed no more than $15 to $30 monthly for such things as clothing, toiletries, stationery supplies, phone and recreational and personal interest needs. The bulk of the salaries is directed to the maintenance of the community and the payment of its institutional debts. Through these specific policies concerning temporalities, American Benedictine women practice Christian stewardship and are a sign of encounter with the Lord.

CONCLUSION

In the 1967 Opinionnaire on Benedictinism some of the sisters had commented that the communities of the Federation had to decide to live either according to the Rule or under an adapted form of it. The data had revealed, however, that the tensions and problems in these communities had not been caused by an infidelity to the Rule of Benedict but by a failure to give expression to it in a manner suited to the needs of its members and appropriate to the culture of the times. The vision of Benedict had become obscured because the modality of expressing it had become an end in itself rather than a means to a living witness. Canonical regulations, the Constitutions of the Federation, and the customaries of each community had frozen the Rule of Benedict in a cultural expression of a preceding age.

In contrast to this, the abbots and communities in primitive monasticism did not write down their rules, much less constitutions and customaries. They realized that this would deny the growth principle so essential to maintaining a living rule and a living tradition. They desired, instead, to have an oral tradition of monastic rules so as not to inhibit those who would follow them from making changes and reinterpretations according to the needs of the time and the circumstances of the locality.

Benedict himself had a tradition of rules which he applied to the communities of his time. This process of renewing and adapting past rules to present circumstances has always gone on in monasticism in one way or another. Since the ninth century, it has occurred in Benedictine communities through the reformulation of Constitutions. During the past decade the efforts of the members of the Federation to give an appropriate expression of Benedict's vision to contemporary American society have therefore been in the best tradition of monastic life.

PART V
The Personal Effects of Change

This chapter substantiates what Chapter One, "We Are Asking For More Voice" describes: the climate of pre- and post-Vatican II religious life. It suggests the principles upon which future structures in religious life must be based if they are to protect the values of the present theology of the Church in the modern world. If the function of a religious is to transcend the world, then pre-Vatican II convent life had a laudable inner logic. If, on the other hand, the function of a religious is to transform the world, then structural changes to enable that have a logic of their own.

The intent of this section of the work is to make a social-psychological assessment of the causes and effects of renewal. Therefore, its content is based almost entirely on the direct responses of the chapter delegates themselves. Of all the facets of this study, it is this type of analysis which researchers of the future will be least able to do because of its personal nature.

In response to a 453-item survey instrument, the participants to this study reported their attitudes, behavioral patterns, motives, beliefs, and private evaluations of the present state of religious life as they now experience it. This chapter attempts to explain the social and psychological factors which generated these and to identify what these religious women value and believe at the present time.

Institutional renewal ultimately depends on the feelings and commitment level of the membership. If women religious are alienated or disillusioned then there is no hope for religious life. No new laws or theories alone can save it. Therefore, this part of the research attempts to find out what the renewal of religious life did to the people themselves. Isn't that what renewal is really all about?

". . . THESE ARE NOT HER ONLY CHILDREN"

Although fear, unrest, and anxiety have been the
offspring begotten by renewal, these are not her only chil-
dren. Renewal is providing religious with the opportunity
for challenge so great that it will test our response to Chris-
tianity in a dynamic way undreamed of by previous genera-
tions of religious. Renewal is inviting, enticing religious to
dimensions of sanctity that are awesome. Therefore, I see
religious life today as a very meaningful form of existence
calling individuals to a freedom and maturity that is truly
"wholeness" . . . holiness. I am optimistic about the future
of religious life. Its form is nebulous and, to a certain ex-
tent, its direction is unclear, but it is moving toward the fu-
ture in a manner worthy of the Christ who leads it.

Delegate's Response to Participant Profile, 1976

AN ATTITUDE STUDY

It is a clear reality that American Benedictine Sisters have made
a massive number of behavioral changes in the last ten years. They
dress differently, both from their past members and now even from
one another. They are involved in different ministries. They are seen
in public more often; they pray more simply. They are less restricted
and less anonymous. They spend money and take trips. They are, for
all practical purposes, very unlike Sisters of a decade ago and yet
they are the same women.

Consequently, it is just as important to determine how these
women feel about their life as it is to describe the changes it has undergone because these are the people who have lived both modes.
Only they can assess with real understanding the impact of change on
their religious lives. Do they consider it as satisfying, as substantial,
as worthwhile in its present form as it was before Vatican II? Are
they happy? And when women enter a convent now, what kind of environment do they find?

A whole generation of Catholics, raised by sober-faced Sisters in
long flowing serge robes and high headdresses, are either openly uncertain or politely quiet about the new images of their former teachers. Whatever their attitude, very few now claim to understand in
what way, if at all, contemporary religious life is related to convent
life as it was once lived. What is more, major writers pronounce

167

doom daily about the fervor or longevity of religious life. The situation raises deep questions. What if even the Sisters themselves now regret the effects of the movement to change?

Every woman who participated as a delegate in the renewal chapters of the Federation of St. Scholastic was asked how she felt about past and present forms of religious life as she lived it. It is interesting to discover that of the ninety per cent who responded to the survey, only one-fifth of them saw themselves as progressive about changes in religious life when they went to their respective chapters. In other words, very few delegates to these renewal assemblies went to those meetings with a strong intention to change much of anything about the patterns of their lives. Some were even declared traditionalists while two-thirds called themselves moderates then and claim to be moderates now. It is impossible to believe that total change would even be acceptable to a population of this composition, let alone their conscious goal. But by the time those Chapters closed, this group of Sisters had effected by 90 to 100% majorities the most sweeping policy changes ever to shape religious life in a single decade. The question is why did they do it and how do they feel about it now?

There are two characteristics of the decision-making process: 1) that discomfort or tension follows rather than precedes change;[2] and 2) that groups make more daring or radical judgments than individuals normally undertake alone.[3] Both concepts are obvious. It is one thing to choose between two unequal situations. To select a new car instead of an old bicycle is, in most instances, an uncomplicated choice. The differences between the two are clear; the advantages are relatively unarguable. But to make a decision between two apparently equal elements, between a new Buick and a new Oldsmobile, for instance, is much less certain a situation. And it is only after the choice has been made that a person can come to know whether or not the decision was sound, whether things are really better as a result of the choice or not. At this point, people often change their minds.

When difficult decisions are made in large groups, the problem may even be compounded. It is easy to be anonymous in the group situation. Someone else does the talking; someone else promotes the idea. Consequently, even though a group, made heady by its own rhetoric and identity, may make grandiose gains together, its individual members left alone and defenseless later may easily be less bold about the issue. The conclusion is that individuals who have made major changes will more than likely be concerned later about whether or not these decisions have indeed been wise choices. If they are uncertain or actually negative about the outcomes, it is highly likely that they will withdraw from the commitment once they are outside the influence of the group in which the decision was made. The General Chapters would seem to have been particularly vulnerable to these circumstances. Some long held customs were certainly to be questioned but many of the proposals for change were equally troublesome. And at home there would be no General Chapter to make the explanations or interpret intent.

As a rule, General Chapters are brief and intense. None of the sessions held during the Renewal Period—'66, '68-'69, '71 or '74—met longer than a week.[4] In 1966, the entire process took less than three days. But in all cases the Sisters met in formal session morning, afternoon and night. The delegates came from across the country, only several from each of the 22 member communities, and strangers to one another. In this rarefied and focused atmosphere, personalities, private histories and local agendas could not intrude on the process or color its outcomes. There is certainly room to believe that in circumstances of this kind the mood of the moment or the prestige status of the consultants who were used, especially in the earlier Chapters, could affect the situation to such a degree that delegates might definitely vote for policies which they would later consider harmful and so regret. Since General Chapters are not stable communities or ongoing groups, there is an even higher likelihood that members would later find it easy to disassociate themselves from its decisions. After all, the delegates didn't really know one another; didn't owe one another anything; would probably never be together again so what could be lost by going back to safer, more familiar ways once they returned to their home communities?

The fact of regret or retraction would be a serious consideration under normal conditions. In this period and in regard to these meetings, the possibility is of even greater concern. If women who have participated actively in two distinct styles of religious life feel negative about the results of the changes, then in that situation alone may lie sobering questions about the immediate future as well as the spirit of any religious life which comes from it.

One of the purposes of this study, therefore, was to determine as clearly as possible how the sister-delegates of this renewal period feel now about pre- and post-renewal forms of religious life. In order to determine those feelings, each respondent was given a mixed list of 54 adjectives, one-half negative, the other half positive in connotation and was asked to indicate which adjectives in the list, in her opinion, applied to pre-Vatican II religious life. Then she was asked to use the same list of adjectives to register her attitude toward post-Vatican II religious life. In each case, the respondent was instructed to indicate whether the adjective given was generally true or generally false of the environment of that period as she knew it. The answers are not reflective of women who are bitter, fearful, regretful or negative.

ATTITUDES TOWARD PRE-VATICAN II RELIGIOUS LIFE

There are some observations about which the group is very sure and very unified. For instance, two-thirds of the respondents agreed that life in pre-Vatican communities of Benedictine women was strong in thirteen areas. (See TABLE I.) They considered the convent life of the past *meaningful, satisfying, effective* and *happy*. They called it *secure, stable, edifying, reverent* and *respectful*. They said it had been for them *hopeful, peaceful, joyful* and *sanctifying*. These word choices are important ones. They convey clearly that pre-Vatican II religious life was purposeful and clear. It gave a sense of meaning to life. Its goals and its structures were steady. Everybody knew what was to be done and why and how. The people who lived this kind of life knew that tomorrow would be like yesterday; that today was under control. Women who lived the life well were enriched by its tranquility and people who observed the life were convinced of its good intentions and sincerity. Nothing was ever much disturbed; turmoil was foreign and order was pre-eminent.

What is even more interesting, perhaps, is the fact that for these respondents past forms of religious life, for all their controls, were not considered ridiculous or demeaning. For all their differences from the culture which surrounded them, most of these sisters nevertheless felt accepted and dignified, committed and fulfilled.

It is certainly legitimate then to wonder why a group who apparently lived a settled and harmonious life—quiet, steady, productive, regular and spiritual—would choose to risk it to change. The an-

TABLE I: ATTITUDES: PRE-VATICAN II RELIGIOUS LIFE

True of PV religious life		*False* of PV religious life	
Stable	96%	Unfaithful	95%
Secure	94%	Scandalous	90%
Reverent	89%	Frightening	79%
Respectful	81%	Indifferent	75%
Sanctifying	81%	Confused	72%
Edifying	81%	Depressing	70%
Happy	80%	Demeaning	67%
Meaningful	77%		
Peaceful	76%		
Hopeful	71%		
Joyful	70%		
Satisfying	70%		
Effective	69%		

swer to that question may lie in the fact that at least two-thirds of the respondents were just as strong in their association of negative qualities with pre-Vatican II religious life. (See TABLE II.) It is true that the group in large part agreed that the religious life of the past was peaceful, stable and secure. It is also true that they considered it *closed, introverted, restrictive,* and *static.* They called it *immature* and *regressive.* They said it was *impersonal.*

Religious life prior to Vatican II was built on a separatist philosophy. The "world" was to be avoided. Few people came into a convent. Few Sisters went out. Only the necessities of food and clothing were permitted and the standards for these were set by other people, not the Sisters involved. Daily schedules, work assignments, even companionship were determined by the superior.

Year after year, place after place, life was always the same. In one convent, a sign went up on the bulletin board to announce the day the sisters were to begin to wear their winter shawls. Another sign went up to tell them when to put them away for the season. A sister was trained to keep her dresser organized like everyone else's; to make her bed the same way. On her desk could be kept one picture of her own selection, the only touch of singularity that was allowed. Color and space and personal responses were all controlled. Life was predictable and sanctity guaranteed. All a sister had to do to gain it was to relinquish her own will. The result was a steady-state environment that had little respect for the rag-tag consequences of personal growth patterns.

TABLE II: ATTITUDES: PRE-VATICAN II RELIGIOUS LIFE

True of PV religious life		*False* of PV religious life	
Restrictive	90%	Liberating	79%
Frugal	85%	Dynamic	74%
Closed	84%	Forward-looking	70%
Introverted	75%	Mature	69%
Regressive	70%		
Impersonal	66%		
Static	64%		

The conclusions to be drawn are that, for many, at least, the peace had a price; sanctification required adherence to the community pattern; effectiveness was measured by old goals; respect was a very formalized thing.

But what may be even more telling in the history of change is the fact that there are a series of adjectives around which the group could come to no consensus at all. (See TABLE III.) Each of the concepts in question has something to do with the effect of environment on the development of persons and indicates what happened to their personalities as a result. The respondents are very divided in their attitudes. There was, in other words, apparently a growing tension over the question of whether or not the emphases of the past on order and transcendence were doing good things to the psychological development of women religious. Almost half the group said they were not. They agreed instead that life in pre-Vatican communities was *adolescent* or *childish*. They said, furthermore, that for them it had been *frustrating, stifling, negative* and *subservient*. They even labeled it *elitist, irrelevant* and *unsensible*. Clearly, a large number of these sisters were beginning to feel cramped by what should have been the most liberating life of all. Consequently, the growing suspicion that rigidity of institutional forms was actually beginning to affect the emotional and social development of the members may easily account for the fact that the group was ready to open itself to radical change.

TABLE III: SOCIAL-PSYCHOLOGICAL EFFECTS OF PRE-VATICAN II RELIGIOUS LIFE

True		*True*	
Lonely	40%	Sensible	44%
Questionable	42%	Relevant	45%
Dehumanizing	46%	Enthusiastic	55%
Negative	49%	Positive	57%
Frustrating	49%	Trusting	57%
Stifling	50%	Supportive	61%
Childish	52%	Loving	64%
Adolescent	56%		
Subservient	59%		
Elitist	60%		

Given these emerging attitudes the General Chapters of the period were ideas whose moments had come. The Vatican Council had closed in 1965 calling for renewal in every area and had even begun the process by officially reconsidering the very nature of the Church itself. Obviously there were no questions which could not be rightly asked, no matter how long previous answers to them had held.

The structuring of the Council, in brief and well-publicized sessions over a four-year period, also prepared people to plan for change or at least to get used to the idea that change was probably coming. Every major publication, Catholic or not, carried commentaries or editorials or reports on those groups who had already begun to adapt. In most communities of women religious, excitement, or at least an aura of expectancy, grew. Frustrations were expressed in small tentative hopes: perhaps sisters wouldn't have to ask for formal permissions any more. Perhaps they would be allowed to use the telephone; to watch feature films on TV; to call one another by names instead of titles. The list was simple and basic but it pointed back ultimately to the question of why these things had ever been done in the first place and what should be done instead. A revolution of ideas had begun.

The Federation of St. Scholastica called itself together and, following the documents of Vatican II and the *Motu Proprio*, began a series of Chapters of Renewal; not because, as the attitudinal responses indicate, they were negative or rebellious or uncommitted women, but because they were in search. And they needed to search. Four hundred sisters, approximately twenty per cent of the professed membership of the Federation, had left religious life between the years of 1963 and 1969.[5] The novitiates and postulancies had emptied too. New applications had dwindled to a trickle. To make the point, one of the consultants to the 1968 General Chapter included in his presentation on the meaning of renewal slide after slide of empty European monasteries.[6] Each abbey, he said, had once been a center of culture, renowned and effective, but was now a museum. A juncture had been reached in the history of American Benedictine women.

It is easy to see why the General Chapters were ready to make changes. What is in question now is whether or not the changes resolved the simmering issues: the development of the members and the rigidity of the institution. Having reshaped an environment which they prized despite its weaknesses, are they more or less happy about it? Do they see their choices as good ones? Are they still committed to the decisions they made as part of a Chapter of Renewal or have they reconsidered those unanimous votes and found them difficult to justify, impossible to live, destructive of religious life? Is the institution alive and its members growing spiritually and psychologically?

The answers to these questions become even more meaningful after an examination of the composition of the group itself because renewal has its myths. There are those who believe that changes would never have taken place in religious life if there had not been immense pressure applied by the young, the defecting and the disobedient. The population of women religious who responded to this study are little or no proof of those opinions.

One comfortable way to account for radical change in community life has been to blame it on the young or the militant middle-aged, as if either age group simply took over the convents and imposed change on all the others. The delegates to the renewal chapters whose responses are reported here, however, give little foundation to that kind of explanation. No single age group dominated the various chapters. In fact, every one of four major age divisions—those under 40 years of age; those between 40 and 50; 50 and 60; and those over 60 years of age—were almost equally represented. If the age of the delegates was the factor effecting change, then coalitions by other age groups could have effectively blocked the passage of any renewal legislation whatsoever. It could certainly have shown significant division. Obviously, renewal was not the fancy of the young.

Nor was it the careless creation of the lukewarm or the uncommitted. Of the 158 delegates who attended the five General Chapters of the Federation of St. Scholastica from 1966 to 1974, only six have left religious life. The women who made the decisions to renew must have intended to live under them.

Finally, the delegates came from very different social backgrounds. They were from eighteen different states. Twenty-seven of them were prioresses, the major superior of the community. Fifty-four were local superiors, coordinators or community council members. Over half of the group, in other words, was directly involved in the administration of the community and therefore the group most likely to lose status or influence as a result of organizational changes. The educational level of the group was extremely high. Sixty-nine per cent had Masters Degrees; ten per cent held Doctorates.

ATTITUDES TOWARD POST-VATICAN II RELIGIOUS LIFE

The delegates were dissimilar in age, backgrounds, responsibilities and education but one thing they all had in common. For years they had been trained in almost exactly the same ways; lived the same routines; read the same spiritual reading books; followed the same program of spiritual exercises; professed the same public vows and practised them in very similar ways. It is hard to suppose that a group such as this would generally or easily adjust to a life pattern that was so unlike the patterns in which they had been formed and had apparently found effective. But their answers to this study show that this is exactly what happened. In every instance but one they show more positive evaluation of post-Vatican religious life than of their previous community experiences. (See TABLE IV.) The feeling is that although they valued religious life in its earlier form they value its present expression even more.

TABLE IV: POST VATICAN II RELIGIOUS LIFE

Qualities affirmed of both post and pre-Vatican II religious life				Qualities affirmed only of post Vatican II religious life	
	True				*True*
	%Post	%Pre	%Dif.		
Hopeful	96	71	(+25)*	Developmental	97%
Respectful	93	71	(+12)	Positive	97%
Effective	92	69	(+23)	Open	95%
Meaningful	92	77	(+15)	Affirming	94%
Sanctifying	90	81	(+ 9)	Liberating	94%
Happy	88	80	(+ 8)	Relevant	92%
Joyful	87	70	(+17)	Sensible	92%
Edifying	83	81	(+ 2)	Forward-looking	91%
Reverent	82	89	(− 7)	Loving	89%
				Enthusiastic	88%
*Figures in parentheses indicate the difference in percentage points between the post and pre-Vatican II responses to the same adjectives.				Trusting	87%
				Supportive	86%
				Mature	83%
				Dynamic	82%

In the first place, the group reaffirmed of post-Vatican II religious life every quality they had said of pre-Vatican community, with only three exceptions. They do not claim that the present period is *stable, secure* or *peaceful.* They do call it *effective, sanctifying, meaningful* and *happy.* What is more interesting, though, is that more sisters report positive attitudes toward religious life in its present state than did of the past. In fact, in the post-Vatican responses these qualities are reported by an average of 13% more people than they were in the pre-Vatican data. The conclusion is that, for these sisters at least, contemporary religious life has not lost the qualities that were valued in pre-Vatican communities but has even gained credibility in these areas and in fourteen additional characteristics as well. Unlike their evaluation of pre-Vatican religious life, they say that life in a religious community now is *dynamic, loving, mature* and *relevant.* In large numbers they say that it is *developmental, positive* and *affirming.* They give a strong notion that a religious community is a very good place for a person to be; that it is a liberating, open, sensible and supportive environment. If people who live a life have any right to rate its depth and vitality, then religious life as it exists at present is definitely a living institution.

Like their responses to pre-Vatican II religious life, there were attributes of the present forms of community which the delegates were able neither to clearly claim nor strongly deny at the present time. There is a difference of opinion over whether or not contemporary religious life is *stable, secure* or *peaceful.* All of these elements had been allowed of the pre-Vatican environment. None of them is overwhelmingly asserted of the present period. What is more, there is considerable disagreement over whether or not religious life in its present forms isn't also *confused, fragmented* and *questionable.* Needless to say, a period which suspends the detail, the conformity and the enclosures of the past would certainly introduce ambivalence into the lives of many religious for whom order had been a premium. And so the kind of peace that comes with certainty and regularity will be threatened, too. It is difficult to find in the older theology of religious life the rationale for new patterns. To stand at the cutting edge of history, in a period of transition, with past ideals blurred and new forms yet unclear creates considerable stress for women who by public vow had promised to live religious life to the hilt. It is small wonder that numbers of them feel insecure and confused. The obvious inference is that when the institution opted for forms which emphasized the development rather than the control of person, religious life became a more challenging but less predictable experience.

It is most revealing, however, that despite the fact that sisters in this era are apparently experiencing more turmoil than they did in their immediate past, almost half report that their lives in the last ten years have been happier than they had ever expected them to be. Only 12%, in fact, say they have been less happy than they had hoped for. If that is actually the case, then whatever effort may be required to redefine and reaffirm religious life is worth the effort since, according to these sisters, the life is psychologically more healthy and potentially as sanctifying as ever before.

The central question then becomes whether or not the redefinition will succeed and if so what form it will take. There is no doubt that a number of factors had converged to facilitate change. A council of the Church itself had called for "renewal." The delegates to the renewal chapters say that they had a great deal of respect for one another's competencies in theology and the social sciences and would, therefore, probably be predisposed to follow the recommendations of their peers in these areas. There were new needs in society: the ghettoes were burning; an undeclared war in Vietnam was dividing the

United States; the political system had become suspect; individuals were being crushed by big city bureaucracies. The new mobility of the population and of the sisters themselves made ideas contagious and global needs more demanding. Worst of all, membership continued steadily to dwindle. After long years of religious life, women had begun in large numbers to leave. But simply because there were pressures in favor of change is no reason to assume that change was inevitable. To accept that position is to leap to the level of determinism. That any of these elements might certainly have led a group of sisters to come together to determine whether or not they did actually need to change is an acceptable conclusion. To conclude that therefore they would actually make changes is a tentative theory at most. The life as it stood had been blessed by the Church; it was a special vocation. People ordinarily approach the major poles of life with great caution and limited designs.

A COMPARISON OF ENVIRONMENTS

The fact that radical change took place in religious communities of women cannot be explained by outside situations alone. Something must have existed within the environment itself which these women felt in the recesses of their own lives and bore in their hearts. A review of the adjectives most commonly associated with both periods may be a clue to the tone of the pre-Vatican II spiritual environment which had come to make it difficult for committed women of this era to experience a fuller possibility of spiritual growth. (See TABLES V and VI.)

A reading of the positive and negative qualities that are most and least affirmed of pre-Vatican II religious life points up a clear picture. The life was stable and ordered but at the same time inert and restrictive. The life was safe and sanctifying but, according to these people, had gone dry and closed itself off. Few questioned that it was edifying but a large number had begun to deny that it was also sensible and maturing. Life was proper but repressive; clear but lacking in energy. Obviously the tension in pre-Vatican life was tension between the maintenance of the institution and the development of the person. It is no wonder that internal pressures rose in favor of change. The question is whether or not the changes eased those pressures or created even more serious problems in their place.

Life in the post-Vatican II community, as far as it can be inferred from the coalescence of general impressions, is very unlike the pre-Vatican profile. The adjectives used to describe this environment

TABLE V: ATTITUDES TOWARD
PRE-VATICAN II RELIGIOUS LIFE

Rank Ordered

POSITIVE		NEGATIVE	
Stable	96%	Restricted	90%
Secure	94%	Frugal	85%
Reverent	89%	Introverted	75%
Sanctifying	81%	Impersonal	66%
Edifying	81%	Static	64%
Respectful	81%	Withdrawn	70%
Happy	80%	Elitist	60%
Meaningful	77%	Subservient	59%
Peaceful	76%	Adolescent	56%
Hopeful	71%	Childish	52%
Satisfying	70%	Stifling	50%
Joyful	70%	Frustrating	49%
Effective	69%	Dehumanizing	46%
Loving	64%	Questionable	42%
Supportive	61%	Lonely	40%
Positive	57%	Fearful	35%
Trusting	57%	Selfish	35%
Enthusiastic	55%	Fragmented	34%
Affirming	53%	Demeaning	33%
Relevant	45%	Depressing	30%
Sensible	44%	Confused	28%
Developmental	37%	Indifferent	25%
Mature	31%	Ridiculous	22%
Forward Looking	30%	Frightening	21%
Dynamic	26%	Scandalous	10%
Liberating	21%	Unfaithful	5%
Open	16%		

by these respondents rank-order in a completely different pattern. Energy words—*open, liberating, forward-looking*—rise to the top of the list. Subservience and restriction have disappeared. Personal development is a conscious reality and hope has been raised. The new environment frightens about one-fourth of the delegates; but, in general, the climate is so positive that the confusion and feeling of fragmentation that is a natural part of any re-orientation or transition period can probably be sustained while the group adjusts to the new definition of itself.

TABLE VI: ATTITUDES TOWARD POST-VATICAN II
RELIGIOUS LIFE

Rank Ordered

POSITIVE		NEGATIVE	
Positive	97%	Confused	56%
Developmental	97%	Fragmented	47%
Hopeful	96%	Frustrating	36%
Open	95%	Frugal	34%
Affirming	94%	Lonely	26%
Liberating	94%	Frightening	25%
Respectful	93%	Fearful	24%
Relevant	92%	Selfish	21%
Sensible	92%	Elitist	18%
Effective	92%	Impersonal	14%
Meaningful	92%	Introverted	13%
Forward Looking	91%	Indifferent	11%
Sanctifying	90%	Scandalous	10%
Loving	89%	Static	8%
Enthusiastic	88%	Adolescent	6%
Happy	88%	Depressing	6%
Joyful	87%	Withdrawn	4%
Satisfying	87%	Ridiculous	4%
Trusting	87%	Negative	4%
Supportive	86%	Unfaithful	4%
Edifying	83%	Subservient	4%
Mature	83%	Restrictive	4%
Reverent	82%	Demeaning	4%
Dynamic	82%	Childish	3%
Peaceful	57%	Dehumanizing	3%
Stable	39%	Stifling	2%
Secure	39%		

The words chosen are a clue to the vitality and endurance of the group. They describe their religious lives now as *affirming* and *respectful, effective* and *trusting* despite the fact that over half of the very group who shaped the new ideals also call the period *confused* and *fragmented*. Many people who once did everything together, and looked alike, and worked in the same place and accepted the same answers about the practice and meaning of life are suddenly at different stages of acceptance or understanding. That has to be a new kind of reality for these religious to bear. And so, though in pre-Vatican religious life, it had to be questioned whether or not persons could be holy without being mature and self-directed, in post-Vatican religious life it will have to be discovered how to make self-direction compatible with community.

At any rate, the attitude analysis allows at least seven possible conclusions:

1. Whatever the fears of others, sisters living in post-Vatican communities consider religious life more meaningful in its present form than they found it before.

2. Delegates to the Renewal Chapters of the Federation of St. Scholastica claim continuing commitment to the changes undertaken.

3. Internal tensions rather than social pressures alone confirmed the need for radical change.

4. The confusion of the transition period is offset by the positive tone of the present environment.

5. Post-Vatican religious life is conducive of personal growth.

6. The basic religious values—sanctity, joy, effectiveness and love—have been augmented by renewal.

7. Life in communities of Benedictine women in the Federation of St. Scholastica has been a change in form rather than in basic values.

The point is that what we have here, it seems, is a band but not an army. Things are a little ragged around the edges but there is spirit in the clay.

BEHAVIORAL ORIENTATION

Since Vatican II five facets of convent life have changed noticeably. In the first place, spiritual practices which have traditionally characterized the vowed life have been modified or completely revised. Secondly, leisure, once considered the enemy of the soul, has taken on value. As a third factor, human relationships are encouraged rather than feared. In the fourth instance, self-direction is considered a priority for the mature religious. Finally, individual identity rather than uniformity has become common. At first glance, the changes seem to be so radical and so total that it is difficult to account for their relatively broad and quick acceptance. But tensions in community life itself as well as circumstances in the society around them had long prepared women religious to make changes in their community structures and practices. The call of the Vatican Documents to update their life styles was a summons they could easily understand.

For years religious sisters had been cast in incompatible roles. In the convent they were to be docile and childlike in their submission and eager for direction from authority. In their ministries they were to be competent professional women. Consequently, they were put repeatedly into situations which were likely to cause either discomfort or guilt: e.g., should they go to school at night to work with student committees and so be good teachers or should they stay in the convent and so be good religious? Should they eat with the "seculars" who drove them long hours to meetings or refuse food as sisters were supposed to do and cause discomfort for everyone in the car?

Role or state of life is an important element in self-development.[7] The positions people have and how they fulfill them tells them something about who they are and what their value is. Since every public position carries with it certain public expectations, it can be both personally distressing and publicly embarrassing not to be able to fill the role as it is commonly defined. For instance, for a sister to leave the Parent-Teacher meeting before refreshments were served because she was not permitted to eat in public or to be out after 9:30 p.m. was to function in ways that were proper for sisters but unprofessional for teachers in the same circumstances. This role conflict is one of the most difficult of all the stress situations of the human condition for a person to be able to sustain, since social approval and self-esteem are bound up in role performance. To be considered an irresponsible teacher or lukewarm religious affected self-confidence as well as social value.

As a result of tensions like these, individuals invariably move to clarify the social expectations which their roles imply. Sisters, too, learned soon to emphasize one position or another. Before Vatican II, a sister had two basic choices: she could be "spiritual" and give professional responsibilities the bare minimum of attention. Or, she could concentrate on the requirements of her ministry knowing that as a result she would be away from the convent more than others, reading professional as well as spiritual journals and talking more to people rather than being silent and enclosed. The dichotomy was false but real. At its base it meant that either convent regulations or public expectations would be countered. Whatever the choice, basic behavioral changes would have to be made. Religious sisters could not be expected to make independent decisions in one area but denied the right to make them in the other.

Looking back, it would seem that the choices would be easy and obvious. But more than a simple culture lag undergirded the practices and structures in religious communities. There was more to the problem than the partial truth that an old institution was slow in adjusting to the professional environment of the twentieth century. At a deeper level lay the fact that a philosophy of spirituality which rested on the assumption that matter was evil and persons unworthy was deeply engrained in the very foundations of religious orders.[8] Out of this approach to the spiritual life had come the notion that sanctity was an individual exercise of special people who tested and proved their commitment to the Gospels by avoiding the world and practicing extreme self-discipline. Renewal, then, pitted present circumstances against a long-term value system which was based on the inherent weakness of the person. In a system like this, restriction and repression of self can be considered good even by the people who are repressed. It could not be certainly presumed, therefore, that the group would really be comfortable with changes which did not preserve the structured asceticisms of the earlier period. So the question to be answered then became: If people have been trained to be dependent and repressed and been told moreover that it is holy to be so, will they really opt for behaviors that require their being able to make choices and assume consequences? In the secret places of their hearts, what actions would sisters intent on living their vows really want to do? Clearly, the intent of the questions was to determine whether or not the sisters tested might not actually have endorsed a new mode of religious life but personally prefer the earlier style of commitment.[9]

THE IMPLICATIONS OF BEHAVIORAL CHOICES

In order to determine whether these delegates to renewal chapters would choose behaviors that coincided with their attitudes toward pre- and post-Vatican religious life, the respondents were asked to select from 30 pair of behaviors the one practice in each pair which they most preferred. The thirty items used in this section were described both in its pre- and post-Vatican form. All of the behaviors were based on prescriptions taken from community customs books in use at least to 1965.[10] In this section, for instance, the respondent was asked to indicate whether she would rather a.) pray in Latin, as she had done before Vatican II, or b.) pray in the vernacular, as she does now; or a.) have her mail inspected as it was in 1965, or b.) have freedom in matters of communication as is the practice now. Then the items were scrambled so that a pair might read: a.) to pray in Latin and b.) to have freedom in matters of communication. Basic to every pair, however, was the fact that one item was traditional practice, the other contemporary.

On the basis of these forced choices, the data was analyzed to determine the general attitudes of the group toward past and present practices. When free to select one or the other anonymously, would these sisters opt for established or emerging forms of community life? Do orientations differ among the five aspects of religious life: spiritual exercise, leisure, personal relationships, authority and individuality? Of the traditional behaviors, which, if any, are still meaningful to a significant portion of the group? Is the group's basic orientation to traditional or contemporary expressions of religious life?

The process of change in religious communities over the past ten years has been emotionally unsettling for most groups and divisive for some. Every new practice brought shock waves and confusion and fear. Friends and families asked questions; the clergy showed concern; the sisters themselves were under the continuing stress of risk and uncertainty, states that were foreign to an institution that had flourished on absolutes. It is reasonable to expect, then, that in their inner selves they might surely wish back a life-style that was more defined, more tried. In every instance, however, an average of two-thirds of the group chose the more contemporary behavior rather than the traditional behavior pattern. (See TABLE VII.)

TABLE VII: PRE- AND POST-VATICAN BEHAVIORAL PATTERNS

%	*	
9.9	T	1a. To take a companion when I leave the premises
90	C	1b. To have freedom in matters of communication
5.6	T	2a. To ask permission to do such things as eat with seculars
94	C	2b. To have a private room
70	C	3a. To make a private on-going assessment of my strengths, weaknesses
29	T	3b. To pray from a common monastic breviary
5	T	4a. To pray in Latin
95	C	4b. To have no specified community customs book
90.7	C	5a. To participate in various forms of communal reconciliation
9.3	T	5b. To use Gregorian Chant in the liturgy

%	*		
91.4	C	6a.	To choose my own time of recreation
8.6	T	6b.	To have only a specific number of home visits a year
64	C	7a.	To have no distinguishing garb as a community
36	T	7b.	To have specific times and places of silence
5.8	T	8a.	To observe the practice of mail inspection
94	C	8b.	To talk at any time and place in the convent
6.5	T	9a.	To sleep in a dormitory
93.5	C	9b.	To have any number of home visits a year
90	C	10a.	To use varied forms of music in the liturgy
10	T	10b.	To set aside a specific period of time each day for particular examen
3.6	T	11a.	To have a book of community customs
96	C	11b.	To pray in the vernacular
2.9	T	12a.	To participate in culpa chapters
90	C	12b.	To use several arrangements of the Liturgy of the Hours
95	C	13a.	To make personal decisions for myself
5	T	13b.	To be present at a specified community recreation every day
19	T	14a.	To wear the same distinguishing garb as the rest of the community
81.2	C	14b.	To go out alone
4.3	T	15a.	To observe rank in community
96	C	15b.	To attend Mass when I am able
98.6	C	16a.	To treat all people with equal respect
1.4	T	16b.	To make an annual inventory of my possessions and submit it to a superior
1.4	T	17a.	To submit Lenten resolutions to the superior for approval
98.6	C	17b.	To develop healthy interpersonal relationships with members of both sexes
32.9	T	18a.	To accept the apostolic assignments assigned by the prioress
67	C	18b.	To decide for myself what kind of personal accessories I need
80	C	19a.	To have money to spend
20.9	C	19b.	To use the television when I want to

%	*		
54.3	C	20a.	To live where I choose even if the motherhouse is in the vicinity
46	T	20b.	To love God only
78.4	C	21a.	To have no assigned rank
21	T	21b.	To work only within the institutional commitments of the community
37.9	T	22a.	To live at the motherhouse if my ministry is in the vicinity
62	C	22b.	To eliminate my surplus possessions
6.4	T	23a.	To use TV only within prescribed times
93.6	C	23b.	To practice appropriate penances
83.5	C	24a.	To discern for myself the form and place of ministry
17	T	24b.	To follow the regulations of the community in the use of accessories (eyeglasses, etc.)
2.9	T	25a.	To avoid associations with members of the opposite sex
97	C	25b.	To live within a budget or allowance
5.7	T	26a.	To treat the clergy with greater respect than is generally shown to others
94	C	26b.	To have human friendships
36	C	27a.	To work outside the institutional commitments of the community
65	T	27b.	To attend Mass daily
6.4	T	28a.	To be assigned by my superior to study in a particular field
93.6	C	28b.	To take time for leisure
85	C	29a.	To exercise discretion in developing personal relationships
15	T	29b.	To fill my time with work and prayer
94.2	C	30a.	To decide on a field of study myself
5.8	T	30b.	To avoid unnecessary contacts with people outside my religious community

*T = traditional practice   C = contemporary

This choice of less restrictive or more choice-provoking behaviors is consistent then with the attitudes expressed toward post-Vatican religious life. Although these forced-choice patterns simply indicate that the group has evidently made a break with the concepts and philosophy of the past and not that they necessarily approve without reservation the present programs, the results are nevertheless revealing. In each choice there is clear evidence that this group expects to take responsibility for its own acts. It appears, too, that neither nostalgia nor regret is operating within this particular body of religious women. Though they go on record saying that pre-Vatican life was meaningful and sanctifying for them when they lived it, they do not, when given specific manifestations of that form of religious life, choose to live it again. What is more, in each of the areas tested —spiritual practice, leisure, social patterns, government and identity —the choices made reflect beliefs or values that are distinct from the traditional principles of formation which were part of each respondent's upbringing in religious life. If these behavioral choices are an indication of anything at all, they are an indication that a whole new philosophy of commitment is affecting the development of modern religious life.

THE NATURE OF SPIRITUAL PRACTICES

Religious life in the Benedictine tradition is a life consecrated to the practice of the Gospel. The Rule provides for stable communities, rooted in the scriptures and devoted to the spiritual and corporal works of mercy which St. Benedict calls "The Instruments of Good Works." Religious life in this spirit is designed then to be a balance between the contemplation of the God-experience in life and a response to its demands. In order to effect the union of the two, it presupposes both prayer and penance. A review of some representative spiritual practices of pre- and post-Vatican religious life reflects two distinct approaches to this prayer-penance concept. In the first mode communal forms are paramount; in the second, individual responsibility is the ideal.

In the pre-Vatican community, prayer was said in Latin from a single authorized text, the monastic breviary, and sung in Gregorian Chant. Central to the environment was the strict regulation of times and places of silence. For most sisters, particularly those who taught, conversation with other members of the community was confined to 45 minutes a day and, with the exception of major celebrations, never during meals. Spiritual reading books, meditation periods and private devotions all developed to provide personal prayer experiences in the vernacular. Prayers got longer, ministries got more taxing and the two situations—convent life and professional demands—got more disparate. The language, the breviary, the musical form and the silence were all foreign to the cultural background and the immediate milieu out of which the American religious came. As a result, pre-Vatican prayer life was formal, stylized and remote from the ordinary conditions of life.

The penitential practices of the period, too, had an aura of formula about them. In weekly Culpa Chapters (in English called a Chapter of Faults) the sisters confessed those personal mannerisms or minor accidents which had become part of a regular community script. Each day time was set aside in the schedule for the examination of conscience, or particular examen, a practice designed to uproot faults by counting daily transgressions and comparing the results to previous counts. During Lent the sisters submitted a Lenten resolution for the approval of the superior, who might accept it or prescribe another if she thought that some other mortification would better suit the person involved. With the penance went an inventoried list of possessions so the superior could indicate what was excessive and call for its disposal. The point is that a person's spiritual choices, too, were controlled.

The respondents to this survey chose in every instance to reject these stylizations of spiritual experiences and asceticism. (See TABLE VIII.) In their stead they selected behaviors that call for personal accountability and cultural relevance.

The philosophy of spiritual growth inherent in this post-Vatican position is geared to the notion that individuals who are sincere in their commitment and devoted to the achievement of their ideals can be trusted to pursue a regimen of prayer and penance that is consonant with community life. It emphasizes response to individual graces rather than a standardization of forms. The fact that these respondents choose to pray in the vernacular; to vary their forms of reconciliation and prayer; to live without what they themselves judge to be surplus; to practice appropriate but not standard penances; and to attend Mass when they are able, not because someone else thinks that it ought to be part of the daily routine, may be the indicator of the emergence of a communal spirituality that is less ordered but more personal. If that is the case, then it is apparently the purpose of this spirituality to lift to another sphere the matter of everyday life rather than to routinize exercises on the assumption that regularity itself is sanctifying.

LEISURE

In Benedictine life, leisure has always been considered an essential element of its scriptural and contemplative dimensions. For the

TABLE VIII: SPIRITUAL PRACTICES:
                    TRADITIONAL AND CONTEMPORARY

%	*	
10	T	To set aside a specific period of time each day for particular examen
70	C	To make a private on-going assessment of my strengths and weaknesses
5	T	To pray in Latin
96	C	To pray in the vernacular
3	T	To participate in Culpa Chapters
91	C	To participate in various forms of communal reconciliations
9	T	To use Gregorian Chant in the liturgy
90	C	To use varied forms of music in the liturgy
1	T	To submit Lenten resolutions to the superior for approval
94	C	To practice appropriate penances
36	T	To have specific times and places of silence
94	C	To talk at any time and place in the convent
29	T	To pray from a common monastic breviary
97	C	To use several arrangements of the Liturgy of the Hours
65	T	To attend Mass daily
96	C	To attend Mass when I am able
1	T	To take an annual inventory of my possessions and submit it to a superior
62	C	To eliminate my surplus possessions

*T = traditional behavior   C = contemporary behavior

Discrepancies in total percentages are accounted for by the fact that each of these items was originally paired with an unlike element rather than its opposite. Consequently, the percentage of choice will depend also on what the item was chosen against. (See TABLE VII.)

American Benedictine sister who is actively involved in professional works, it is also a psychological priority. The daily horarium, though, provided for little common recreation and no private relaxation at all. Even meditation and spiritual reading were done in common under

prescribed circumstances. If the data from the delegates who participated in this study can be taken to signal a trend, then the concept
of leisure, too, has apparently taken a major turn in contemporary
religious life. (See TABLE IX.) Despite the conditioning of the earlier period, it has come to be regarded as a personal and private act of
high value.

TABLE IX: THE NATURE OF LEISURE: TRADITIONAL AND CONTEMPORARY

%	*	
5	T	To be present at a specified community recreation every day
91	C	To choose my own time of recreation
6	T	To use the television only within prescribed times
21	C	To use the television when I want to
15	T	To fill my time with work and prayer
94	C	To take time for leisure

*T = traditional behavior   C = Contemporary behavior

Discrepancies in total percentages is accounted for by the fact that
each of these items was originally paired with an unlike element
rather than its opposite. (See TABLE VII.)

Of equal interest, perhaps, is the fact that the work ethic, once as
pronounced in religious life as it was in the society around it, has
given way to a respect for the productive effects of non-labor and
private space. The attitude that an individual should take time for
leisure and that this might best be done outside the context of the
total community is a post-Vatican development which at first created
a considerable amount of concern. The fear of some that, without a
common and daily recreation period during which the group sat in a
common room together for a prescribed amount of time, certain
members, particularly the old, would be isolated or community spirit
destroyed is not borne out by the cross-section of experiences brought
to this study. Almost a total majority affirm the notion that leisure is
a private or at least a personal matter and opt to retain it in its present form. The fact, furthermore, that over 90% of the group value
leisure at all is a clear departure from the philosophy of spiritual
growth which reduced religious life to work, prayer and common exercises.

THE NATURE OF HUMAN RELATIONSHIPS

The fact that human love is a necessary element of the Christian and celibate vocation has been affirmed repeatedly in the writings of the spiritual masters. In the behavioral sciences, the ability to establish and maintain deep personal relationships has been identified as one of the necessary elements of personal development and mental health.[11] In religious community, however, it is the risk of personal relationships rather than their value which has been traditionally stressed. The argument was, of course, that having no special love for anyone enabled the religious to love everyone. The result was the creation of a high level of protocol—rank, community recreation, companions—but minimal affective growth. Emotions and the manner of handling or profiting from them were suppressed in favor of control. Consequently, of all the changes which have taken place in religious life in the last decade, one that is least apparent to non-religious but which may be one of the most significant in terms of the renewal of community life is the contemporary attitude toward the nature of human relationships in the lives of women religious. (See TABLE X.)

Despite the fact that according to the Declarations and Constitutions of the federation, religious life was "founded on love for all and one another,"[12] the life style was structured in such a way as to preclude to a great extent the personal contacts or private sharings that form the basis for human bonding. The assumption seemed to be that perfect community existed when all relationships were equal. To that end all personal relationships were discouraged. In order to protect the community from disintegration and to insure the practice of detachment, a virtue considered basic to union with God and reflected in a person's ability to withdraw from all things human or material, the association of the sisters with one another as well as with relatives or acquaintances had become highly specified. Sisters spent a great deal of psychic energy attempting to remain "unattached," a process that drained more and more satisfaction out of their increasingly pressured lives. Whether or not the common life could also be community under these circumstances had emerged by 1965 as a pressing question. Among the respondents to this study, over two-thirds cited rank, restricted associations and need for experimentation in areas of community life and government as matters of major importance to their communities at the time of the chapters of renewal.

The constitutions and customs books of the period regulated every possible social situation. The underlying intent was that sisters were to love God only and so should not risk attachment to anyone

TABLE X: HUMAN RELATIONSHIPS AMONG RELIGIOUS WOMEN: TRADITIONAL AND CONTEMPORARY

%	*	
9	T	To take a companion when I leave the premises
81	C	To go out alone
9	T	To have a specific number of home visits a year
94	C	To have any number of home visits per year
4	T	To observe rank in the community
78	C	To have no assigned rank
6	T	To observe the practice of mail inspection
90	C	To have freedom in the matters of communication
6	T	To treat clergy with greater respect than is generally shown to others
99	C	To treat all people with equal respect
3	T	To avoid associations with a member of the opposite sex
99	C	To develop healthy interpersonal relationships with members of both sexes
48	T	To love God only
94	C	To have human friendships
6	T	To avoid unnecessary contacts with people outside my religious community
85	C	To exercise discretion in developing personal relationships

*T = traditional behavior   C = contemporary behavior

Discrepancies in total percentages is accounted for by the fact that each of these items was originally paired with an unlike element rather than its opposite. (See TABLE VII.)

else. The regulations were designed to guard them from that pitfall.

Relations among the sisters themselves were regulated by the custom of having assigned companions and defined ranks. In that way it was always clear where the sisters were to be and with whom. Spontaneous relationships between like-minded people were very difficult to develop and easy to identify as violations of detachment.

Relationships with people outside the community were even less free. Mail was inspected to make sure that the contents were neither frivolous nor personal. In order not to give scandal, the sisters were never to be alone with a man, including their fathers. In order not to disturb the cohesion of the community or the spirit of recollection, they were not to associate with outsiders whom they called seculars. Only priests were received with special openness. For them the schedule could be changed and the rules mitigated somewhat.

In the name of community, contemplation, and chastity the communal dimensions of celibacy had been abandoned. The phenomenon of enclosure that had never fully and completely been part of the American Benedictine tradition had become an attitude of mind.

When confronted with these experiences again, the participants to this study rejected the withdrawal patterns that had characterized the religious life of the 1960's. Almost unanimously they made choices that allowed them to go out alone, rather than to have assigned companions; to visit their family homes freely; to mingle in community rather than to have places and works assigned by rank or their dates of entrance; to develop interpersonal relationships; to have freedom of communication. The picture that emerges as a result is a tendency toward a kind of community that is alert to individual experiences and accepting of the human dimensions of the spiritual life rather than cut off from them.

DIRECTION AND CONTROL

Obedience has long been considered the cornerstone vow of religious life and for centuries the practice of it has not been much distinct from the authority systems of the monarchical or feudal societies in which it existed. In these systems authority was hierarchical and centered ultimately in a single individual who by virtue of position or education or economic influence controlled whole bodies of people. But the democratic environment of the United States, the rising educational level among women and the call of the Church itself in Vatican II for collegiality and subsidiarity all brought pressures to bear on the authoritarian structures of religious life. Factors other than the plans or insights of a single person in a privileged position began to shape the practice of the vow. Responsible obedience rather than blind obedience became the norm. The era of specialization, even in the elementary classroom, created a new social situation for superiors who had customarily assigned sisters to any one of a variety of corporate works. Communities were no longer systems of interchangeable parts; academic certification programs had given uniqueness to every profession and, plagued by financial problems or loss of sister personnel, community-owned institutions to which sisters had been routinely assigned had begun to disappear. Ministry and commitment had become very individual decisions.

The essential mandate of St. Benedict to the Benedictine religious is simply "to seek God." However, since the Benedictine religious searches in the context of community, it is obvious that the welfare of that group as well as social needs and her own abilities must come to bear upon the search. In this new milieu, the basic problem lies in the weighing and ordering of the three elements—community, self and society—in such a way that neither the individual nor the group is destroyed in the process. The transition from communal conformity to communal cohesion is a delicate one. Too much structure can make it impossible for groups of people to achieve their own ends because environments that make individuals dependent do not at the same time make them creative or adult.[13] On the other hand, groups without structure may lack effect as well as efficiency.[14]

As part of the renewal process, therefore, communities dispensed with structures which they considered to be irrelevant to this era or repressive of human development: asking permissions, mandating "customs," assigning works, for instance. This study asked the respondents to determine whether it might not really be better for religious to restore those elements which had in the past given certainty and security both to the members and the institutional apostolates that were served through them. By margins as high as ninety percent, the respondents negated the idea of returning to institutional structures that controlled religious for their own sake. (See TABLE XI.)

The effect of such choices is an active assertion of the notion that people do not exist for institutions but that institutions exist for people. The ramifications of that philosophy for the profession of obedience are sweeping. Authoritarianism has given way to the process of discernment in which the administrator, the sister and the community itself consider together the risks and reasons for major decisions. Individual adulthood rather than childish dependency has become a prime value. Communities stress peer relationships rather than hierarchical structures. In most communities, for instance, the title "Mother" for the community leader has been abandoned for that very reason. The conclusion is that if the responses to this survey are

TABLE XI: CONTROL ELEMENTS:
TRADITIONAL AND CONTEMPORARY

%	*	
6	T	To ask permission to do such things as eat with seculars
95	C	To make personal decisions for myself
4	T	To have a book of community customs
95	C	To have no specified community customs book
33	T	To accept the apostolic assignments assigned by the prioress
84	C	To discern for myself the form and place of my ministry
21	T	To work only within the institutional commitments of the community
36	C	To work outside the institutional commitments of the community
6	T	To be assigned by my superior to study in a particular field
94	C	To decide on a field of study myself

*T = traditional behavior   C = contemporary behavior

Discrepancies in total percentages is accounted for by the fact that each of these items was originally paired with an unlike element rather than its opposite. (See TABLE VII.)

in any way indicative of a trend or general philosophy of contemporary religious life, then it can be assumed that the character of obedience in the future will lose its parental overtones. The luxury of knowing what will happen in every standard instance of every day will have to give way to the vagaries of grace and the growth process.

IDENTITY

Of all the traditional understandings of the salvation myth taught by the Church, one of the most central is that God is a personal God: that Jesus became incarnate for each and every individual;

that the individual is highly valued by the Creator; and that Christian community is the interdependence of responsible people. Of all the findings of social psychology and psychiatry, one of the most basic is that self-image and self-esteem are directly related to human development and interaction.[15] What people think of themselves, in other words, regulates to a large extent the way they deal with others— openly, securely, defensively—as well as their sense of personal well-being or achievement. It is important to be somebody who is noticed by others and accepting of self. Together, these two concepts of incarnation and person may have had the single most profound effect on the total renewal of religious life.

In one section of this study, the participants were asked to identify which of 25 possible catalysts of change had the most effect on them as chapter delegates. Almost half of the respondents said that they had been considerably influenced by the fact that "total human development had emerged as a cultural value and replaced self-denial as a primary value for religious." Another one-third owned that they had been at least somewhat influenced by the same factor. But, though theology and psychology were compatible in their emphasis on the individual, they differed fundamentally in their understanding of what factors actually effected the development of responsible persons.

There had been a consistent strain within the Catholic tradition that effacement and the repression of self were signals of personal strength as well as virtue.[16] To "offer things up," sisters were trained, was a sanctifying process which gained merit and built character. That continual stress or self-repression might also weaken personal fiber was a finding not yet part of the formation philosophy. Furthermore, the findings of psychology indicated that a positive self-image and a high sense of self-esteem were essential to the development of mental health and the creation of community. Conformity and false humiliations were found to breed hostility, dependence and tension.[17] With those discoveries went much of the support for the permission system; the assumption of anonymity; or culpa practice, the "confession" of natural characteristics like "making mistakes in spiritual reading" or "spilling food and water." It became clear that the Christian ideal, the supportive interdependence of mature adults, was not completely possible among stunted personalities. One of the functions of renewal, therefore, became to reestablish the personal identity of the woman religious and to develop an environment where the emergence of individuality was a strength rather than a threat to the on-going dynamism of the group. In five basic examples, the respondents to this survey chose behaviors that allow for the expression of self and the recognition of uniqueness. (See TABLE XII.)

TABLE XII: IDENTITY FACTORS: TRADITIONAL AND CONTEMPORARY

%	*	
19	T	To wear the same distinguishing garb as other members of my community
64	C	To have no distinguishing garb as a community
7	T	To sleep in a dormitory
94	C	To have a private room
80	C	To have money to spend
97	C	To live within a budget or allowance
38	T	To live at the motherhouse if my ministry is in the vicinity
45	C	To live where I choose even if the motherhouse is in the vicinity
17	T	To follow the regulations of my community in the use of accessories (eye-glasses, earrings, etc.)
67	C	To decide for myself what kind of personal accessories I need

*T = tradition behavior   C = contemporary behavior

Discrepancies in total percentages is accounted for by the fact that each of these items was originally paired with an unlike element rather than its opposite. (See TABLE VII.)

It had been the custom for sisters to wear uniform clothes, to take new names (many of them male), to sleep in curtained dormitories of fifty or one hundred beds, and to beg the smallest items in limited numbers from a superior. By affirming the individual's right to make personal choices in these matters, the respondents effectively dispose of a religious life that submerges human beings into an anonymous corps. They would apparently strongly resist the restoration of an environment that blurs all of its members into standard-brand people who dress exactly the same and live in large rooms together even though the life style was explained as an attempt to live the vow of poverty.

The choices of these participants indicates instead an attempt to create a community that respects personality, i.e., the total individual as she was, is and can be. There will be problems in this orientation, too, since both individualism and institutionalism have their extremes. The extreme expression of individualism is self-centeredness. To make personal decisions without regard for their effects on community is to shirk responsibility to others, to exploit the group by using it as a base to satisfy personal desires without giving in return and to foster a selfishness contrary to the Gospel to "lay down one's life for one's friends." On the other hand, the extreme expression of institutionalism is depersonalization.[18] Groups that expect their members to forfeit personality and self-determination and maturity for whatever reasons are psychologically suspect to begin with and sanctity that must be bought at these prices is a far cry from a respect for the mystery of creation. The balance of individualism and institutionalism, however, is a community life where growth toward uniqueness as well as interdependence is possible.

CURRENT QUESTIONS

Finally, a review of the selection pattern of the forced-choice behaviors underscores three elements of pre-Vatican religious life which still have meaning or question for a significant portion of the population responding. These issues were identified by comparing the responses to the traditional and contemporary expression of each item. In this section, if there was not at least twice the amount of acceptance of the contemporary behavior as there was for the traditional expression, the conclusion was made that the element itself has independent influence, that that particular behavior is still an important factor or question among the women religious represented by this sample, and not just affected by the nature of the item with which it was paired in the instrument. This type of analysis yielded three areas of philosophical difference: the nature of a sister's apostolic activity; the importance of daily Mass and the desirability of residency options. (See TABLE XIII.) Basic to these behavioral choices are the effects of current circumstances and dissimilar attitudes toward the nature of corporate witness, Eucharistic orientation and community.

TABLE XIII: CURRENT QUESTIONS

%	*	
21	T	To work only within the institutional commitments of the community
36	C	To work outside the institutional commitments of the community
65	T	To attend Mass daily
96	C	To attend Mass when I am able
38	T	To live at the motherhouse if my ministry is in the vicinity
54	C	To live where I choose even if the motherhouse is in the vicinity

*T = traditional behavior   C = contemporary behavior

Discrepancies in total percentages is accounted for by the fact that each of these items was originally paired with an unlike element rather than its opposite. (See TABLE VII.)

Institutional Apostolates. The effect of corporate ministries and community-owned institutions on the development and renewal of religious life is hard to estimate but integral to the kinds of changes that have taken place in communities of women religious in the past decade. The movement into new ministries, whatever their value and however visionary they may be, is affecting the character of ministries that were begun and institutionalized by past generations. The buildings and structures which were raised to implement these works still exist and must be dealt with. Many of them have formed the economic base as well as the principal activity of the community. Some of them are less than twenty years old. Some of them are still mortgaged. All of them were once seen as the community's greatest and most appropriate work. Whole generations of sisters were educated to staff them. Closings mean that large numbers of upper middle-aged women will have to be retrained for other areas, perhaps, and adjust to new environments. The question then of whether or not sisters ought to work only in institutional commitments has pragmatic as well as parochial overtones.

There is, in addition, the fundamental question of whether or not religious should function in institutions which do not also give corporate Catholic witness. Should sisters work as counselors in state prison systems or as writers of farm legislation or in any public arena? Or should they stay in the convent school or the Catholic hospital in order to maintain it for the community and to witness to the pastoral function of the Church through the existence of a parallel Catholic institutional system?

In the final analysis, the resolution of the question may depend both on the financial resources of the community, its commitment to a new world order, and the group's understanding of the meaning of witness. In this present age, however, it is apparently still an unresolved issue for women religious.

Eucharistic Orientation. The traditional understanding of Eucharistic orientation was that the sisters were to attend Mass daily. There is obviously a growing acceptance of the notion—if the population of this study may be regarded to be a barometer of general attitudes—that readiness and quality of celebration is a more essential part of a Eucharistic mode than quantity or regularity. There is even the implied understanding that dailiness under certain conditions may contribute more to routinization or weariness in the spiritual life than it enriches it. Furthermore, this trend is surely not unrelated to other significant developments. The concerted effort to move away from formalism in spiritual practice supports the notion. Then, too, the liturgical movement, which preceded the renewal of religious life, heightened awareness among sisters of the expressive function and participatory nature of the mass. Finally, the continuing effect of past training patterns encourages people to create and maintain personal rather than group patterns. Now, too, the woman's movement has raised new consciousness about the relationship between liturgy, clericalism and the role of women in the Church. It is clearly easy to account for the fact that the question has yet to be resolved.

Community. Finally, the understanding of what constitutes community itself is still in flux. At one time, sameness was an essential criterion. Now that the era of uniform dress is over, however, there is need to examine the issue in more depth. The fact of the matter is that sameness has disappeared but communities have not. The question in the wake of this experience is the principal one: how much difference can a group sustain and remain a group?

The cloister, too, was once considered an essential part of the definition of community, much as the homestead or the estate or the village identified families. People who were not community members were kept out; people who were stayed in. Consequently, a natural manifestation of the traditional definition is that at least everyone who can should live together at the motherhouse, but the history of religious communities in the American experience clouds the conclusion. Unlike the enclosed European convents from which they came, Americans moved quickly to establish "missions" or branch houses which were staffed by two or more community members miles from the founding community but dependent on it for resources, government and personnel. Some communities even had two or three branch houses in the same city as the motherhouse for the sake of convenience.

With the emergence of renewed respect and trust for individuals, the creed of conformity has begun to disintegrate in favor of spiritual and psychological bondings. This emphasis on relational community has led to a move to separate home and work environments and the sudden rise of small "primary" communities. Some arise within the central group itself and organize themselves in such a way that they have separate prayer, meal and community patterns that are distinct from other residents of the same large institutions. Some move out of the large group entirely. Unlike the branch houses of the past, common work is not the unifying element in the group and sisters are not assigned to their living conditions. Fear for the cohesion of the larger community and concern for whether or not a high level of commitment to the total group can be sustained under these conditions is a continuing problem for some sisters. Whatever the shape of future structures or networks, it is clear that the acceptance of individual differences will make it necessary for communities to define their group boundaries in ways other than sameness or living space or the whole notion of person as well as community may be lost.

CONCLUSIONS

Pre-Vatican II religious life was ordered largely by the 1922 Constitutions of Federation of St. Scholastica and the customs books of the individual priories. The practice of these prescriptions was considered essential to the proper expression of religious life and sanctions were applied in order to maintain them. Since the Vatican Council and the General Chapters of the renewal period, most of these practices have been suspended or revised. In order to determine whether or not the delegates to the chapters which legitimized these changes were themselves comfortable with the new experiences, they were given the opportunity to select a traditional or contemporary custom from each of thirty pair of possible behaviors. The behavioral choices made by this group point to the following assumptions:

1. There is overwhelming preference for contemporary forms of

behavior among this particular group of women religious.

2. Contemporary spirituality is based on and grows out of a conscious commitment to the demands of everyday life rather than on the use of structured or stylized penances.

3. Formalism in prayer and penance has been abandoned.

4. The concept of leisure as a private and essential element of religious life is strongly affirmed.

5. Increased emphasis is being given to the development of human relationships as an acceptable element of celibate community.

6. Community control is rooted in the discernment process rather than in authoritarian structures.

7. The affirmation of personality has replaced conformity as a central value of religious life.

8. Three questions have arisen as a result of behavioral changes in post-Vatican religious life: the place of corporate apostolates in the life of women religious and the community; the nature and obligations of a Eucharistic orientation in religious life; the nature of community in an open society.

Whatever the questions, however, it is obvious from the general pattern of behavioral choices that religious life is done with old forms, at least for a significant portion of the membership. What the new forms will eventually be and how they will affect religious life in the next century is still uncertain; but what is becoming increasingly clearer is that, whatever the pain of renewal, there are many who are beyond the winter of their discontent.

MOTIVES FOR CHANGE

Changes in religious life become both more easy and more difficult to understand as the realization dawns that the Chapters of Renewal did not mandate change. What the chapters did was to research the history of Benedictine monasticism, the theology of the vows, the psychology of human development and the state of contemporary religious life; and then, on the basis of these findings, to identify certain areas of community life which could be lived out differently, if the members so chose, without departing from the essential elements of the religious vocation and the monastic tradition.[19] What is more, the basic principle of renewal in local communities of women during the entire period was also to permit experimentation, but not to prescribe it. So, although anyone might change once an area had been declared open for experimentation, no one had to. For instance, an individual could modify her clothing style or she could retain the traditional uniform; she could request a specified allowance from which to buy personal articles or she could continue to request them from the general supply; she could take an active part in the selection of a ministry or she could request to be assigned in the traditional manner. These circumstances give rise to a compelling question: if the legislative assemblies did not require change, then did people actually do so and if they did, what kinds of factors most prompted the adaptations?

Since the changes proposed confronted the ingrained beliefs of their entire lives, it is entirely possible to expect that many of the delegates, too, though they had affirmed the right for others, would not themselves choose to change. In fact, the greater part of this group described itself as basically moderate or even traditional in their attitudes toward renewal rather than eager for change.

It is true that these same respondents did claim to have very positive attitudes toward the climate and effectiveness of post-Vatican II religious life and that in a paper and pencil test they selected contemporary rather than traditional forms of religious practices when given the opportunity to make anonymous choices between the two situations. Research has discovered, however, that it is relatively common for people to say that they feel one way but continue to act in an entirely opposite fashion.[20] In classic experiments, for instance, subjects who claimed not to be racist nevertheless refused in their daily practice to rent rooms to blacks.[21] Obviously attitudes are not always reflected in behaviors.

In this case, however, over 90% of the delegates actually engage in at least one of the major behavioral changes which have been adopted since the beginning of the renewal period: the participation in social-cultural events; adherence to a personal allowance; divestment from the traditional habit; the practice of communal discernment; and the sharing of spiritual reflections. (See TABLE XIV.)

In every area of community life then—in spiritual practices, the uses of leisure, the mode of authority, the manner of interpersonal relations, and the choice of identity symbols—past delegates to the General Chapters of Renewal have made newly endorsed behaviors a part of their own life patterns. In other words, most of the respondents to this study actually demonstrate behaviors in their own lives that are clear departures from past models of convent culture despite the fact that in an earlier period of their lives they had publically opted for an entirely different life style. Why? What led responsible women, authority figures in fact, to make such significant modifications in the very system for which they were responsible?

TABLE XIV: CURRENT BEHAVIORAL PRACTICES

	*More	Same	Less	Neither
1. Share spiritual reflections with others	62.2	25.4	2.8	4.9
2. Talk with Sisters about our life together	71.8	25.4	.7	2.1
3. Seek and welcome insights of other sisters in matters of community life	83.8	12.7	2.8	.7
4. Seek and welcome the insights of other sisters in matters concerning ministry	69.0	22.5	2.8	5.6
5. Seek ways of reconciliation in community and in my places of work	64.8	31.7	2.1	1.4

	Yes	No
6. Use contemporary clothing	75.4	23.9
7. Live within an allowance	87.3	12.0
8. Take regular vacation periods	69.0	30.0
9. Work in a self-chosen ministry	62.7	36.6
10. Attend cultural events	93.7	5.6

*More = more than before; Same = about as much as before; Less = less now than before; Neither = neither in my pre-Vatican religious life nor now.

In order to surface the factors which most contributed to the personal decision of these various delegates to accept change-patterns in their own life, they were asked to rank-order five of twenty possible situations which they recognized as having affected them. The twenty items reflect four general areas of influence: ecclesiastical affirmation; communal relationships; social pressures and personal stress factors. (See TABLE XV.)

TABLE XV: IMPACT ANALYSIS GRID

Ranked 1-5 by			
86%	*EA	1.	The Vatican Documents called for change.
30%	PS	2.	I felt that much of pre-Vatican religious life inconvenient.
7%	CR	3.	The superior expected the community to change.
27%	PS	4.	I felt that sisters were elitist, triumphalistic and out of touch with contemporary society.
17%	SP	5.	The sisters I lived with had changed.
80%	PS	6.	I felt that change was necessary if religious life was going to survive.
47%	CR	7.	Our local chapter voted to permit the change.
95%	PS	8.	Personal convictions flowing from new understandings of the essence of religious life required change.
3%	SP	9.	My family encouraged me to change.
22%	PS	10.	I felt I should change to support others.
10%	SP	11.	My best friends were changing.
3%	CR	12.	The prioress was not changing.
3%	SP	13.	The students I taught expected me to change or made fun of sisters who didn't.
63%	PS	14.	Our past behaviors were becoming meaningless to me.
7%	EA	15.	The priests with whom I worked encouraged change.
18%	SP	16.	I had argued for change for a long time and so felt that I should adopt the changes when they came.
4%	CR	17.	The younger sisters were changing.
4%	CR	18.	The prioress changed.
2%	CR	19.	The older sisters were changing.
30%	PS	20.	I came to believe that it was all right for me to do it.

*EA = ecclesiastical affirmation; CR = community relationships; SP = social pressure; PS = personal stress.

To the question of why the sisters changed a number of answers have been assumed by others: that they succumbed to the pressure of liberal dissidents; that they were doing what the Church said to do; that seculars chided them until they gave in; that they couldn't live in their own communities unless they did. To have these sisters themselves answer the question makes it possible to look at these various kinds of influence-agents and to speculate on the depth and duration of decisions that emanate from one kind of influence rather than another. That kind of information is of no small importance to the continuing renewal of religious life.

ECCLESIASTICAL AFFIRMATION

The two instances of ecclesiastical influence which were included on the list of impact items represent official church contact as sisters know it best: through Roman documentation and through contact with local priests.

TABLE XVI: ELEMENTS OF
ECCLESIASTICAL AFFIRMATION

	Ranked 1-5 by
1. The Vatican Documents called for change.	86%
2. The priests with whom I worked encouraged change.	7%

Although 86% of the respondents rank the call of the Vatican Documents among the five circumstances which influenced them most, less than ten per cent indicate that encouragement from local priests was any factor at all. (See TABLE XVI.) In another part of the survey, in fact, over a third of the respondents maintain that obstruction by the clergy was actually an obstacle to change. It is of course unclear whether the remaining delegates were in dialogue with local priests about change or not. But whatever the case, it is relatively certain that one of the major factors influencing this group as individuals was the fact that the official Church at its highest level had mandated renewal. It may be exactly this commitment to the universal Church and the clear inappropriateness of the local clergy to address the situation that empowered religious women to proceed for themselves.

In the main then it is clear that these delegates took the Vatican Documents to heart regardless of any forces to the contrary.

COMMUNAL RELATIONSHIPS

Among the impact items were six circumstances which could conceivably have motivated change in sisters whose concept of religious life revolved around acceptance by significant groups or authority figures in the community.

TABLE XVII: COMMUNAL RELATIONSHIPS

	Ranked 1-5 by
1. Our local chapter voted to permit change.	47%
2. The superior expected the community to change.	7%
3. The younger sisters were changing.	4%
4. The prioress changed.	4%
5. The prioress was not changing.	3%
6. The older sisters were changing.	2%

Very few of the delegates claim that reference groups or authority figures had much to do with their private decisions to make behavioral changes in their own lives. (See TABLE XVII.) On the contrary, they discount almost entirely the notion that the changes they now participate in were undertaken in order to identify with any particular element of the community. The legitimation of change by older members or the expectations of change by younger ones may indeed have been present in each situation but the delegates do not own these factors as having contributed to their individual acceptance of behavioral change.

The single communal element, in fact, which is held as having been important in the delegates' personal decision to participate in new forms of religious life is the influence of the community chapter as the authorizing element in the renewal process of the local community. Almost half of the respondents attest to the fact that the approval of change by their own chapters or community assemblies had had considerable effect on their own actions.

The fact is an interesting one. In the first place, it indicates that change was not simply an individual decision but one made in the context of community. In the second place, it reflects a sensitivity to the local group and high affirmation of the respect for the autonomous character of each priory. For these women, changes were made not simply because other groups of women religious were changing but because their own groups had ratified the movement. It is also possible, however, that this dependence on the vote of the local chapter may also be indicative of a need of these women for legitimation by authority, a conclusion not inconsistent with research data attesting to the fact that peoples in any authoritarian structure are likely to look to others for direction.[22]

Whatever the underlying reason, the statement "Our local chapter voted to permit change" masks years of struggle and confusion in the member priories during this renewal period. Although the General Chapters of the Federation had authorized experimentation in every area of community life, factions arose in each community. In some cases, the prioresses, acting out of the content of the Vatican documents and the Chapters of Renewal, simply permitted change. In others, every item was expected to be taken to the community for approval. As a result, in many instances, individual sisters grew frustrated by the refusals and changed of their own accord or left the community entirely, wearied by the internal tensions and opposition. Eighty percent of these respondents, in fact, said that experimentation in community life and government was a central issue to them, to their communities, and to the General Chapter during this period. Obviously, the vote of the local chapter to permit change was an important part of the renewal process and no minor factor in the life of the individual religious.

SOCIAL PRESSURE

The impact analysis also included six examples of social situations to which most sisters would have been exposed during the period of the Renewal Chapters and which could conceivably have triggered the need to be socially acceptable or consistent. Some of the items described circumstances within the community itself which could have brought social pressure to bear on the individual's decision to adopt change. It could be difficult, for instance, to continue to live the traditional religious life if others in the same living group did not want to or if friends or associates who for years had been a source of support and identity also chose to do otherwise.

On the other hand, the expectations of those outside the community might also have affected the decision of large numbers of sisters to accept change even though privately they would have preferred not to have had to make the transition. The attitudes of family members or school students perhaps might certainly have been the decisive factor for sisters who wanted to be effective in their ministries or respected in their homes.

In other cases, the fact that some sisters, in theoretical fashion, might have argued for renewal or even defended it before the general chapters approved it could have felt obligated to change in order to give public proof that they were stable and consistent personalities. (See TABLE XVIII.)

There is very little evidence in this study to support the idea that this was actually the case. Pressure from others, whether expressed or not, is owned by less than twenty percent of the respondents as factors which had any considerable effect on their decisions to adopt new forms of religious life.

TABLE XVIII: SOCIAL PRESSURES LEADING TO CHANGE

	Ranked 1-5 by
1. I had argued for change for a long time and so felt that I should adopt the changes when they came.	18%
2. The sisters I lived with had changed.	17%
3. My best friends were changing.	10%
4. My family encouraged me to change.	3%
5. The students I taught expected me to change or made fun of those who didn't.	3%

These responses lead to the conclusion that forces outside of the community—family and students, for instance—were either not actively supportive of change, not conscious of it at all, or simply indifferent to the renewal of religious communities. At least the respondents to this study did not consider these groups as having exerted influence on their actual decision.

On the other hand, a small portion, 18%, do relate their final move to the fact that living groups or their own past record of public positions did affect the decision to make changes in their own behavior patterns. Consequently it seems that for some members, at least, the need to identify with the community or its opinion leaders as well as to maintain a role consistent with their own established reputation or public image was of priority.

Since one of the functions of a group is to provide norms and identity for the individual members there is absolutely nothing unusual about these responses. What is of interest, however, is that more of these respondents—the average of whom had been members of the community from 26 to 35 years—did not report the same influence. One possible explanation may be that the strong emphasis on individual sanctification and relation to authority in the past had succeeded in weakening the natural network of relations within the group. The other explanation is simply that even more salient influences than group expectations existed. The remaining responses indicate that this might indeed be the case.

PERSONAL STRESS

It probably goes without saying that women who commit themselves to celibate community life for the purpose of prayer and ministry see great value in it. For an institution to continue to be effective, however, its value must continue to remain clear, both to its members as well as to those whom it serves.[23] A hospital may have a reputation as the best medical center in the region among those who receive medical aid there but if the staff itself feels that the administration or philosophy of the facility actually stifles the practice of creative medicine, then it is unlikely that the institution will maintain its vitality and effectiveness for very long. Doctors and nurses committed to the profession will soon find more challenging or developmental environments to practice in. The application of the example to communities of American religious women is clear.

Unlike other periods of history or other nations of people, the culture of contemporary America offers security, comfort and independence to women as well as to men. Unmarried women do not have to go to religious communities to justify the value of their existence nor do they have to stay in a community for economic support. They can leave and do something else if leaving seems the better thing for them to do. Consequently, tensions between the purpose, personal value and structures of religious life will make the religious institutions more vulnerable to change and sensitive to persons than ever before in history.

In this case, it seems to have been exactly these tensions which most influenced the delegates to the Chapters of Renewal to make changes in their life styles. (See TABLE XIX.) Seven items of the impact scale related directly to the nature of religious life itself and its level of effectiveness. The responses of the delegates indicate that discrepancies between the purpose of religious life and its current state had apparently generated frustration, disenchantment with past practices and concern for the survival of the institution itself.

TABLE XIX: STRESS FACTORS LEADING TO BEHAVIORAL CHANGE

	Ranked 1-5 by
1. Personal convictions flowing from new understandings of the essence of religious life required change.	95%
2. I felt change was necessary if religious life was going to survive.	80%
3. Our past behaviors were becoming meaningless to me.	63%
4. I came to believe that it was all right for me to do so.	30%
5. I felt that sisters were elitist, triumphalistic and out of touch with contemporary society.	27%
6. I felt that much of pre-Vatican life was inconvenient.	30%
7. I felt I should change to support others.	22%

Three stress points emerge strongly. In the first place, for most of these women, there had obviously been a period of philosophical demarcation. Concepts held for life and considered almost absolute had suddenly been opened to question. The ideas of Church, government, community and person had been scrutinized and reordered, not only by theoreticians but apparently by these women themselves. A full 95% of the delegates claim to have come to new understandings about the very purpose of their lives. Whatever they had been told in the past about the function and form of religious life had apparently become impossible to accept. What is more, 80% of these same respondents came actually to doubt that religious life could possibly survive in the form in which for years they themselves had lived it. The number of dispensations from every community every year only confirmed the fear. Finally, for two-thirds of the group the past behaviors, clear and constant though they had been, had lost all meaning. But to discover new belief patterns, to fear for survival if the old ones should maintain and to have personal reservations about the value of their own behaviors was disparity too disturbing to bear. The whole situation "required change."

IMPACT ANALYSIS

It is useless to attempt to identify exactly the single most effective influence which prompted change.[24] It is even harder to believe, in the face of the responses, that there was only one. According to the members themselves, the communities were filled with tension, frustration, overwork and repression. In addition to these problems, the secular society to which they were expected to relate was democratic, educated, pluralistic and person-oriented. It seems that there were more than enough forces operating to make sisters, most of all, open to new forms of religious life. But of all the factors which led these sisters to make major adjustments in their lives, instances of personal stress, ecclesiastical affirmation and communal ratification were obviously paramount. An analysis of the data designed to determine the relative influence of the five factors most frequently named, however, gives a slightly more specific profile of the impact items. In this case the factors were ranked in order of the number of responses to each item in each of the five categories.

Of the 136 valid responses to the impact scale, two items were ranked by equal numbers of respondents as having had the greatest or most conscious influence on the decision to make behavior changes in the expression of their own religious life style: the development of new understandings about the nature of religious life and the convictions to which these led, and the call of the Vatican Council to renew. (See TABLE XX.)

TABLE XX: ITEMS HAVING THE GREATEST EFFECT
ON THE DECISION TO CHANGE

Ranked 1		
new understandings convictions	Call of Vatican II	other
0 43%	43%	14% 100%

Ranked most often as having had the second greatest effect on their private decisions to change were those same factors: personal conviction and the call of the Church; and another concept, the concern for survival of religious life itself. (See TABLE XXI.)

TABLE XXI: ITEMS HAVING THE SECOND GREATEST
EFFECT ON THE DECISIONS TO CHANGE

Ranked 2

new understandings	survival	Vat. Doc.	other
30%	25%	19%	26%

0   30%   25%   19%   26%   100%

Indicated by most of the respondents as having had the third greatest effect on the change process for each of them were these three same concepts again and an additional factor: the realization that behaviors they had practised all their lives had become a meaningless part of their vowed commitment. (See TABLE XXII.)

TABLE XXII: ITEMS HAVING THE THIRD GREATEST
EFFECT ON THE DECISIONS TO CHANGE

Ranked 3

survival	meaning	under-standing	Vatican Doc.	other
22%	20%	19%	14%	25%

0   22%   20%   19%   14%   25%   100%

In the fourth factor, other issues begin to emerge. In addition to a sense of the meaninglessness of past behaviors and a continuing concern for survival, the elements of community approval and a disassociation with what the delegates perceived to be the elitism, triumphalism or irrelevance of religious communities come into play. (See TABLE XXIII.)

TABLE XXIII: ITEMS HAVING THE FOURTH GREATEST
EFFECT ON THE DECISIONS TO CHANGE

Ranked 4

mean-ing	chapter vote	survival	elitism	under-standing	other
21%	14%	14%	11%	9%	31%

0   21%   14%   14%   11%   9%   31%   100%

Finally, as the fifth factor, these same ideas are repeated or reinforced by like concepts. The questions of survival and meaning remain. The fear of elitism and the desire for community justification become even clearer. The notion of the inconvenience incurred by women who functioned in one culture but lived as if they were of another appeared. The feeling of personal conviction and commitment to past promises collected around the item: I came to believe that it was all right for me to do it. (See TABLE XXIV.)

TABLE XXIV: ITEMS HAVING THE FIFTH GREATEST
EFFECT ON THE DECISIONS TO CHANGE

Ranked 5

	V*	B*	M*	E*	S*	I*	other	
0	14%	14%	13%	10%	10%	9%	30%	100%

*V = Chapter Vote; B = I came to believe that it was all right for me; M = meaninglessness; E = elitism; S = survival; I = inconvenience

In both analyses then it is the development of new ideas, the call of the Church, the function of community and the meaning of the life itself which prompted the personal expressions of a whole new philosophy of religious life.

CONCLUSIONS

1. Personal needs and feelings of disparity between the purpose and effects of religious life exercised considerable influence on the decision of delegates to the General Chapters to initiate change in their own lives.

2. Affirmation by legitimate authority was an important element of the change process for this particular group.

3. Personal social pressures by family, friends or associates wielded little general influence on this group of federation delegates.

4. No specific group in the communities was of special significance for these respondents as they contemplated personal change.

5. The attitudes expressed and the behaviors chosen indicate that the individual group members were personally committed to change rather than simply in compliance with it.

In general, then, this group of federation leaders reject the notion that a desire to be liked or a need to maintain reference group relationships motivated them much at all. They do show a strong need, on the other hand, to be personally correct about their conception and expression of religious life as well as to maintain the group itself.

Consequently, the picture which emerges is hardly one of careless rebellion. Crowded by personal tensions, concerned about the very survival of religious life, intent on preserving its meaning and approved by legitimate authority—the chapters of the order and the documentary if not the personal authorities of the Church—these women religious instituted changes designed not to destroy but to energize religious life. Seventy per cent of them say that as a result of renewal they experience an increased commitment to the vowed life, 48% of them "to a great extent."

Obviously the needs, the ideas, the call, the chapters and the vision were of a piece.

BELIEF PATTERNS

There is no sympathetic observer of religious life who cannot but be concerned about its present period. Either it has gone aground or it has turned a corner; either a new creation is building or the old one is shifting on sand. The sisters who value religious life, who have stayed with it despite its past and present stresses are surely most concerned of all. What data, if any, are there to indicate whether or not the changes of the last ten years have been anything other than a fad or a momentous mistake that has passed the point of no return? The answer to the question depends on why people changed in the first place and to what degree the changes have been integrated into their own belief systems. To this point, the research has surfaced three findings which have considerable bearing on that question.

To review: In this study, the respondents were asked to report their attitudes to religious life as they had experienced it both in its pre-Vatican and post-Vatican II forms. Then they were given the opportunity to select again from a list of traditional and contemporary behaviors those forms of religious practice with which they would feel most comfortable or authentic. Finally, they were asked to select and rank those items which they recognized to have had a major influence on their personal decisions to make actual changes in their private life styles. The responses were revealing.

In the first place, it was significant to note that though the participants reported a positive attitude about pre-Vatican II religious life, they were considerably more positive about their post-Vatican experiences, even in the same categories. Though there were negative attitudes and negative evaluations of religious life in its present form, the negative responses were made by far fewer people in far fewer dimensions than the number or kinds of negative evaluations of the pre-Vatican mode.

Secondly, it was also telling to discover that the behaviors selected by the group correlated with the attitudes that had been expressed: the respondents had said, in essence, that post-Vatican religious life was a good thing—sanctifying, liberating, positive—and consistently selected behaviors that showed commitment to this life-style rather than nostalgia for one past.

Finally it was the delineation of impact items that most suggested the notion that these respondents had not only changed their behaviors but apparently had also broadened their beliefs. This new notion, that beliefs about the nature of religious life as well as its behavioral forms have changed, warrants close attention. One of the theses of the social sciences is that, in general, people make changes in their basic behavior patterns for one or more of four reasons: to be accepted; to create relationships; to be correct or to satisfy the goals of the group. Depending upon which of these influences is paramount, it is possible to speculate about the depth and longevity of the change.[25]

If a person changes in order to be liked or accepted in a group, and the group ceases to exist or makes new demands, it is highly probable that the person will either readjust the behavior to meet new expectations or revert to previous patterns. The person has, in other words, conformed to group pressure. When the pressure vanishes, the behavior may very well vanish too.

If, on the other hand, a person changes some basic behaviors in order to identify with people whom she loves or holds in respect, then the behavior may alter when the relationship ends. In this situation, no pressure has been applied. The changes are made in imitation of a respected other. But people grow into independent adults, tensions arise or new models appear to replace the borrowed belief pattern of the first. The identification ends and the adopted behavioral pattern with it.

In both of these situations, the permanence of the change depends on factors outside the subject. In the first case, the person has conformed; in the second, she has complied. In neither circumstance, however, is there much guarantee that the behavior will maintain once the settings which generated it are removed.

There is another level of acceptance, however, that is deeper than either of these. It comes out of personal conviction and conscious-ness of the goals of the group rather than as a response to social pressures or personal models. It is the adoption of behaviors because they are consonant with internalized beliefs.

For example, a sister could have chosen to accept contemporary clothing because people she had to work with let her know that they would include her in their social life more easily if she did; or because the principal of the school whom she admired had; or because she felt that the very nature of religious life, which she valued and was at-tempting to pursue, demanded the use of other forms of apparel to communicate its meaning. In the third case, it is a central belief that prompts the behavior.

It is exactly this type of change base that is claimed by delegates to the Chapters of Renewal. The sister-respondents to this study deny the notion that they may have changed their previous life styles be-cause people expected them to. They deny that they made changes in order to protect their social positions in their communities. They maintain instead that they made major changes in the manner of liv-ing religious life because they had internalized new insights, come to new convictions, adopted new beliefs. Ninety-five per cent claimed as one of the five major items which led them to participate in new forms of religious life the fact that "personal convictions flowing from new understandings of the essence of religious life required change."

The implications of the statement are profound. If the present behaviors of contemporary religious are actually based on new be-liefs, then the present style of religious renewal is a great deal more than a passing phase of American religious life. Beliefs that have become part of a personal value system lead to behaviors that are in-dependent of an external source and are therefore more resistant to change. Furthermore, since beliefs, attitudes and values are so in-tegrated in the human psyche that change in any one of the elements affects the other parts of the system and leads eventually to behav-ioral change, it is absolutely essential to know what people believe in order to predict the nature or permanence of their behaviors.

In order to determine whether or not the attitudes expressed and the behaviors chosen by the participants to this study really related to the emergence of new ideas rather than to social pressures as the respondents had claimed in their selection of influence items, they were asked to identify from a list of thirteen belief statements about religious life those concepts which they themselves hold true.

The statements were of two types: six reflected a pre-Vatican II theology of religious life and seven expressed a post-Vatican orientation. (See TABLE XXV.) The items were derived by paraphrasing the philosophy statements of two major groups of religious superiors in the country who, shortly after Vatican II, issued public documents which defined religious renewal from these two points of view.[26] One group sought to affirm or enliven the existing structures of the institution but to keep religious life and its established constructs pretty much intact. The other claimed that the renewal of religious life demanded the formulation of new goals and the creation of whole new response patterns.

TABLE XXV: BELIEF STATEMENTS: TRADITIONAL AND CONTEMPORARY

Traditional Beliefs:　　　　　　　　　　　　　　　　True

1. Religious are called to special holiness because they have vows. — 34%
2. The Holy See has the right to interpret the norms of religious life for the universal Church and within each diocese. — 32%
3. The best work a religious community can do will take the form of an institutional corporate apostolate under the guidance of the hierarchy. — 7%
4. The purpose of religious life is to witness to the existence of another world than this one. — 60%
5. Religious owe their obedience to a duly chosen superior. — 72%
6. Poverty demands the wearing of a distinctive religious habit as a sign of consecration to God and commitment to the world. — 6%
7. Religious life presumes regular community life within a program of communal and liturgical prayer. — 72%

Contemporary Beliefs:

1. I think of religious life as gospel life, no more no less. — 60%
2. The religious community reflects the Church, and therefore must be outgoing and open to the secular. — 92%
3. Religious witness involves a manifestation of social concern and civic involvement characterized by charity, simplicity and compassion. — 92%
4. The interpersonal relationships in a community affect community prayer. — 94%
5. Non-institutional ministries provide a dynamic way to respond to the needs of the times. — 82%
6. Small communities contribute to self-awareness and growth toward maturity and an enriched relationship with Christ and are therefore authentic forms of religious life for these times. — 92%

All of the items in the scale were stated positively in order to facilitate their acceptance. The purpose of the section was to identify 1) what new ideas, if any, had actually been accepted by this group; 2) what traditional ideas had been rejected or retained; 3) what relationship existed between the beliefs, behaviors and attitudes of these participants and 4) what implications of these postures can be drawn for the future.

Like the behavior patterns before them, the belief statements given relate to five major facets of religious life: the nature of the religious life and the practices which express that character; the forms of relationship which it regards; the authority it recognizes and the kinds of control it exercises; the manner of its mode of witness or identity; and the characteristics of its ministries. In each case, the belief which is held affects the kinds of behaviors chosen to reflect it and are distinct in this way from the counter position.

THE NATURE OF RELIGIOUS LIFE

The religious who responded to this survey apparently believe three things about the purpose or essence of religious life. They believe that it is no higher or better a way to do the will of God than any other form of Christian life. They believe that the measure of its meaning is to be determined by its adherence to the gospel message. And they believe that the very existence of religious life attests to the reality of the coming Kingdom of God. (See TABLE XXVI.)

TABLE XXVI: BELIEFS CENTRAL TO THE ADOPTION OF SPIRITUAL PRACTICES

T.	1. Religious are called to special holiness because they have vows.	34%
T.	2. The purpose of religious life is to witness to the existence of another world than this one.	60%
C.	3. I think of religious life as gospel life, no more no less.	60%

T = traditional belief   C = contemporary belief

These delegates make an obvious break with the traditional concept of religious life that defines it as apart from the rest of humankind. The fact explains in large part why the participants in other questions of the study claimed no special privilege or special place.

Signs of preference, attempts at separation and extraordinary pieties or penances are clearly difficult to reconcile with a real belief that religious life is a different but not a superior way to work out God's will.

The other two major issues, however, are less clearly defined. On the one hand, religious life is said by these delegates to be "gospel life, no more no less." On the other, it is seen as existing to give witness to another world. Both ideas are affirmed in the Rule of Benedict. The Benedictine is told that the Rule is "a little rule for beginners" the goal of which is to attain "some degree of virtue and the rudiments of the religious life." She is also told "to seek God" and "to hasten to the heavenly homeland." What is more, the two concepts are not necessarily antithetical. The "gospel life" surely implies commitment to the transcendent as well as to the incarnational aspects of the religious vocation. What is puzzling in the data, however, is the fact that only 60% of the respondents clearly yoke the two notions of involvement in this world and witness to the next.

When confronted with both belief statements, the group was free to do three things: to affirm both statements—that the purpose of religious life is to be a "gospel life, no more no less" and also that it is "to give witness to another world"; to affirm neither; or to support one of these statements but not the other. First, if both statements had been highly affirmed by the group, it would have been possible to conclude that the concepts of transcendence and incarnation were integrated parts of the definition. But, if neither concept had been asserted, it would seem legitimate to assume that some other purpose of religious life—one which included the notion that both this world and the next were the proper ends of religious life or which posed an entirely different thesis—was consciously operating among them. If, thirdly, one statement had received a great deal more support than the other, it would seem clear that one orientation more than another was determining their attitudes and selection of behavioral choices. But none of these was the case. (See TABLE XXVII.)

Forty per-cent of the group said both statements were true. In their minds, then, both this world and the next are the proper concern of religious.

Twenty per cent of the respondents said neither statement was true as it stood. For these people, both statements are either inadequate or inaccurate.

Nineteen per cent of these sisters said that the purpose of religious life is to witness to the existence of another world.

Finally, twenty per cent said only that the purpose of religious life is to manifest "the gospel life . . ."

TABLE XXVII: THE PURPOSE OF RELIGIOUS LIFE	
1. I think of religious life as gospel life, no more no less.	21%
2. The purpose of religious life is to witness to the existence of another world than this one.	19%
3. Both statements are true.	40%
4. Neither statement is true.	20%

The point is that fewer than half of respondents (40%) linked both ideas—the relationship of religious life to this world and the next—by affirming both statements. Some others (20%), if their understanding of the gospel life consciously includes the idea of the transcendent as well as the incarnational, did so by accepting that statement alone. But an agreement level of only 60% about the very reason for a group's existence is a slim certainty on which to renew an entire institution, let alone to direct the private lives of its members.

Some possible conclusions are that at least two theologies of religious life are still operating; that they may be at odds; and that the implications of the disparateness may be serious. If religious life is gospel life "no more no less" then it calls also for immersion in the immanent. It is rooted in the now—human and involved, Christian to the utmost. If on the other hand, religious life is primarily heaven-centered then humanity demands less attention since eventually all things human pass away. What gains primary attention in this orientation is private devotion and the pursuit of personal perfection. One emphasis leads to a sense of concern for the responsibilities of today; the other looks primarily to the promise of the world to come.

Since no single statement of purpose received more than marginal consensus, it is hinted that the aim of contemporary religious life may be still unclear; that still to be developed is a manner of living that reconciles these transcendent and incarnational elements. Whether the differences in belief derive from multiple educational experiences, the ambivalence that results from cultural upheaval, or the new teaching of the Church itself, the fact remains that purpose is central to the cohesion of any institution.[27]

It is interesting to note, too, that of the attitudes expressed, 59% of the participants feel "confused" about post-Vatican II religious life. Perhaps it is just this question about the purpose of religious life itself—the only statement in the entire belief grid on which the group did not achieve high consensus—which unsettles them. At any rate, it is certain that the situation must be resolved if religious life in the

Benedictine tradition is to be able to effect renewal and its members to make behavioral choices with ease and conviction.

RELATIONSHIPS

Of the belief statements controlling the existence or development of human relationships in the life of the woman religious, three contemporary convictions are common to over 90% of the group. (See TABLE XXVIII.)

TABLE XXVIII: BELIEF STATEMENTS GOVERNING THE EXISTENCE OF RELATIONSHIPS		
C.	1. The religious community reflects the Church and therefore must be outgoing and open to the secular.	92%
C.	2. The interpersonal relationships in a community affect community prayer.	94%
C.	3. Small communities contribute to self-awareness and growth toward maturity and an enriched relationship with Christ and are therefore authentic forms of religious life for the times.	92%
T.	4. Religious life presumes regular community life within a program of communal and liturgical prayer.	72%

T = traditional belief   C = contemporary belief

It is clear that a large proportion of delegates feels strongly that religious must be outgoing and, by inference therefore, not closed off from the people of God. They agree that the community can be open to the secular rather than protected from it. It is easy to see, then, how the same group could so freely opt for the right, if not the obligation, to communicate with non-religious or to make contacts and develop personal relationships with people outside their religious communities.

What is more, these representatives see interpersonal relationships as directly related to the quality of community prayer. Small wonder then that they were also willing to forego standardized prayer forms in favor of new modes of reconciliation and dialogue among themselves.

These past delegates believe, too, that small communities prod personal development in ways conducive to maturity and spiritual completeness and so affirm these growing forms of convent life. The fact that numbers of the delegates claimed the right to choose their own form and place of residence is congruent with this belief and seems then more than a desire for convenience or a groundless move away from the traditional type of convent life. On the contrary, there is apparently some new conviction about the effect of environment on the development of spiritual maturity.

The one traditional concept in this category—that religious life presumes a regular pattern of community life within a specified program of prayer—is also affirmed but by 20% fewer delegates than had agreed with the other belief statements which control the sisters' relational patterns. The fact that the statement presumes "regularity" and "patterns" may account for the decline of support, especially since 75% to 95% of the population rejected in earlier questions the specification of time slots for personal activities like periods of recreation, silence or examen, and the daily examination of conscience.

The notion of community life itself, however, is an abiding element in the Benedictine way of life. The question of how much pattern this implies is a real issue but, if the responses of this group are to be trusted as a general indicator, not a polarizing one. The question of the quality of community life, on the contrary, is certainly the more demanding concern and almost all of the respondents had already called post-Vatican II community life "positive."

In each of these elements, then, there is the kernel of a new belief. The belief that sisters are to live lives protected from the world has been abandoned. In its stead is a belief that God is in history and indeed to be sought and served there.

The belief that human relationships are irrelevant to the sisters' approach to God has been abandoned. In its stead is the conviction that growth in prayer is directly related to the quality of interaction in a community.

The belief that the achievement of religious community is independent of the size of the group and personal needs has been abandoned. In its stead is the judgment that small group living can affect personal development in ways necessary to religious life and thus suited to a culture that is alienated and individualistic.

The belief that a prayerful life in community has both form and content as a constant and essential element of Benedictinism is reaffirmed by almost three-quarters of the group. The fact that 30% of the respondents did not accept the statement as it stands, however, may be indicative that the structure of community life itself may be in the process of new definition.

AUTHORITY AND CONTROL

In the area of obedience or authority there is a pronounced movement away from the belief system of the immediate past history of American religious women. (See TABLE XXIX.)

TABLE XXIX: BELIEFS RELATED TO THE NATURE OF AUTHORITY AND CONTROL	
T 1. The Holy See has the right to interpret the norms of religious life for the universal Church and within each diocese.	32%
T 2. Religious owe their obedience to a duly chosen superior.	72%
T = traditional belief	

Two separate types of authority are at issue in these statements. One deals with the relationship of the local and autonomous community to the universal Church through the specific agency of the Sacred Congregation of Religious in Rome. The other brings in to question the whole notion of obedience itself. Both statements reflect a traditional orientation toward religious life.

Elsewhere in the study over three-quarters of these respondents claimed the privilege of autonomy or the right to contribute to the creation of policies that affect the local experession of religious life but denied that overemphasis on autonomy in the local priory is obstructionist. It is perfectly consistent then for 70% of the delegates to negate the right of the Holy See to interpret norms that are made by religious women in their own federations or local chapters. The fact that the 1918 Code of Canon Law did specify some internal matters; that these specifications were more stringent or particular for religious women than they were for religious men; and that American religious women have since gained the professional experience and education to make their own evaluations of the factors affecting their lives may all have something to do with the resistance to this notion. At any rate, Benedictine communities are defined as autonomous and exempt. The move to clarify or acclaim that status for women as well as for men is clearly a contemporary development of an historical reality.

On the other hand, the notion of obedience to "duly chosen superiors" is a traditional concept of religious life which over 70% of the group accepts. The fact that the statement specifies two factors—the necessity of obedience and a choice of superiors—puts it, unlike the reference to the function of internal authority by the Holy See, squarely in the mainstream of Benedictine history. Recent explications of the nature of obedience, though, may have made the statement ambiguous for some.

In the first place, the suggestion that religious owe obedience to a superior in the manner of the medieval or feudal allegiance of a vassal to a king completely diminishes the responsibility of the individual for her own commitments and spiritual obligations. In a previous part of the Profile, 72% of the group had already indicated discomfort with the nature of the "superior-subject relations" of community life.

In the second place, both the Rule and the Vatican Documents direct the religious not to the will of the superior but to the will of God as it is expressed communally. The statement may falter for some then in that it calls for obedience but neglects to define its mode, especially in a group that by margins as high as 84% chose discernment processes over authoritarian mandates by the superior. If discernment too had been rejected then the degree of respect for obedience held by this group would certainly and properly be open to question. Since that is not the case, it is possible to conclude that it is not the vow itself that is problematical but the form of obedience that is being called for or the motive behind it that accounts for the evidence of dissent.

Nevertheless, the fact that the statement even in its most traditional form was claimed by so many is clear proof of the centrality of the concept in Benedictine mentality.

In the areas of obedience and authority, then, there is at least one new canon. The idea that outside agents may interpret local norms for women's communities has been contradicted. The obvious outcome of such a persuasion is a rising desire for self-direction and a consciousness of local responsibility, a far cry from the passive dependence on external authority in the past.

IDENTITY

Two statements of the belief scale dealt directly with the aspect of religious witness. One of the principles defined the essential elements of religious witness as an involvement in areas of human need that is marked by love and authentic feeling. The other statement required the use of uniform garb as a sign of consecration and commitment. (See TABLE XXX.)

TABLE XXX: BELIEF STATEMENTS RELATING TO MODES OF RELIGIOUS IDENTITY

C. 1. Religious witness involves a manifestation
   or social concern and civic involvement
   characterized by charity, simplicity, and
   compassion   92%
T. 2. Religious poverty demands the wearing of
   a distinctive religious habit as a sign of
   consecration to God and commitment to the
   world   6%

C = contemporary belief   T = traditional belief

In a sweeping way, 93% of the respondents manifest high social consciousness but disclaim a distinctive habit as a sign of religious life, a function of poverty or a mark of engagement with the world. The whole viewpoint is directly contradictory to the older ideal of enclosure or withdrawal. The implications of the new perspective are evident in the respondents' denial that renewal has secularized their lives and may explain their contention that sisters had become elitist and out of touch with contemporary society.

In any event, the traditional belief that the mark of a religious is that she wears a uniform dress has been supplanted in the delegates' minds by the assumption that the sign of religious life in the world is the degree of its genuine Christian presence.

MINISTRY

Ministry is at the very root of the foundation of communities of Benedictine women in the United States. Benedictine communities in the United States were founded by European motherhouses who were suspect for being a useless burden to the societies of which they were a part and in a period when state governments decreed apostolic work as a condition for their continued existence. What is more, Abbot Boniface Wimmer requested the presence of women religious for the express purpose of caring for the needs of a German immigrant society.[28] In the context of their history, then, corporate ministry in direct response to ecclesiastical or federal authority is a constant, as the ownership or staffing of large institutions—schools or hospitals primarily—by every community attests.

In the belief scale of the Participant Profile, this tradition is explicitly included. (See TABLE XXXI.)

TABLE XXXI: BELIEF STATEMENTS RELATED TO CHOICES IN THE FORMS OF MINISTRY

T.	1.	The best work a religious community can do will take the form of an institutional corporate apostolate under the guidance of the hierarchy.	7%
C.	2.	Non-institutional ministries provide a dynamic way to respond to the needs of the times.	82%

T = traditional belief   C = contemporary belief

Despite the past order of things, 80% of the delegates contend in this study that non-institutional ministries are valid and effective. A full 93% moreover deny that corporate institution in a diocesan system is the best work a religious can do.

Clearly, the old belief that religious are the work force of the diocesan structure has been superseded by a more charismatic or individual mode of response to the needs of modern society. It is obvious, then, why so many of these respondents made behavioral choices which were designed to allow for a measure of personal choice in the kinds of professional preparation needed or the ministries performed.

Ministry, it seems, may be seen by many as personal involvement rather than corporate obligation, a concept that will undoubtedly raise the entire question of the nature of corporate witness. The concept may also account for the fact that over 75% of the respondents see the investment of corporate monies and responsible use of natural resources as well as the sharing of personal talents and skills as matters of high priority for religious communities of this period.

IMPLICATIONS OF A CHANGE OF BELIEFS

Whatever the specific implications of the belief system described, two conclusions may be drawn from the response patterns of these participants. In the first place, new ideas about the nature and expression of religious life have indeed been internalized by these religious women. In the second place, they are consistent with the behaviors and attitudes that were also expressed by the group. But there is something to be said for that fact that all the beliefs espoused were not contemporary only.

It is a truism of social-cultural dynamics that successful social development or change depends on the compatibility of new behaviors with existing values and beliefs.[29] In the situation of change in religious life, the value and belief base is broad and basic as well. Of the thirteen belief statements presented, at least four-fifths of the delegates affirmed five out of six contemporary concepts. Of the seven traditional premises, the group rejected four but accepted the two whose relationship to mainstream Benedictinism runs deep: the necessity of obedience and the centrality of community. One issue, an integrated expression of the purpose of religious life, is yet to be concluded in each.

The point is that instead of revolution in the ranks, a growth of perceptions has been grafted to some very deep roots. Not only is the group bonded by affection and covenant but by the commitment of self as well, by sign and by tradition, by growth together and growth alone. It is hard to argue then that American Benedictine women in their continuing commitment to the ministry, to community, to the spiritual life and to the will of God have destroyed American Benedictine life even though they have certainly changed its form.

CONCLUSIONS

1. The internalization of new beliefs about the essence of religious life led the participants to this study to make major changes in their behavioral expression of religious life.

2. Basic traditional beliefs have been retained and enable the group to continue a historical tradition.

3. The integration of the transcendent with the immanent elements of religious life is creating tension in this group of contemporary religious women.

4. New concepts of ministry, authority, identity and relationships have been adopted.

5. The traditional concepts of community, obedience and prayer have been affirmed.

6. Traditional concepts of identity, religious life, authority and ministry have been negated.

7. Behaviors and attitudes expressed in other sections of the study are consistent with the beliefs listed here and may therefore be expected to maintain in relatively stable fashion unless or until additional belief patterns replace them.

EMERGING ISSUES

Major institutional change is not accomplished without consequences. Each stage of the institutional life cycle has its special
qualities and its special pain.[30] In the period of origin, new groups
have great vision and high aims, a sense of liberty and unbounded
energy for the task. In the first 25 years after Benedictine sisters
came to the United Stats, between 1852 and 1877, they established
foundations in states from New Jersey to Nebraska. Time and space
and numbers seemed to be no deterrent at all. There was, of course,
little security, not much money, very little help, a very great work to
be done.

But the sisters did it. And the period of expansion began. They
went from diocese to diocese, opening schools, caring for children, affecting parish life and development all across the country. Vocations
increased, the mission system flourished, organizational structures
began to be refined in order to maint in the effectiveness of the
apostolate as well as the monastic tradition.

The network of the religious institutional system as it had been
founded in 1852 reached its peak between 1940 and 1960. There were
2400 sisters in the federation. Schedules and prayerbooks and works
and formation patterns and pieties had all become standardized.
Flexibility had to be sacrified for the sake of size and efficiency.
Fewer and fewer women found it possible to fit the old patterns. The
decline had begun long before the Council called for renewal and renewal is no small undertaking under the best of conditions.

To reorient an entire institution, to return it to its driving purpose, to refound it is a radical task. American sisters undertook to do
just that. The effort has not been without struggle, nor is it without
accomplishment. As the delegates to the Chapters of Renewal of the
Federation of St. Scholastica see it, there have been clear gains. (See
TABLE XXXII.)

It is clear that individual development, participation and commitment have been a direct result of the reorientation process. A
sense of themselves as women and a concern for all the oppressed of
the world is apparently also a characteristic of this new period. But
indifference about religious life or despair about its future seems
hardly to exist at all. Least of all do they feel guilty about what
they've done to hasten or implement change.

Given the fact that these respondents are almost entirely sisters
who have chosen to remain in their communities at a time when
many others are leaving, what trends for the future of American

TABLE XXXII: CONSEQUENCES OF CHANGES SINCE 1966

As a result of renewal, I experience:

	Grtly	Usually	Some	None
1. Greater individual responsibility	74	18	6	1
2. Changes in modes of decision-making in community	73	19	8	0
3. Increased involvement in the creation of local community policy	60	20	19	2
4. A desire for the increased autonomy of women in the Church	51	13	31	4
5. A heightened awareness of social responsibility	49	31	18	2
6. An increased commitment to the vowed life	48	22	23	8
7. Greater respect for individuals in community	40	34	18	8
8. A feeling that my view is sought in community matters	38	38	19	4
9. A feeling of hopefulness about the future of religious life	30	35	26	9
10. Increased polarization in my community	16	12	60	11
11. A lack of community cohesion	9	14	66	11
12. Confusion due to the psychological pressures of change	6	9	70	14
13. A feeling that my religious life has become secularized	6	4	30	56
14. Loss of respect from lay people	5	2	38	51
15. A feeling that there have been too many changes in religious life	5	2	27	63
16. Loss of respect from clergy	4	4	45	43
17. A feeling of fear for my future security	4	3	30	58
18. A feeling that renewal will be accomplished only by beginning new foundations	4	1	18	73
19. A feeling of indifference about the present or future state of religious life	3	.7	16	77
20. A feeling of despair about the present state of religious life	3	4	31	57
21. A feeling that the pace of renewal is too slow	2	6	40	48
22. A feeling of hostility toward those who obstruct change	.7	9	44	43
23. A feeling of resentment toward people who have changed	.7	13	81	6
24. A feeling of resentment toward people who have not changed	.7	4	29	63
25. A feeling of guilt that by participating in change I have contributed to the deterioration of religious life	.7	1.4	7	86

Grtly = Greatly   Usually   Some = Somewhat   None = Not at all

Benedictine communities of women can be gathered from this data?

It is obvious that the communities have been resilient enough to adapt their government structures so that the entire membership is to some degree involved with policy and decision making. The individual sister has assumed more responsibility for her own life, and in addition, is aware of her responsibilities, not only to the institutional Church, but to all people. And finally, the sister is not only committed to her type of life, but is hopeful about its future.

The very resiliency with which priorities have adapted to new modes of government and life style is evidence of the vitality present in Benedictine communities of women. This vitality would seem to be the basis for the sisters' optimism regarding the future of their communities.

Their awakened social consciousness and desire for the increased autonomy of women in the Church will undoubtedly lead them into new types of ministry in accord with the needs of the times and the resources available to their communities.

The sister's life within her community promises to be increasingly satisfying as a new generation works out the age-old tension between individual needs and community needs in an environment which emphasizes the dignity of the person. But the new period is exactly that, a new period. It has its own questions, its own concerns, and sisters are not unmindful of their presence or unconcerned about their effects on the future of religious communities and the Church.

In addition to the questionnaire data in its formal and structured forms, the delegates were given the opportunity to respond to three open-ended questions. In this section they were asked: In your opinion, what are the problems facing your community at the present time? In what ways do you feel these will affect the future of your community? And is there anything else you care to tell us about religious life as you see it? In this section, therefore, the present issues of religious life will be explained by the sisters themselves and largely in their own words.

The answers are revealing both for the issues they identify and for the tone they reflect. Two responses speak well for two different orientations.

One sister is obviously disapproving of the whole contemporary condition. She not only prefers a previous life pattern but suspects that the present one is motivated by selfishness. She considers it scandalous and unreligious. She writes: "As I observe Religious in general today, I am inclined to say that too many are suffering from a severe attack of pride and materialism. They are trying to give the impression that they know all the solutions and answers to the world's ills.

They have suddenly acquired a tremendous wisdom somehow. "Their incessant traveling hither and yon, for example, to find a solution to the poverty problem is a scandal to many lay people who wonder how anyone who professes poverty can waste so much time and money with really very little to produce as a result. What the world is hungering for is witness to a simple, humble life style that isn't concerned about relevancy and needs not the wisdom of the sages, but the wisdom of the handmaids of the Lord. Religious have become too involved, even in affairs that it were better for them to leave alone."

Another of the responses, on the other hand, speaks of personal spiritual growth as a result of renewal. Involvement is seen as a result of community, not a betrayal of it. There is a sense of responsibility here rather than withdrawal, a feeling of empowerment. This religious wrote:

"I feel very strongly that I need to say what the changes in religious life have meant to me.

"I believe I was a good religious in pre-Vatican days, more or less faithful to the rules, saying all the prayers (though not scrupulously) we were supposed to say—even if at times counting the minutes or hours it would take to get them in, rather conscientious about my teaching, seeing the ideal religious as one who did not 'mix' too much with 'worldly' people, etc.

"After a transition period of throwing aside much of the traditional practices and even minimizing prayer life to simply community prayers—and even these were frequently not attended. (sic) It was a period of experiencing a new found freedom during which most things associated with the past were judged as 'irrelevant.'

"I've come now to a wholly new experience of commitment both to my community and the Church, an awareness of the need for my own active involvement, a realization that much of what the future will be depends on what I am willing to do now. This means an acceptance of an almost wholly different conception of my role and witness—it involves the desire and efforts to be as fully human as I can be, as aware as possible of my own needs and strengths and weaknesses and a desire to meet others at the human level in the manner of Christ in the gospels—being ready and willing to respond to needs however they may manifest themselves. Persons outside the community have become a very important part of my life and the days are long and filled with busy hours (including long evenings) because there are many people who seek meaning in the Church and in their lives. All this has been fortified by a much deeper prayer life —both community prayer which has become very important and a source of support, and personal prayer which means spending a fairly long period daily just reflecting and praying especially the Scriptures. This has become an absolutely essential foundation for me—without which the involvement would be too draining.

"I know today I am a religious living life much closer to the example given us by Christ—a life much more filled with pain as well as joy than ever dreamed possible before—convinced that I can share truly in the ministry of the Church.

"This is what the renewal has meant to me—and it is the reason I remain committed to the Benedictine life."

Out of these two attitudes and experiences and hopes have grown all the issues of the present era. The current problems as this group defines them are more than situations. They are focal points around which collect tangible expressions of differing philosophies of religious life. For every thesis, there is its opposite understanding.

By large margins, the respondents agreed in another part of the profile that the issues of rank, restricted association with seculars, clothing, enclosure, permissions, chapters of fault, and scheduled periods of community silence—all of which were once "really important items" on the renewal agenda—have largely disappeared as community pressure points.

At the same time, they identified new items which they say are affecting the development of religious life as they know it at the present time. These are, they say, questions of ministry, tradition, community life and government. In their responses to the open-ended questions, the delegates confirm the fact that these are indeed the issues which they and their communities are presently facing and in most instances illuminate to some degree what is really implied for them by four general topics: the ministry, the meaning, the cohesion and the survival of religious life.

MINISTRY

Of the 138 responses to the open-ended question, 37 sisters made specific reference to different aspects of ministry as being crucial to the future of religious life. Of these four were distinctly negative of the new trends in ministry; twelve were positive and the remaining 17 chose only to present the topic as a present problem. Ministry, "the laying down of one's life for one's friends," involves service to the community as well as to external society. These responses, consequently, deal with both aspects of the question.

Several of the respondents refer simply to the fact that "manual labor" or "internal service to the community" is on the decline. In the past, sisters spent a great deal of time doing domestic work in the convent itself and this work was regularly rotated among all the members. In the present period less time and attention is apparently being given to household tasks than was true of the past. "Household tasks at the priory are weighing heavily on those who live there," a delegate wrote. "The need to cook and clean on top of full-time school work (is too much.) . . . Active people are withdrawing to help out at the priory. I do not see (that) as good for the future of us as a group."

Whatever the actual expenditure of time, however, the development is seen by some as an indicator of irresponsibility or a violation of community, and by others as a necessary attempt to bring a balance of leisure into their lives. One sister described the problem in detail and explained the tension this way:

"Every active sister is the 'good sister'; the one who seeks leisure to re-order herself, her program, to pray, to think, to breathe, to be aware, in order to be of better service, is the lazy 'not good sister.' It's the old agonizing strain of active vs. contemplative (but we're) work oriented (and get) guilt feelings in regard to any suggestion of need for leisure."

The struggle, if it exists in significant measure, is an easy one to understand. Hard work built American communities and hard physical labor has maintained them. The very success of those institutions, however, had led to over-extension of the personnel. One sister said clearly: "Our apostolate has increased—our vocations have not, and this ministry absorbs us in such a way that we don't often have time for leisure, or preparing community prayer."

It is the other side of the ministry question that was given the greatest amount of attention and that is the problem of corporate commitments. Most communities own large plants or staff parochial systems. The practice has been to accept a work in the name of the community and assign members to fill the positions. The theological rationale was that an essential part of the religious vocation was to be "sent," to be disposable. In the last decade, though, the rising degree of specialization in each area has made the assignment system increasingly more difficult. Specialists are at a premium or positions are unavailable. What is more, numbers of sisters have begun to move outside the community school systems to use their specialties in new areas and among the poor.

The moves, whatever the motives, affect the traditional ministries in numbers as well as in costs and cause tension among the community members themselves. For some, the movement of sisters into individual ministries is a sign of waning commitment, an "unrealistic and selfish response (which places) personal likes . . . over the needs of the people of God or demands for personnel."

Seventeen of the respondents see the move as an extension of community and a responsibility of the celibate vocation to perform functions or engage in ministries for which other parts of the church are unprepared or unfree to go. As one participant put it: There is need (in my community) for a greater involvement in the ministry . . . and larger needs of the Church (which) are often ignored."

Another comment pointed to what may be another kind of situation confronting communities when she wrote "we feel we need a community apostolate at the motherhouse but lack of personnel and decrease in enrollment . . . are making us examine if we should change that apostolate." It is clear, then, that the shift in the type of ministries being performed by these communities today is the result of external as well as internal circumstances.

All of the 32 responses, for instance, refer in some way to the fact that the number of personnel has declined, the cost of maintaining older institutions has risen, the desire to maintain traditional commitments is in question, and the call to new ministries has increased. Each of these factors—some a direct result of the renewal period, others an outgrowth of culture—is apparently a pressure point for a number of communities in the Federation of St. Scholastica.

One of the respondents indicated that in her situation, at least, there is "an unwillingness to consider . . . the personnel shortage and a lack of response to requests by sisters to serve in new ministries. In a word," she says, "we play the ostrich game."

On the other hand, another participant feels that in her community there is "suspicion . . . tension and defensiveness (about those) who choose ways other than those honored at the motherhouse" but, rather than immediate resolution, asks for "a lot more study, a lot more living experience and a lot more patient sharing (because) we've come some way on it, but need to keep it open."

It is obvious that more than the ideology of corporate ministry or leisure is the issue. Very tangible questions of income, service, witness and community are at stake and may now need to be addressed, not from the point of view of philosophy but of consequences.

MEANING

In 35 of the 142 responses to the open-ended question, there was some reference to the fact that the very meaning of religious life had been blurred somewhat by the process of renewal. The remarks are not so much either positive or negative as they are a call for definition. Implied in many of the statements yet is a declared dichotomy between involvement and community. In the others, the suggestion that what is needed to close the communication gaps among the membership is a general theological updating. In the final analysis, the two may be very much related.

One past delegate reiterated the continuing question: "Is it possible to live the Benedictine way of life with its emphasis on worship and community and still be involved in the problems of the Church and the world, for we are now a global village?" Another statement read: "I fear for the future for the docile person who comes to religious life for quiet, security, prayer in peace and quiet. (Now) one must be mature, prayerful and yet quite able to go 'into the world' and to spread the 'Good News.' This makes me wonder about the 'monasticism' of the Benedictine way of life. Shall it not be dropped as our way of life?"

Years of semi-enclosure have apparently left the impression on some, at least, that Benedictinism is in essence incompatible with ministry; that a contemplative experience of reality is incompatible with reality itself. In that case, the questions of ministry take on even wider significance than simply a transition from one form of service to another. At the base may be the continuing issue about the very purpose of Benedictine life itself and this may account for the fact that other respondents cited as a current problem "the lack of scriptural and theological training of our sisters . . . (of whom) only a few have done any theological study whatsoever and, as a result, are looked upon as ultraliberal, if not renegades." The question remains then, as one respondent put it, of how to "translate communal monastic understanding and purpose into effective life in contemporary society."

For one of the participants, the answer is to regain esteem by being different; for three others it is to wear the habit or some recognizable dress so people know that we are different; for another it is "to be wholly human because the world needs holy humans." For the greatest number, however, the priority of the period seems to be to internalize *Call to Life*, the Constitutions of the federation that developed in the course of the renewal period, and to integrate the elements of the charism statement which says that it is the vocation of a Benedictine "to seek God in community and to respond to Him through praise and ministry."

For those sisters for whom the issue exists, the struggle is a real one. For the greater number of respondents, however, there are two much more consuming questions at the present time: the nature of community cohesion and the question of survival.

COMMUNITY COHESION

Over half of the sisters who responded to the open-ended question made at least one comment about the issue of community life itself. Some identified more than one facet of the problem. In general, however, the comments concentrated on three subjects: the nature of community life, the place of interpersonal relationships within community life and the present level of polarization or frustration in the post-renewal period.

After the Council one of the most immediate indicators of a community in the process of renewal was the decline of uniformity or emergence of diversity in the life style of the sisters. The public image of the sister was a woman who looked, walked, lived and worked like every other sister in her community. Almost immediately after Vatican Council II the picture changed. Lay people were astounded and the clergy disconcerted but it was within the community itself that the greatest effects were felt. The weakening of the strong physical bonds of community left many sisters themselves fearful and insecure.

Thirty-one of the respondents addressed themselves directly to the results of this movement from large to smaller community groupings. In the first place, the answers indicate that the very meaning of community is now at issue. Some members are still committed to the model of the common life. Four delegates took that viewpoint. One wrote: "We need more stress on 'community.' In unity there is strength." Another said: "Much has been stressed on the individual, but there should be a better understanding of the relation of the individual to the community. This should take into consideration that we are to think, work, pray and do all as a community." The third said directly: "I long for the shared and enjoyable recreation of community living we used to have."

The remaining 32 comments on this particular facet of the subject present views that are exactly the opposite of these but which suggest that in each of the communities represented, there is a similar difference of opinion among the membership. One of these comments traced the edges of the entire subject. It read: "Each of us is called (to be) first of all a *monachus,* a woman alone, devoted to making Him central in her life, to praising Him in prayer. Cenobitic life, life in common, is a means to that end, a support, not an end in itself."

The notion that there is great need for a new or broadened understanding of what it means to be a community surfaced repeatedly. One delegate confronted present forms with past structures to indicate that inconsistency in the practice of physical community has been part of the American tradition. "Stability," she wrote, "was not 'stable' when sisters were moved frequently and somewhat arbitrarily; neither is it 'stable' when sisters choose to move out of a group at any time. (In the same way) sisters who live without a sense of collegiality are not obedient, etc. . . ."

Others point out that community members resist becoming involved in policy-making or committee work because the trust level is low in community, because dialogue is suppressed or because "individuals rather than issues become the subject of discussions." Trust is the essence of community life, one respondent said, and "Sisters will continue to leave religious life . . . until we learn more about relating . . . more personally, sensitively and lovingly."

One response to the problem of alienation, rejection, or bureaucratization of community living has been the emergence of small group living experiences. These tend to take one of two forms. In one instance, large numbers of sisters living in the same building subdivide for prayer, meals or recreation but in many instances attend Mass and large group discussions together. In other instances, groups set up community life in touch with the larger community but in physically separate living circumstances.

For those for whom "community" means the sharing of the same living space by all the members "in common," the move is a threatening one. For others it is an attempt to establish a community life that is more personal, flexible or supportive than the patterns of larger groups allow and to form a network rather than a single institution.

One delegate explained: "Truly, I feel our 'institution' has grown to be a burden and ceases to be a communion."

Another described the position in greater detail. She wrote: "I think it extremely important that we don't let any structure or tradition deteriorate into a stylized, meaningless 'rule' or ritual. I personally believe this can only be achieved if religious accept small groups within the larger community. I feel this because I'm convinced that it has to be such things as responsibility, accountability, prayer-sharing, confessing, forgiving and other signs of love and support that replace former concepts of obedience, rules, schedules, examen, (or) Chapter of Faults, etc., and this kind of in-depth sharing can only be accomplished with small numbers. This love and support then can and should overflow to the larger community, and greatly affect our dealings with one another and all others with whom we come into contact."

Though most of the respondents who raised this topic indicated that in the community represented by her there is tension around the question, only three delegates themselves rejected the notion of small communities within the larger context. One said that these life-styles "affect the community's need of support and concern for one another (in order) to be free and not accountable to the community." Another stated: "I'm not sure that some of those wanting a small group community are capable of the sacrifice and unselfishness involved in the necessary give and take. . . . I hear so much 'give me,' 'I want' and 'I need.' "

What is of greater concern, perhaps, than the fact that there is yet uncertainty about the validity of either or both styles of community life is the inference by five of the delegates that in their membership a distinction is made between those at the priory, who consider themselves "the community" and those in small groups who are spoken of separately. The attitude is particularly crucial and problematic when it becomes clear that American communities of Benedictine women have been traditionally structured in a satellite system. In other words, ever since the sisters began to staff parochial schools it was the custom to erect "branch houses" or convents in the parishes or cities served that were directly subject to the central motherhouse rather than to create each as an independent foundation. Some section of every community has always lived in small groups away from the priory. The only difference between the past system and the present circumstances, then, is that many of the small groups that are forming at the present time come together in houses or apartments that are not owned by the parishes and regardless of whether all the members of the group work in the same circumstances and parish or not.

Obviously there is need to clarify the nature of community and its various kind of bondings. Love, commitment to common ideals, mutual benefit and common enterprise are the factors which cause groups to cohere. Clearly, the greater the number of these strands that hold a group together, the less likely it is to disintegrate, the more impregnable it is to destruction, and the more likely it is to express its unity in physical ways. The internal strength of a group, then, depends on a great many more factors than physical contact. In fact, it is possible that a group can have contact but no community at all, as armies, factories, and prisons long ago found out.

Out of this struggle for meaning and bonding has come division in some instances and frustration in others. Twenty-eight of the delegates made reference to a continuing struggle within their communities to resolve the philosophical differences. They describe the difficulty encountered in attempts to free the frightened or to support those weary of explaining themselves. A number of them talk about "the search for common values" or the amount of personal suffering that exists for those who resist change or those who seek it even more fully.

As a result, there is repeated reference in one way or another to communication gaps between large blocks of the community and "fragmentation that comes from operating out of different stances." One delegate is happy that in her community "we have lost (Deo Gratias) most of our 'rabble rousers' (and) have come back together for the most part stronger than we were before the 'wars.' " Another one has exactly the opposite interpretation of a similar experience. She wrote: "The biggest problem is that a large number of the 33-48 age bracket and the most progressive and educated members have left. In one sense this is good because it has lessened the polarization. But as far as the future goes it makes for a static, unchanging way of life. . . ."

From three other delegates there is a suggestion of impasse. One wrote: "We've done some of the 'easy' things, made a few changes but we are at a standstill renewal wise . . . (which) could result in division . . . another surge of departures . . . and eventual death."

In general, the responses of the delegates indicate that in a number of communities there is a small core of passive resistance to renewal that weighs down or divides the group, but that, in most part, progress and healing is steady and growing. One sister wrote: "From the beginning of renewal, our community has had the complete gamut of overly-conservative to overly-liberal, so we had the freedom to fit in somewhere and struggle things out." And another one described the process as the very essence of renewal. "Many community members," she said, "are still 'opposing' changes but we have to accept this if we really believe in plurality. We each arrive at a stage at a different time. Because of this, we are still feeling tensions. Each of us must be very understanding of others."

SURVIVAL

Finally, another group of responses clustered around circumstances which the delegates feel will affect the form of religious life in the very near future. Sixty-four delegates made one or more comments about four major issues: the current membership profile; the financial situation which this creates; the effects of institutional ownership and the need for leadership at the local level.

Of the 64 respondents who identified these circumstances as having great effect on the current state of religious life, 45 cited the fact that the present membership is aging, numbers of middle-aged have left and new vocations are few and far between. The other situations seem to be directly related to this single factor. As a result of this imbalance in the age level of the membership, there are fewer active members to support the number who are retired. Community costs, then, have increased but the traditional apostolates from which support has come until this time lack the staff or the enrollment to continue. In some instances, the original mortgage was not paid before the institutional apostolate began to decline. Consequently, debt and maintenance problems weigh heavily on communities as they search for new sources or ministries that reflect the call to social justice.

Of more impact on the future than these logistical issues, however, may be the fact that 23 of these respondents also cite as a crucial current issue a lack of leadership committed enough to renewal to be able to face the institutional questions with new solutions.

In the first place a number of them worry that younger members avoid leadership positions or "romanticize monasticism," a phrase that is apparently meant to refer to exaggerated notions of leisure and contemplation and withdrawal. Others are concerned that segments of their communities fail to take part in policy-making or collegial processes. One explained: "There is a lack of involvement in assuming leadership positions that requires intense goal setting, objectives and evaluation. . . . (But) failure to anticipate the future, or unconnected ideas that are not unified into a common goal and end cannot but have future consequences (in) departures from religious life, lack of total commitment and a smug security that is divorced from the needs of the Church today." Fourteen others cite conservatism, lack of long-range planning or a reluctance to function collegially on the part of the prioress to be militating against the ability of the group to deal with its present issues.

One respondent wrote: "Our leadership is lacking in the spirit and vision of Vatican II. . . ." In another place, a delegate said: "For the past decade the administration has preferred the traditional expressions of community, liturgy and ministry while maintaining a permissive attitude toward new approaches. Those confusions promise to persist into the 80's. The inability of the official leadership to give personal endorsement to new forms may be decisive for the future. As I see it, the question is whether the members' personal sense of responsibility and autonomy is sufficiently strong that the active members will gain and maintain their freedom as vowed religious to shape and live the life as it is interpreted in *Call to Life*, even when the official leadership does not offer clear direction."

Through the comments, though, run a strain of quiet persistence; a sense of commitment; a consciousness of error and risk. "The temptation to give up," another sister wrote, "must be consciously resisted,—especially when those in administrative positions aren't as receptive to change as to tradition and the future-oriented vision is merely tolerated. Sometimes," she goes on, "the strain shows in inter-community relationships. We need to keep liberating ourselves, and to find ways to honor the good of the past without letting it dominate judgments attuned to the necessities of the present."

Clearly, the authority question has diminished in communities of American Benedictine women and in its place has emerged a call for a leadership that honors the present but moves toward the future. And indeed it seems that in this transitional period someone must continue to lead if the renewal and revitalization of religious life in the present religious communities is to actually be accomplished. The confusion and questions raised by the 1967 opinionnaire on Benedictinism have largely disappeared but in their stead are larger matters. It was one thing to lighten the prayer load, another to share faith. It was one thing to be a work force, another to be prophetic. It was one thing to train women to conform, another to call forth personal and communal commitment. It was one thing to build the institutions, another to rebuild or raze them.

So the renewal period in communities of American Benedictine women brought turmoil and future uncertainty. It would seem that women who see these things happen in spite of their efforts and vision and hopes would be at least depressed, if not discouraged. But most affirming of the future perhaps is the ring of the answers themselves. Of the 142 responses, not one said that either renewal had failed or that religious life was failing. Many alluded to the idea that religious life in the form most of them were trained in, is over; that communities of the future will be smaller, less institutional, more open, more identified with the marginal of the society and with prayer, which many of them say is "richer than ever before" in their communities. Almost all of them give testimony to the value of the life for them as individuals; call it "happy" and even "exciting." They ask for "challenges rather than guidelines"; they say they'd "do it all over again"; that it is "a great time for religious life" and that they're "glad to have been a part of the change."

One of them, in fact, may have stated the whole present reality as well as given a signal of the future when she wrote: "Taking a high rank among our needs now, I feel, is to drive a stake through that ever-buried and ever-resurrecting question, 'When is all this going to be over with?' We have said all the right words and printed them in documents, acknowledging that our religious vocation is a call to life *now*—to a part in social and cultural revolution that has made us ideological and occupational pilgrims, with our service life and our worship life again as portable and adaptable as all those tent poles and hangings and knock-down gilded beams that went through the desert in O. T. days. We keep saying all this, but the malaise is still felt and expressed even by those in the vanguard of change—the wish to 'get it right this time around'—presumably to keep it and not want to change it. . . . When in the light of the Holy Spirit we internalize acceptance of our state of continuing change, we can probably begin again to enjoy one another's company on the road, and establish a Benedictine community in transit, and recognize some newly-growing 'traditions' that we can carry right along with us. We may then realize in a new way what it has always been to 'run in the way . . . with unspeakable sweetness.' "

What emerges from all this, then, is the profile of an institution in transition. It claims great traditions and is deeply rooted in the past. It has opened itself to the present and so bears a great responsibility for the future. There are problems which face it, both from within and without, and though it might easily have been smothered by decay it may yet be destroyed by risk. Even in that case, there are several things strongly in its favor at present which are evident in the data out of which this work was written: There is a high level of commitment to celibate community and the spiritual life; the sisters are happy and uncommonly concerned to do the work of God among the people of God. Formalism has gone from their daily lives and with it a single catechesis. And all of these may be the very reason they will be able to meet the problems of ministry and meaning and cohesion and survival in this culture today where single answers to complex questions are usually suspect and often unsound. What is more, like scores of Benedictines before them, they call over and over again for a simple life, centered in prayer and responsive to the world around them.

EPILOGUE

As this study developed, several factors emerged in relief. First, renewal and change in religious communities had not been a rejection of religious life but a rejection of a European or medieval way of living it. Secondly, it became obvious, too, that women religious maintained past patterns of convent culture as long as the ecclesiology supported the mode but, given a new model of the Church, they moved quickly to adapt. In the third place, a study of the monastic tradition, stripped of the cultural accretions of nearly fifteen hundred years, had confirmed their own application of the essential elements of the Benedictine tradition—community, prayer and ministry—to local circumstances. And finally, it grew clear that the pre-Vatican II structure of religious life had come to be a direct contradiction to the new ideas and personal needs of these American Benedictine women.

Everything had come together: facts, feelings and framework for change. The measure of the impact of renewal will depend in the long run on whether or not the Benedictine monastic tradition can be lived by American women in American ways. If not, an even more demanding question must be raised: Is the Benedictine charism simply an agrarian or medieval life-style that depends for its character on withdrawal, conformity, and European social forms whose model of woman and sanctity and community depends on the standards of past times?

American Benedictine women have pursued the renewal of their religious communities firmly convinced that the answer to that question is no but that the answer to Benedictine life is yes.

Appendix A

PARTICIPANT PROFILE (1976)
of the
Delegates to General Chapters
of the
Federation of St. Scholastica—1966-74

Dear Sister,

This questionnaire is an invitation to the chapter delegates of the Federation of Saint Scholastica to make a personal contribution to a current analysis of the renewal period, 1966-1974.

This has been a significant period in the history of our communities. What has happened in the last 10 years will affect a number of Sisters for a long time to come. We should reflect some, it seems, and ask ourselves in what ways each of us brought the Federation to its present point in the renewal process: what were our goals; what were our motivations; what are our feelings now. In this way we can provide an accurate record of what we ourselves thought we did as we revised policies that directly affected religious life as we experience it.

Such a record can be a guide to future generations. It can also help us at the present time to identify the issues surfacing now.

It is easy to grow weary at a time like this. The old vision has been blurred and the new one is unclear. We sometimes wonder if there is present value or future hope in our own lives. We forget that a people chosen before us also wandered, wondering about the wisdom of their past decisions and the presence of God, but they went on anyway. Going on was their contribution. We may forget that it can also be ours.

We are grateful for the journey of all of us. Your participation in this study is important.

Sincerely,

Sister Joan Chittister, O.S.B.
President, FSS

INSTRUCTIONS

1. Please answer all questions on the answer sheets enclosed, not in the survey booklet.

2. Do not put your name on the answer sheet; do not fill in any part of the name grid.
3. Use only a No. 2 ½ pencil or softer. The pencil is enclosed.
4. There are 3 answer sheets in this booklet. *Be careful* to use them in this order: 1A, 1B, 2A, 3A, 3B. Each sheet is identified in the upper right hand corner.
5. You may erase any answer, provided you do so thoroughly.
6. Please note that the directions for each section vary. The instructions for each part or question will explain how to choose a response for your answer. Please read these directions carefully before beginning to work on each section.
7. Do *not* fold, bend or staple the answer sheets.
8. Please answer questions number 212-13, the open-ended questions on the yellow paper labeled Answer Sheet 3A—3B. If your answer exceeds the space provided, use as much additional paper as you need.
9. Please return your three answer sheets by *February 18*. All participants whose response has not been received by that time will be contacted again.
10. The code number on the return envelope will enable us to determine that your response has been received. This way we won't have to bother you with letters of reminder. This code number appears on the envelope rather than on the answer sheet so that complete anonymity can be maintained. It will in no way be used to identify the response sheets themselves.
11. Do not return the Profile booklet with your answer sheets. The pre-postage covers only the cost of returning the answer sheets.

PART I.   CATALYSTS OF CHANGE

There are many factors that brought about change in the world, the church and religious life at the time of the Renewal Chapters—1966-74. Some of these factors are listed below. You are asked to say to what degree YOU as a chapter delegate were influenced by these factors. On the answer sheet please mark the letter that corresponds to your choice:

**Mark: A) considerably   B) somewhat   C) very   little
D) not at all**

1. My voting pattern in the Renewal Chapter I attended was influenced by the Constitution on the Church, Lumen Gentium.
2. My voting pattern in the Renewal Chapter I attended was influenced by the Constitution on the Sacred Liturgy.
3. My voting pattern in the Renewal Chapter I attended was influenced by the Constitution on the Church in the Modern World, Gaudium et Spes.

4. My voting pattern in the Renewal Chapter I attended was influenced by the Decree on the Appropriate Renewal of Religious Life, Perfectae Caritatis.

5. I feel that the Vatican Documents influenced the voting pattern of the delegates to the Renewal Chapter which I attended.

6. Delegates to the renewal chapters had the competence to make the decisions in matters which affected our lives.

7. The sexual revolution cast doubt on the values and normality of celibate life and influenced the discussions and attitudes at the General Chapter.

8. Total human development emerged as a cultural value and replaced self-denial as a primary value for religious.

9. The educational level of the delegates and resulting competence in the humanities and social sciences influenced the agenda, the process, and the results of the renewal chapters.

10. The educational level of the delegates in Scripture and theology influenced the agenda, the process, and the results of the renewal chapters.

11. The experience of pluralism in the United States contributed to the acceptability of diverse modes of living in a single community.

12. Life in a democratic society contributed to the acceptability of a broadened base of decision-making.

13. The influence of mass media and the resulting impact in the chapter of the free flow of information promoted a greater sense of involvement among the chapter delegates.

14. The influence of democratic principles in educational methods generated independent thinking among the chapter delegates.

15. The changing needs in contemporary society necessitated a reevaluation of community modes of service by the delegates.

16. The ability to create and satisfy needs in a consumer society led to the realization that society was not static.

17. The influence of easy mobility in transportation resulted in greater exchange of ideas.

18. New theological insights led to different understandings of the Gospel, the nature of the Church and religious life.

19. The rapid rate of change in society contributed to the chapter's flexibility in accepting the revision of religious life.

20. The liturgical movement contributed to the creation of varied forms of corporate worship among the chapter delegates.

21. The numbers of professed sisters leaving religious communities led to a reassessment and clarification of values.

22. Regular meetings of major superiors increased awareness of common problems shared by all religious and affirmed the impulse toward change.

23. Committee structure fostered greater involvement in the decision-making process.

24. Experiences on professional levels led delegates to realize that existing community structures inhibited mature human development.

25. Rapid influx and withdrawal of new members in the early 60's increased

internal stress and heightened the awareness of the need for institutional renewal.

PART II.   A.   ISSUES

NOTE: You will be asked to respond to the items that follow THREE separate times.

First, indicate how important these issues have been TO YOU during the renewal period (1966-1974). On the answer sheet please mark the letter that corresponds to your answer.

A) Was really important to me for awhile but not now
B) Was always of little importance to me.
C) Was never important to me at all.
D) Was of continuing importance to me
E) Is becoming more important to me at the present time.

26. Rank in community
27. Daily horarium
28. Restricted association with family and seculars
29. Limited availability of health care
30. Experimentation in Divine Office and Liturgy
31. Adoption of clothing changes
32. Self-chosen apostolate; open placement
33. Environment fostered by superior-subject relationship
34. Preserving concept of monastic enclosure
35. Practice of obtaining permissions
36. Custom of chapter of faults
37. Preservation of silence in the daily horarium
38. Government in local priory
39. Government on Federation level
40. Preservation of monastic tradition in the American Benedictine experience
41. Enlargement of representation of delegates to General Chapter
42. Suspension of Federation Constitutions to allow for experimentation
43. Autonomy of individual priories
44. Concept of allowing experimentation in areas of community life and government
45. Revision of policies in initial formation program (from entrance through final commitment)
46. Extension of formation policies to include continuing programs for all community members

47. Changes in corporate and individual use of money
48. Assignment of chaplains and confessors

PART II. B. ISSUES

Now, indicate how important these issues were TO YOUR COMMUNITY AS YOU PERCEIVED IT during the renewal period. On the answer sheet please mark the letter that corresponds to your answer.

A) **Was really important to my community for awhile but not now.**
B) **Was always of little importance to my community.**
C) **Was never important to my community at all.**
D) **Was of continuing importance to my community.**
E) **Is becoming more important to my community at the present time.**

49. Rank in community
50. Daily horarium
51. Restricted association with family and seculars
52. Limited availability of health care
53. Experimentation in Divine Office and Liturgy
54. Adoption of clothing changes
55. Self-chosen apostolate; open placement
56. Environment fostered by superior-subject relationship
57. Preserving concept of monastic enclosure
58. Practice of obtaining permissions
59. Custom of chapter of faults
60. Preservation of silence in the daily horarium
61. Government in local priory
62. Government on Federation level
63. Preservation of monastic tradition in the American Benedictine experience
64. Enlargement of representation of delegates to General Chapter
65. Suspension of Federation Constitutions to allow for experimentation
66. Autonomy of individual priories
67. Concept of allowing experimentation in areas of community life and government
68. Revision of policies in initial formation programs (entrance through final commitment)
69. Extension of formation policies to include continuing programs for all community members
70. Changes in corporate and individual use of money
71. Assignment of chaplains and confessors

PART II.   C. ISSUES

Finally, indicate how important these issues were TO THE
CHAPTERS YOU ATTENDED. On the answer sheet
please mark the letter that corresponds to your answer.

A) Was really important to the General Chapter for
   awhile but not now.
B) Was always of little importance to the General
   Chapter.
C) Was never important to the General Chapter at all.
D) Was of continuing importance to the General Chapter.
E) Is becoming more important to the General Chapter at
   the present time.

72. Rank in community
73. Daily horarium
74. Restricted association with family and seculars
75. Limited availability of health care
76. Experimentation in Divine Office and Liturgy
77. Adoption of clothing changes
78. Self-chosen apostolate; open placement
79. Environment fostered by superior-subject relationship
80. Preserving concept of monastic enclosure
81. Practice of obtaining permissions
82. Custom of chapter of faults
83. Preservation of silence in the daily horarium
84. Government in local priory
85. Government on Federation level
86. Preservation of monastic tradition in the American Benedictine experi-
    ence
87. Enlargement of representation of delegates to General Chapter
88. Suspension of Federation Constitutions to allow for experimentation
89. Autonomy of individual priories
90. Concept of allowing experimentation in areas of community life and gov-
    ernment
91. Revision of policies in initial formation programs (from entrance through
    final commitment)
92. Extension of formation policies to include continuing programs for all
    community members.
93. Changes in corporate and individual use of money
94. Assignment of chaplains and confessors

PART III.   ORGANIZATIONAL RESTRUCTURING

This section is concerned with federation structures which
have been adopted by the renewal chapters. Please read

the statement and respond to it in one of the four ways below. Mark on the answer sheet the response that best fits your current thinking.

A) strongly agree   B) agree   C) disagree   D) strongly disagree

95. The creation of the pre-chapter sessions to determine the chapter agenda facilitated renewal.
96. The expansion of the federation council by six community elected members provided a broader base of opinion at the executive level of government.
97. By increasing the number of delegates from priories the work of the chapter was representative of more views.
98. The development of committees at the General Chapter facilitated re- - newal.
99. The use of consultants provided an in depth perception for the background of agenda items.
100. Structurally, the Conciliation Board is an effective way to deal with individual grievances within the Federation membership.
101. The publication of interim Constitutions (Blue Book) facilitated renewal.
102. The publication of CALL TO LIFE facilitated renewal.

PART IV.   ATTITUDES

Do the following adjectives reflect your attitude to PRE-VATICAN II religious life? Please respond to each item.

I believe that life in the pre-Vatican religious community was:
Mark each: A) Generally true   or   B) Generally false

103. positive	116. supportive	129. confused
104. restrictive	117. indifferent	130. adolescent
105. stifling	118. hopeful	131. scandalous
106. meaningful	119. questionable	132. loving
107. effective	120. trusting	133. unfaithful
108. demeaning	121. depressing	134. negative
109. open	122. stable	135. sanctifying
110. satisfying	123. peaceful	136. sensible
111. happy	124. subservient	137. relevant
112. secure	125. joyful	138. liberating
113. fearful	126. reverent	139. ridiculous
114. frustrating	127. selfish	140. impersonal
115. childish	128. mature	141. frugal

142. introverted
143. withdrawn
144. lonely
145. fragmented
146. dynamic

147. elitist
148. dehumanizing
149. respectful
150. forward-looking
151. enthusiastic

152. developmental
153. affirming
154. edifying
155. static
156. frightening

Do the following adjectives reflect your attitude to POST-VATICAN II religious life? Please respond to each item.

I believe that life in the post-Vatican religious community is:

Mark each: a) Generally true or B) Generally false

157. positive
158. restrictive
159. stifling
160. meaningful
161. effective
162. demeaning
163. open
164. satisfying
165. happy
166. secure
167. fearful
168. frustrating
169. childish
170. supportive

171. indifferent
172. hopeful
173. questionable
174. trusting
175. depressing
176. stable
177. peaceful
178. subservient
179. joyful
180. reverent
181. selfish
182. mature
183. confused
184. adolescent
185. scandalous

186. loving
187. unfaithful
188. negative
189. sanctifying
190. sensible
191. relevant
192. liberating
193. ridiculous
194. impersonal
195. frugal
196. introverted
197. withdrawn
198. lonely
199. fragmented
200. dynamic

201. elitist
202. dehumanizing
203. respectful
204. forward-looking
205. enthusiastic
206. developmental
207. affirming
208. edifying
209. static
210. frightening

Below are 30 pairs of statements about different aspects of religious life. If you had to choose, which circumstance would you prefer. It will be difficult in some cases to make a clear choice between the items given, but try to select the one you feel you would be most inclined toward in most instances.

Mark either: A or B

211. a) To take a companion when I leave the premises
     b) To have freedom in matters of communications
212. a) To ask permission to do such things as eat with seculars
     b) To have a private room

213. a) To make a private on-going assessment of my strengths and weak-
     nesses
    b) To pray from a common monastic breviary
214. a) To pray in Latin
    b) To have no specified community customs book
215. a) To participate in various forms of communal reconciliation
    b) To use Gregorian Chant in liturgy
216. a) To choose my own time of recreation
    b) To have only a specific number of home visits per year
217. a) To have no distinguishing garb as a community
    b) To have specific times and places of silence
218. a) To observe the practice of mail inspection
    b) To talk at any time and place in the convent
219. a) To sleep in a dormitory
    b) To have any number of home visits per year
220. a) To use varied forms of music in the liturgy
    b) To set aside a specific period of time each day for particular examen
221. a) To have a book of community customs
    b) To pray in the vernacular
222. a) To participate in culpa chapters
    b) To use several arrangements of the Liturgy of the Hours
223. a) To make personal decisions for myself
    b) To be present at a specified community recreation every day
224. a) To wear the same distinguishing garb as other members of my com-
     munity
    b) To go out alone
225. a) To observe rank in community
    b) To attend Mass when I am able
226. a) To treat all people with equal respect
    b) To make an annual inventory of my possessions and submit it to
     superior
227. a) To submit Lenten resolutions to the superior for approval
    b) To develop healthy interpersonal relationships with members of both
     sexes
228. a) To accept the apostolic assignments assigned by the prioress
    b) To decide for myself what kind of personal accessories I need (Eye-
     glasses, earrings, and other items)
229. a) To have money to spend
    b) To use TV when I want to
230. a) To live where I choose even if the motherhouse is in the vicinity
    b) To love God only
231. a) To have no assigned rank
    b) To work only within the institutional commitments of the commu-
     nity
232. a) To live at the motherhouse if my ministry is in the vicinity
    b) To eliminate my surplus possessions

233. a) To use TV only within prescribed times
    b) To practice appropriate penances
234. a) To discern for myself the form and place of my ministry
    b) To follow the regulations of my community in the use of accessories (eye-glasses, earrings, and other such items)
235. a) To avoid associations with a member of the opposite sex
    b) To live within a budget or allowance
236. a) To treat the clergy with greater respect than is generally shown to others
    b) To have human friendships
237. a) To work outside the institutional commitments of the community
    b) To attend Mass daily
238. a) To be assigned by my superior to study in a particular field.
    b) To take time for leisure.
239. a) To exercise discretion in developing personal relationships.
    b) To fill my time with work and prayer.
240. a) To decide on a field of study myself.
    b) To avoid unnecessary contacts with people outside my religious community.

PART V.   CONSEQUENCES OF CHANGES SINCE 1966

On the answer sheet please mark the letter that corresponds to your answer.

Mark: A) To a great extent   B) Usually   C) Somewhat   D) Not at all
As a result of renewal, I experience

1. Changes in the modes of decision-making in community
2. A desire for the increased autonomy of women in the Church
3. Increased polarization in my community
4. A lack of community cohesion
5. Confusion due to the psychological pressures of change
6. Increased involvement in the creation of local community policy
7. Greater respect for individuals within community
8. A feeling that my religious life has become secularized
9. Greater individual responsibility
10. Loss of respect from lay people
11. Loss of respect from the clergy
12. A feeling that my view is sought in community matters
13. A heightened awareness of social responsibility
14. A feeling of hopefulness about the future of religious life
15. A feeling of despair about the present state of religious life
16. A feeling that the pace of renewal is too slow
17. A feeling that there have been too many changes in religious life

18. An increased commitment to the vowed life
19. A feeling of guilt that by participating in change I have contributed to the deterioration of religious life
20. A feeling of resentment toward people who have changed.
21. A feeling of fear for my future security.
22. A feeling of resentment toward people who have not changed.
23. A feeling of indifference about the present or future state of religious life.
24. A feeling of hostility toward those who obstruct change.
25. A feeling that renewal will be accomplished only by beginning new foundations.

PART VI. THEOLOGY OF RELIGIOUS LIFE AND PURPOSE OF RENEWAL

A. Many changes in understanding and the practice of Benedictine life were discussed at the renewal chapters. Indicate the degree to which your own religious life has been modified since the beginning of the renewal period. On the answer sheet mark the letter that corresponds to your answer.

A) more than before   B) about as much as before   C) less than before
D) neither then nor now

26. reading and reflecting on Scripture
27. spending time in current theological reading
28. spending time in personal prayer
29. attending community prayer
30. participating in shared prayer groups or devotional prayer gatherings
31. attending Mass
32. integrating prayer into my life
33. sharing spiritual reflections with others informally
34. sharing spiritual reflections with others in formal ways like giving renewal days, conferences, and homilies
35. fasting voluntarily
36. spending time getting to know sisters in community personally
37. talking with the sisters I live with about matters affecting our life together
38. responding to th daily and also the changing circumstances in the lives of the Sisters I live with
39. seeking and welcoming the insights of other sisters in matters concerning community life
40. seeking out and welcoming the insights of other sisters in matters concerning ministry
41. seeking ways to bring about reconciliation in community affairs and in my work relationships
42. thinking about leaving religious life

B. To what degree do the following behaviors have something to do with the essence of religious life according to the Rule of Benedict as an expression of the gospel? On the answer sheet please mark the answer that corresponds to your answer.

A) a great deal B) somewhat C) very little D) not at all.

43. Fasting voluntarily as a form of personal discipline or recollecting oneself.
44. Modifying eating habits in response to world hunger needs.
45. Using natural resources responsibly.
46. Restricting the use of products that are considered harmful to personal health or the environment.
47. Sharing community temporal resources (building and property) and human resources (professional competence, leadership skills, and political expertise) especially in behalf of the poor or deprived of the area.
48. Sharing community temporal resources (building and property) and human resources (professional competence, leadership skills, and political expertise) with any people of the area who can benefit from their use.
49. Investing surplus community monies in a manner that contributes to the common good of society rather than increasing community financial security.
50. Considering the consequences for society in making choices about ministries.
51. Considering the special needs of the poor or deprived in making choices about ministries.
52. Actively withdrawing community support from or involvement in businesses or institutions that do not operate from the principles of social justice.
53. Publicly supporting the peace movement.

PART VII. IMPLEMENTATION

This section concerns itself with items which may have contributed to or been an obstacle to implementation of the decrees of the general chapter.

How much did each of the following factors CONTRIBUTE to the implementation of the decrees of the General Chapter in your community. On the answer sheet mark:

A) greatly B) to some degree C) not at all

54. Leadership at the administrative level in the priory
55. Leadership at other levels in the priory, formal or informal.

56. Willingness of members to assume leadership.
57. Willingness of members to adopt changes.
58. Organizational changes at both the Federation and local levels.
59. Support of changes from the diocese.
60. Support of changes from the lay community.
61. Mandate of Vatican II
62. Flexibility of the Rule
63. Personal commitment of delegates to implementation
64. Communication skills at the priory level
65. Communication workshops to develop these skills
66. Mandated period for experimentation
67. Continuing education of Sisters in areas pertinent to the General Chapter
68. Facility in long-range planning at priory level
69. Community self-study prior to visitations
70. Study of Call to Life
71. Development of committees to study and call for implementation of chapter decrees
72. Revision of Canon Law concurrent with the chapter
73. Diocesan needs' assessments studies concurrent with community planning
74. Enlargement of representation to General Chapter
75. More frequent involvement of Prioresses at Benedictine and National/Diocesan meetings within and without the Federation
76. Ability of delegates to articulate their experiences
77. Continued presence in the community and participation in implementation of those committed to change

How much of an **OBSTACLE** has each of these factors been in the implementation of the decrees of the general chapter in your community? On the answer sheet mark the answer that corresponds to your answer.

A) great obstacle   B) somewhat of an obstacle   C) no obstacle

78. Fear of change
79. Lack of total involvement in the chapter experience on the part of most of the community
80. Inability of delegates to communicate the rationale for change
81. Confusion between a person's values and her behavior
82. Lack of personal and financial resources to create programs leading to change
83. Lack of values clarification skills
84. The notion that changes in the forms of religious life were destructive of the essence of religious life
85. Overemphasis on autonomy in priories

86. Obstruction by clergy
87. Lack of commitment by delegates
88. Confusion about the meaning of the monastic tradition
89. Age profile of membership
90. Lack of theological preparation as a basis for spirituality
91. The existence of large buildings and/or debts
92. Inability to attract new membership
93. Decline in membership
94. Overdependence on the approval of others
95. Psychological pressures created by the adaptations in religious life
96. Lack of familiarity with current Benedictine scholarship
97. Over extension of personnel
98. Institutional commitments
99. Calling for chapter votes on matters which did not require it
100. Lack of organization skills

PART VIII.   BELIEF STATEMENTS

All the following statements are ways of thinking about religious life. If you accept the statement as written, on the answer sheet, mark the letter A for True. If you do not accept the whole statement, consider your response a disagreement and mark the letter B for False.

101. I think of religious life as gospel life, no more no less.
102. The religious community reflects the Church and therefore must be outgoing and open to the secular.
103. Religious are called to special holiness because they have vows.
104. Religious live together in a believing celibate community and are dedicated to the service of the people of God.
105. The Holy See has the right to interpret the norms of religious life for the universal church and within each diocese.
106. The best work a religious community can do will take the form of an institutional corporate apostolate under the guidance of the hierarchy.
107. Religious witness involves a manifestation of social concern, and civic involvement, characterized by charity, simplicity, and compassion.
108. The interpersonal relationships in a community affect community prayer.
109. The purpose of religious life is to witness to the existence of another world than this one.
110. Non-institutional ministries provide a dynamic way to respond to the needs of the times.
111. Religious owe their obedience to a duly chosen superior.
112. Small communities contribute to self-awareness and growth toward maturity and an enriched relationship with Christ and are therefore authentic forms of religious life for these times.

113. Poverty demands the wearing of a distinctive religious habit as a sign of consecration to God and commitment to the world.
114. Religious life presumes regular community life within a program of communal and liturgical prayer.

PART IX. THE A-G SCALE

Mark the letter of your response on the answer sheet:

115. How happy has your life been over the past 10 years?
    a. much happier than I expected
    b. somewhat happier than I expected
    c. about as happy as I expected
    d. somewhat less happy than I expected
    e. much less happy than I expected

116. Compared to you, how happy do you think most of the Sisters of your community are?
    a. much happier than I
    b. somewhat happier than I
    c. about as happy as I
    d. somewhat less happy than I
    e. much less happy than I

117. How happy do you expect to be 10 years from now?
    a. much happier than I am now
    b. somewhat happier than I am now
    c. about as happy as I am now
    d. somewhat less happy than I am now
    e. much less happy than I am now

118. In Aesop's fable "The Ant and the Grasshopper", the ant spent his time working and planning for the future, while the grasshopper lived for the moment and tried to make things as bearable or enjoyable as possible. Which are you MORE LIKE?
    a. the ant
    b. the grasshopper

119. How confident are you that your guiding values are right for you and will last?
    a. very confident
    b. considerably confident
    c. somewhat confident
    d. not at all confident
    e. I'm questioning my values constantly

120. How optimistic or pessimistic about your life would you say you are?
    a. very optimistic
    b. optimistic
    c. pessimistic
    d. very pessimistic

121. How optimistic or pessimistic are you about the future of your community?
    a. very optimistic
    b. optimistic
    c. pessimistic
    d. very pessimistic

122. I feel that my life has meaning and direction.
    a. strongly disagree
    b. disagree
    c. agree
    d. strongly agree

123. How do you feel about the pace of your life?
    a. always feel rushed
    b. sometimes feel rushed
    c. almost never feel rushed

Compared to the average Sister, I generally consider myself:

Mark: A) strongly agree   C) disagree
**   B) agree   D) strongly disagree**

124. More intelligent
125. More likeable
126. More assertive
127. More conscientious
128. More impressionable
129. More confident
130. More conforming

Of the following attitudes, which were most characteristic of your overall participation in the FIRST renewal chapter you attended.

On your answer sheet mark: A) True   B) False

131. serious   133. frightened
132. sensitive   134. negative

135. upset
136. calm
137. affirming
138. angry
139. quiet
140. timid

141. articulate
142. open-minded
143. passive
144. analytical
145. relieved
146. close-minded

147. If you were a participant in more than one renewal chapter was there a significant change in your attitude between the first and the last chapter you attended?
   a. True
   b. False
   c. does not apply

148. If yes, was this change   A) positive   B) negative

C. Since the renewal period, Sisters have begun to make various changes in their behaviors. Do you participate in the following behaviors?

On your answer sheet mark A) True   B) False

149. small group living in newly established community residence
150. the use of contemporary clothing
151. the use of an allowance
152. a regular vacation period annually
153. the personal use of a community car
154. a work outside the institutional ministries
155. self-chosen ministry or open placement
156. attendance at social/cultural events (e.g. theaters, restaurants, concerts, athletic events, etc.)
157. living alone

People have various reasons for changing or not changing their behaviors. In this section there are 19 statements. You are to choose only the five items which you feel led you to make the changes you have. After you have identified these items, rank them according to their effect on you.

Mark: A) had greatest effect on me
      B) had the second most effect on me
      C) had the third most effect on me
      D) had the fourth most effect on me
      E) had the fifth most effect on me

REMEMBER, you are to select and rank only five statements. Please leave the other fourteen numbers blank on the answer sheet.

158. The Vatican Documents called for change.
159. I felt that much of pre-Vatican Religious life was inconvenient.
160. The superior expected the community to change.
161. I felt that Sisters were elitist, triumphalistic and out of touch with contemporary society.
162. The Sisters I lived with had changed.
163. I felt change was necessary if religious life was going to survive.
164. Our local chapter voted to permit the change.
165. Personal convictions flowing from new understandings of the essence of religious life required change.
166. My family encouraged me to change.
167. I felt I should change to support others.
168. My best friends were changing.
169. The prioress was not changing.
170. The students I taught expected me to change or made fun of Sisters who didn't.
171. Our past behaviors were becoming meaningless to me.
172. The priests with whom I worked encouraged change.
173. I had argued for change for a long time and so felt that I should adopt the changes when they came.
174. The younger Sisters were changing.
175. The prioress changed.
176. The older Sisters were changing.
177. I came to believe that it was all right for me to do it.
178. At the time of the renewal chapter, how did you perceive yourself in relation to the changes in religious life?
179. How did your community perceive you?
180. How do you perceive yourself now?
181. How does your community perceive you know?

PART X.   DEMOGRAPHIC PROFILE

On the answer sheet please mark the letter that corresponds to your answer.

A) True   B) False

182. I attended the chapter sessions of 1966.
183. I attended the chapter sessions of 1968-69.
184. I attended the chapter sessions of 1971.
185. I attended the chapter sessions of 1974.

On your answer sheet, mark the letter of your response to each of the questions below;

186. Your age now: a. 21-30   b. 31-40   c. 41-50   d. 51-60   e. over 60
187. Your educational level now:
    a. less than high school
    b. high school graduate
    c. college graduate
    d. master's degree or equivalent
    e. doctoral degree or equivalent
188. Number of years in community from first vows to now:
    a. 1-10 years
    b. 11-25
    c. 26-35
    d. 36-50
    e. over 50

189. Which best describes your administrative position when you were a delegate to the chapter:
    a. Prioress
    b. Local superior/coordinator/council member
    c. Major administrator of Catholic Institution
    d. Major administrator of a Public/Private Institution.
    e. No major administrative position.

190. Which best describes your ministry at the time of the chapter:
    a. internal to community
    b. education
    c. health care
    d. social welfare
    e. other

191. Which best describes your residence now:
    a. priory
    b. traditional community mission/branchhouse
    c. newly established community residence

192. Which comes nearest the size of your total community:
    a. fewer than 50
    b. 51-100
    c. 100-200
    d. over 200

193. Which comes nearest the size of your present living group:
    a. 21-or more
    b. 10-20
    c. 3-9
    d. 2
    e. 1

194. Which best describes the geographical environment of your priory:
     a. rural
     b. small city/town
     c. suburban
     d. large city
     e. inner city

195. Which best describes your father's religious affiliation when you were growing up:
     a. Catholic
     b. Protestant
     c. Jewish
     d. other
     e. none

196. Which best describes your mother's religious affiliation when you were growing up:
     a. Catholic
     b. Protestant
     c. Jewish
     d. other
     e. none

197. What portion of your education in grade school was in a Catholic school?
     a. all
     b. part
     c. none
     d. not applicable

198. What portion of your education in high school was in a Catholic school?
     a. all
     b. part
     c. none
     d. not applicable

199. What portion of your education in college was in a Catholic school?
     a. all
     b. part
     c. none
     d. not applicable

200. How many children were there in your family including yourself?
    a. one
    b. 2-3
    c. 4-5
    d. 6-8
    e. 9 or more

201. What is your position in the family?
    a. oldest
    b. between oldest and youngest
    c. youngest
    d. only child

202. How would you describe the occupational status of your father?
    a. blue collar laborer
    b. white collar clerical
    c. small business man
    d. professional
    e. agricultural

203. How would you describe the occupational status of your mother?
    a. full time job outside the home
    b. part time job outside the home
    c. full time at home

204. Indicate the highest level of education achieved by your father:
    a. 8th grade or less
    b. part high school
    c. high school graduate
    d. beyond high school but no degree
    e. college graduate

205. Indicate the highest level of education achieved by your mother:
    a. 8th grade or less
    b. part high school
    c. high school education
    d. beyond high school but no degree
    e. college graduate

206. Do you have more or less education than most of your brothers:
    a. more than
    b. less than
    c. about the same
    d. does not apply

207. Do you have more or less education than most of your sisters:
    a. more than
    b. less than
    c. about the same
    d. does not apply

208. Before the renewal chapters my participation in the affairs of my community was:
    a. very involved
    b. somewhat involved
    c. uninvolved

209. Since the renewal chapters my participation in the affairs of my community was:
    a. very involved
    b. somewhat involved
    c. uninvolved

210. In preparation for the Renewal chapters I was on:
    a. one Federation committee
    b. two Federation committees
    c. more than 2 Federation committees
    d. no Federation commitee

211. Are you still a member of a religious community?
    a. True
    b. False

Answer the following questions on the yellow sheet.

212. In your opinion, what are the problems facing your community at the present time?
    In what ways do you feel these will affect the future of your community?

213. Is there anything else you care to tell us about religious life as you see it?

Appendix B

RENEWAL CHAPTER DATA

SITES OF RENEWAL CHAPTERS

1966	St. Scholastica Priory Covington, Louisiana
1968 and 1969	The Cenacle 513 Fullerton Parkway Chicago, Illinois
1971	Holy Name Priory San Antonio, Florida
1974	Mount St. Scholastica Atchison, Kansas

CHAPTER DELEGATES

	1966	1968	1969	1971	1974
Atchison, Kansas					
Blacet, Sr. Jeanne Marie				X	
Collins, Sr. Mary				X	X
Curry, Sr. Kieran					X
Ege, Sr. Mary Paul		X	X	X	
Gampper, Sr. Madonna		X	X		
Harrington, Sr. Lillian				X	
Hansen, Sr. Regina				X	
Hurter, Sr. Noreen					X
Kennedy, Sr. Malachy	X	X			
Schirmer, Sr. Mary Austin	X	X	X	X	X
Schroll, Sr. Alfred		X	X		
Van Dyke, Sr. Mary Jane	X	X	X		
Walter, Sr. Mary Noel			X	X	X
Wolters, Sr. Dorothy					X
Benet Lake, Wisconsin					
Anheuser, Sr. Placida	X	X	X		
Huyck, Sr. Cecilia		X	X		

	1966	1968	1969	1971	1974
Irish, Sr. Benedict					X
Ladner, Sr. Bernadette					X
McCaffrey, Sr. Mary Hugh		X	X		
Miller, Sr. Patricia				X	
Nielsen, Sr. Margaret Mary			X	X	X

Boerne, Texas

	1966	1968	1969	1971	1974
Dashiell, Sr. Elizabeth Ann				X	
Goertz, Sr. Aloysia					X
Goertz, Sr. Mechtilde	X			X	
Goertz, Sr. Walburga		X	X		
Kallus, Sr. Henrietta Marie		X	X		
Kunz, Sr. Madeleine	X	X		X	
Stewart, Sr. Mary Martin					X
Van Golen, Sr. Antoinette Marie					X

Bristow, Virginia

	1966	1968	1969	1971	1974
Altman, Sr. Ethelreda	X	X	X	X	
Black, Sr. Mary Ellen				X	X
Bliley, Sr. Antoinette		X	X		
Hudert, Sr. Mary Clare					X
Johann, Sr. Ernestine	X	X	X	X	X
Muller, Sr. Gertrude				X	X
Sherwood, Sr. Anita				X	
Zimmerman, Sr. Henry Marie					X

Chicago, Illinois

	1966	1968	1969	1971	1974
Lynch, Sr. Catherine				X	
Matern, Sr. Jean Marie	X	X	X		X
McCarry, Sr. Barbara				X	
McKinney, Sr. Mary Benet					X
Moore, Sr. Mercedes			X		
Newman, Sr. Joanne		X	X		
Reilly, Sr. Jane		X	X	X	X
Smith, Sr. Jane				X	
Walker, Sr. Laura	X				

	1966	1968	1969	1971	1974
Westrick, Sr. Colette	X	X	X	X	X
Wilson, Sr. Miriam					X

Mexico City, Mexico

	1966	1968	1969	1971	1974
Armstrong, Sr. Althea				X	
Henry, Sr. Patricia		X	X		
Knoebber, Sr. Mildred	X	X		X	
Markiewicz, Sr. John Marie					X
Swearinger, Sr. Mechtild		X	X	X	X
Watson, Sr. Simone	X				

Colorado Springs, Colorado

	1966	1968	1969	1971	1974
Hays, Sr. Alice Marie		X	X		
Law, Sr. Marita					X
Liston, Sr. Diane				X	X
McGarity, Sr. Clarita	X	X	X		
O'Grady, Sr. Therese				X	
Rosenberger, Sr. Naomi			X	X	X
Sullivan, Sr. Liguori	X	X	X	X	X

Covington, Kentucky

	1966	1968	1969	1971	1974
Bunning, Sr. Benedict	X	X	X		
Collopy, Sr. Andrea		X	X	X	
Franxman, Sr. Justina					X
Henry, Sr. Donna					X
Kirk, Sr. Mariana				X	
Quinlan, Sr. Joyce			X		
Rust, Sr. Renee					X
Saelinger, Sr. Irmina		X	X	X	
Yost, Sr. Ruth	X	X	X	X	X

Covington, Louisiana

	1966	1968	1969	1971	1974
Federico, Sr. Juanita			X	X	
Gallant, Sr. Edna		X			
Gavin, Sr. Patricia	X				
Pravata, Sr. Maris Stella				X	X

	1966	1968	1969	1971	1974
Putnam, Sr. Johnette		X	X	X	X
Simoneaux, Sr. Eugenia	X	X	X		
Simoneaux, Sr. Lucy					X
Cullman, Alabama					
Allen, Sr. Maurus		X	X	X	
Crawford, Sr. Mary Frances	X	X	X	X	X
Frederick, Sr. Margaret			X		
Hamel, Sr. Augusta					X
Heinberg, Sr. Treva					X
Karibo, Sr. Patricia Ann	X	X	X		
Sevier, Sr. Mary Susan	X	X	X	X	
Elizabeth, New Jersey					
Bailey, Sr. Theresa Paul				X	X
Boyle, Sr. Cornelia	X	X	X	X	
Campbell, Sr. Stephanie		X	X		
Garley, Sr. Louise		X	X		
Grant, Sr. Clarence Marie	X	X	X	X	X
Maurer, Sr. Ann Veronica		X	X		
Sharkey, Sr. Kathleen				X	X
Erie, Pennsylvania					
Chittister, Sr. Joan		X	X	X	X
Lavin, Sr. Agnes Jean	X				
Kraus, Sr. Mary Margaret	X	X	X	X	X
McGreevy, Sr. Patricia		X		X	X
Pruchniewski, Sr. Rita		X	X		
Tobin, Sr. Maureen				X	X
Weaver, Sr. Phyllis		X	X		
Glendora, California					
Couhig, Sr. Mary Hope		X	X		
Foley, Sr. Mary Angela	X				
Hartnett, Sr. Padua		X	X		
King, Sr. Joan		X	X	X	X
Marnell, Sr. Francita					X

	1966	1968	1969	1971	1974
Parle, Sr. Augusta	X	X			
Stein, Sr. Serena				X	X
Wellsbacker, Sr. Barbara				X	
Lisle, Illinois					
Bratrsovsky, Sr. Mary Paul				X	
Francl, Sr. Mary Generosa					X
Hartwig, Sr. Mary Louise	X	X	X	X	
Heble, Sr. Judith Ann					X
Laketek, Sr. Celine		X	X		
Lidinsky, Sr. Eleanore	X				
Sebo, Sr. Irene				X	X
Sincak, Sr. Josephine		X	X		
Vesely, Sr. Charlotte		X	X		X
Oak Forest, Illinois					
Dziolek, Sr. Joann			X	X	
Gajniak, Sr. Geraldine	X	X	X		
Kadlub, Sr. Ethel	X				
Machalica, Sr. Mary Methodia		X			
Munoz, Sr. Dolores				X	X
Omastiak, Sr. Mary Ann				X	
Rafac, Sr. Gaudentia			X		
Rafac, Sr. Imelda					X
Pittsburgh, Pennsylvania					
Dettling, Sr. Evelyn				X	X
Farabaugh, Sr. Michelle		X	X		
Hemberger, Sr. Bernardine		X	X	X	
King, Sr. Demetria	X	X	X	X	X
Mack, Sr. Kathleen			X		
Stevens, Sr. Pauline	X	X	X	X	X
Ubinger, Sr. Maura					X
Ubinger, Sr. Theresa Clare				X	
Ridgely, Maryland					
Becker, Sr. Marie					X

	1966	1968	1969	1971	1974
Biskach, Sr. Anselma	X	X			
Dugan, Sr. Mary Ann				X	
Gamgort, Sr. Patricia			X		
Gerstenberg, Sr. Miriam Thomas				X	
Houtman, Sr. Immaculata			X		
Hussey, Sr. Mary Ellen					X
Kern, Sr. Augustine		X			
Murray, Sr. Jeannette		X	X	X	X
Quinn, Sr. Hildegarde	X	X			

St. Marys, Pennsylvania

Bridge, Sr. Teresita					X
Heberlein, Sr. Celestine				X	
Hoffman, Sr. Jane Frances		X	X	X	X
Krellner, Sr. Rose Mary	X	X	X		
Revak, Sr. Martina					X
Roth, Sr. Claudia		X	X		
Schaut, Sr. Romayne					X
Schneider, Sr. Callista	X				
Wegemer, Sr. Gertrude				X	

San Antonio, Florida

Bailey, Sr. Roberta					X
Driscoll, Sr. Patricia Ann			X		
Ducuing, Sr. de Chantal	X				
Leavy, Sr. Jerome				X	X
Martin, Sr. Frances	X	X	X		
McDonald, Sr. Margaret		X	X	X	
Neuhofer, Sr. Dorothy					X
Young, Sr. Carmen		X	X	X	
Zilles, Sr. Jane				X	

Tulsa, Oklahoma

Dorado, Sr. Jacinta	X			X	X
Fleming, Sr. Pierre					X
Gilpin, Sr. Anita Marie		X	X	X	X

	1966	1968	1969	1971	1974
Mohr, Sr. Marie Denise	X				
Mundell, Sr. Mary Edward		X	X		
Sokolosky, Sr. Veronica		X	X	X	

Warren, Ohio (1969)

	1966	1968	1969	1971	1974
Chuchvara, Sr. Ambrose			X		X
Dobos, Sr. Marion			X		X
Konkus, Sr. Judith			X	X	X
Pavlik, Sr. Barbara				X	
Schima, Sr. Margaret Mary			X	X	X

Appendix B

CONSULTANTS TO THE
GENERAL CHAPTERS OF THE CONGREGATION
OF SAINT SCHOLASTICA

June 1968

Rev. Matthew Benko, O.S.B., (Canonist), St. Vincent's Archabbey, Latrobe, Pa.

Dr. Leonard Borman (Anthropologist), Stone-Brandel Center, Chicago

Rev. Ambrose Clark, O.S.B., (Canonist), St. Mary's Abbey, Morristown, N.J.

Mr. Patrick Crowley (Attorney—Crowley, Sprecher, Barrett & Karaba), Chicago

Sister Dunstan Delehant (Philosopher), Mount St. Scholastica Convent, Atchison, Ks.

Rev. Demetrius Dumm, O.S.B., (Scripture scholar), St. Vincent's Archabbey, Latrobe, Pa.

Rt. Rev. John Gorman (Theologian), St. Mary of the Lake Seminary, Mundelein, Illinois

Sister Jeremy Hall, O.S.B., (Sociologist), St. Benedict Convent, St. Joseph, Minn.

Dr. Anthony Iezzi (Philosopher), St. John College of Cleveland, Cleveland

Rev. Eugene Kennedy, M.M., (Psychologist), Maryknoll Seminary, Glen Ellyn, Illinois

Rev. Eugene McClory (Secretary to the Cardinal for Religious Affairs for the Archdiocese of Chicago)

Mrs. Guy Pelton (Parliamentarian), Evanston, Illinois

Rev. Charles Schleck, C.S.C., (Theologian), Holy Cross College, Washington, D.C.

Most Rev. Rembert Weakland, O.S.B. (Abbot Primate), Collegio S. Anselmo, Rome, Italy

June 1969

Consultant	*Special Area*
Benko, Rev. Matthew, O.S.B. (Canonist), St. Vincent's Archabbey, Latrobe, Pa.	(Canon Law)
Blecker, Rev. Michael, O.S.B., (Historian), St. John's Archabbey, Collegeville, Minn.	(Evangelical Counsels)
Borman, Dr. Leonard (Anthropologist), Stone-Brandel Center, Chicago, Illinois	(Obedience)

Breitenbeck, Most Reverend Joseph (Auxiliary Bishop of Detroit, Liaison Person between the Sacred Congregation for Religious, the United States Conference of Bishops and the Religious Women of the United States)

Delehant, Sister Dunstan, O.S.B. (Philosopher), Mount St. Scholastica, Atchison, Kansas   (Apostolate)

Dumm, Rev. Demetrius, O.S.B. (Scripture Scholar, Rector of St. Vincent's Seminary, St. Vincent's Archabbey, Latrobe, Pennsylvania)

Emery, Dr. Andre (Superior, Society of Our Lady of the Way, Los Angeles, California)   (Evangelical Counsels)

Fogarty, Brother Ronald, S.M. (Psychologist), Marist College, Clayton, Victoria, Australia

Iezzi, Dr. Anthony (Philosopher), St. John College of Cleveland), Cleveland, Ohio

Jegen, Sister Carol Frances, B.V.M., Mundelein College, Chicago, Illinois   (Poverty)

McClory, Rev. Eugene (Secretary to the Cardinal for Religious Affairs for the Archdiocese of Chicago), Chicago, Ill.

O'Shea, Sister Joan, O.P., (Theologian), Rosary College, River Forest, Illinois

Pelton, Mrs. Guy (Parliamentarian), Evanston, Illinois

Penet, Sister Mary Emil (Member of the Board of Directors of the Religious Education Association and of the National Sister Formation Conference), Detroit, Michigan   (Formation)

Seasoltz, Rev. Kevin, O.S.B. (Theologian), St. Anselm's Priory, Washington, D.C.   (Formation)

Thole, Rev. Thomas, O.S.B. (Sociologist), St. John's Archabbey, Collegeville, Minn.   (Evangelical Counsels)

June 1971

Benko, Rev. Matthew, O.S.B. (Canonist), St. Vincent Archabbey, Latrobe, Pa.   (Gospel Poverty in 1970's)

Collins, Sister Mary, O.S.B. (Theologian), Mt. St. Scholastica Convent, Atchison, Kansas   (Prayer)

Brother Frank, Taize, France   (Gospel Poverty in 1970's)

Gelston, Mrs. Arthur   (Parliamentarian)

Iezzi, Dr. Anthony (Philosopher), St. John College, Cleveland, Ohio   (Polarization)

Johnson, Sister Margaret Mary, O.S.B., Mt. Angel, Oregon   (The Aging Process and Adaptation)

Putnam, Rev. G.J., New Orleans, Louisiana   (Race Relations)

Steindl-Rast, Brother David, O.S.B., Mt. Saviour Monastery, Elmira, New York   (Prayer)

Tkacik, Rev. Arnold, O.S.B., St. Benedict Abbey, Atchison, Kansas   (Prophetic Community)

June 1974

Benko, Rev. Matthew, O.S.B., (Canonist), St. Vincent Archabbey, Latrobe, Pa.   (Canon Law)

Carton, Sister Francis Regis, S.S.N.D., Provincial, Baltimore, Maryland   (Liberation Theology)

Raabe, Sister Marie Augusta, O.S.B., Mt. Angel, Oregon   (Benedictinism)

Appendix C

OPINIONNAIRE ON BENEDICTINISM (1966)

Dear Sister,

Typed below is an opinionnaire on Benedictinism. The purpose of this opinionnaire is to ascertain the general thinking of the Benedictine Sisters of the Congregation of St. Scholastica about Benedictinism in the modern world. The information gathered from this opinionnaire will be used as part of a study on Benedictinism being conducted by the Congregation Committee on Benedictinism. The findings of this opinionnaire will be synthesized in a report to be given to the Congregation during the second meeting January in preparation for the General Chapter. We will be deeply appreciative of your efforts in answering this opinionnaire as thoroughly as possible.

I. *General Information:*

Differences in background will influence the interpretation of this opinionnaire. Please check the following:

1. Community status:

   _____ postulant _____ novice _____ scholastic _____ Perpetually professed

2. Years in community:

   _____ 0-5 _____ 6-10 _____ 11-20 _____ 21-30 _____ over

3. Education:

   _____ high school _____ up to 90 hours _____ bachelor's _____ master's

4. Apostolate

   _____ teaching _____ nursing _____ administration (school

   _____ administration (community) _____ social work _____ CCD _____ Other

II. *Opinionnaire:*

1. One of the difficulties facing Benedictines today is an understanding of the basic elements of their life. Which of the following do you consider to

be *absolutely essential* elements of Benedictinism?

_____ liturgical prayer
_____ common life
_____ choral office
_____ enclosure
_____ lectio divina
_____ Scriptural orientation
_____ contemplative orientation
_____ work
_____ ascesis
_____ a certain amount of solitude and leisure

Comments:

2. According to the guidelines set down by St. Benedict, the rhythm of life in his monasteries is regulated by a balance of prayer, lectio divina, and work. Is the life of the American Benedictine Sister a balance of these three?

_____ Yes _____ No

Comments:

3. Do you believe that there is a difference in Benedictine life and the life led in other religious institutes?

_____ Yes _____ No

If "yes," how are we different?

If "no," do you think we should be different?

_____ Yes _____ No

Comments:

4. Is any apostolate commensurate with a Benedictine orientation:

_____ Yes _____ No

Comments:

5. Do you think that the Benedictine life of work and prayer with a communal, Scriptural, liturgical, and contemplative orientation can be an authentic and powerful Christian witness in the "secular city"?

_____ Yes _____ No

Comments:

6. In keeping with the view of the world as a sacramental rather than a profane reality, do you think that our concept of enclosure needs to be redefined?

_____ Yes _____ No

Comments:

7. With the possibility of phasing out certain areas of Catholic education because of financial and other problems looming before us, what new areas of apostolic involvement consonant with the monastic ideal do you believe Benedictines should be planning for?

8. Do you think that the Benedictine apostolate must be carried on within a limited radius of the monastery to be true to the Benedictine ideal?

_____ Yes _____ No

Comments:

9. Do you think that the ideal of stability is being realized by American Benedictines in the light of the whole system of mission houses as we have them today?

_____ Yes _____ No

Comments:

10. Do you feel that our first apostolate as Benedictines is to give witness as a monastic community to the real meaning of the Church and that any work we undertake must fall within the scope of that primary end?

_____ Yes _____ No

Comments:

11. Do you think that the Benedictine familial ideal is possible in large communities?

_____ Yes _____ No

Comments:

12. In the light of modern thought on religious life, do you think that St. Benedict's concept of the monastic community as a family has value today?

_____ Yes _____ No

Comments:

13. Do you think that there should be one or more Benedictine communities within the Congregation that live a purely contemplative life so that the needs of certain members who feel drawn to this type of life may be met?

_____ Yes _____ No

Comments:

14. Do you feel that the Rule of St. Benedict in its overall vision is relevant today?

_____ Yes _____ No

Comments:

15a. Do you feel that certain areas of the Rule are irrelevant today?

_____ Yes _____ No

Comments:

15b. If your answer is "yes" to question 15a, which areas do you feel are irrelevant?

16. The following is the plan proposed by the Congregational Committee on the study of Benedictinism:

1) Conduct a survey of current thinking on Benedictinism in the Congregation by means of this opinionnaire.
2) Tabulate this opinionnaire and prepare a report of its findings to be given to the Congregation at the January meeting in preparation for the General Chapter.
3) Synthesize the progress reports on the study of Benedictinism submitted by each Priory by December 16. The Congregational committee will follow the outline given below. The committees on Benedictinism at the individual Priories are invited to follow it if they wish to do so.

I. Nature of Benedictinism based on the study of:
   A. Human life (see *Gaudium et Spes*, Chapters 1-2 (#12-24)
   B. Christian life (see *Lumen Gentium*, Chapter 5)
   C. Religious life (see *Lumen Gentium*, Chapter 6)
   D. Monastic life (see *Perfectae Caritatis* and *Ecclesiae Sanctae*)
      1. Theology of monastic spirituality
      2. Basic elements of monastic spirituality
   E. Benedictine life

II. Relevance of Benedictinism:
   A. Relevancy of the Rule of St. Benedict
   B. Benedictinism in America Today
      1. The concept of "separation from the world" in the twentieth century
      2. The value of the witness of monastic community today
      3. Benedictines and ecumenism

III. Implementation of the above principles to the following:
   A. The Apostolate
   B. Beatitudinal life (Evangelical counsels)
   C. Sister Formation
   D. Community life
   E. Religious life
   F. Temporalities
   G. Other

4) Present a position paper on Benedictinism based on this outline at the General Chapter in June. This paper will be a synthesis of the on-going studies conducted at each Priory throughout the year.

16a. Do you think that this is a good plan?

_____ Yes _____ No

Comments:

16b. Would you have any suggestions for changes in the plan?

_____ Yes _____ No

If so, what are they?

16c. Do you think an entirely different approach is necessary?

_____ Yes _____ No

If so, explain below.

17. Since this committee would like to function as a channel of resource material to all members of the Congregation, would you list below any books, articles, information on tapes, and names of lecturers on Benedictinism and related topics which you think would contribute to this study.

Appendix D

GLOSSARY

American Benedictine Academy: An association of Benedictine women and men founded in 1940 for the purpose of the advancement of scholarship in the monastic community in the United States.

Benedictine Order: The term used to identify all communities who follow the Rule of Benedict. It does not, however, designate the organization of these communities under one central authority since each Benedictine foundation is autonomous.

Canon Law: The Code of Canon Law is a mandatory and sovereign codification of church laws which have for part of their subject matter the organization and government of religious orders. The 1918 codification is under revision as a consequence of Vatican II.

Cenobitic: The form of monastic life in community that is characteristically Benedictine and distinguishable from other styles of monasticism that are eremitical or semi-eremitical.

Chapter: The legislative body of each local autonomous priory. It is composed of all the perpetually professed members of the community and meets to decide specific matters of a juridical nature or to give counsel and advice to the local prioress.

Choral Office: See Opus Dei.

Collegiality: Shared responsibility or participatory government.

Congregation: A canonically recognized association of religious communities having a central governing authority. There is a single American congregation of Benedictine Sisters, the Benedictine Sisters of Perpetual Adoration. Formerly, the term was used officially if inaccurately to designate also the three federations of American Benedictine women's communities.

Constitution on the Church: See *Lumen Gentium.*

Constitution on the Church in the Modern World: See *Gaudium et Spes.*

Constitution on the Sacred Liturgy: See *Sacrosanctum Concilium.*

Constitutions: The body of laws by which the Federation of St. Scholastica is governed. The current constitutions promulgated in 1974, in the Congregation of St. Scholastica, are entitled *Call to Life.*

Culpa: Literally, fault. A monastic practice of acknowledging one's failings either to the community when assembled for a chapter of faults or to the superior.

Customary: A compilation of local community practices which governed rules of behavior.

Declarations: A series of statements by means of which the Rule of Benedict was either authoritatively interpreted or legitimately circumscribed so as to be appropriate to contemporary conditions. The last declarations were published in 1953.

Decree on the Appropriate Renewal of Religious Life: See *Perfectae Caritatis.*

Divine Office: See Opus Dei.

Federation: An association of autonomous priories with canonical authority to convoke general chapters and to write and implement the constitutions to which the member houses subscribe, but not to govern the internal affairs of the community. The three federations of American Benedictine women are the Federation of St. Scholastica, the Federation of St. Gertrude the Great, and the Federation of St. Benedict.

Federation Council: The council of the federation is the governing body of the federation between sessions of the general chapter. It is composed of eleven persons: four persons elected by the general chapter, six elected from within the member houses who serve on a rotating basis and the president of the Federation. The council meets at least once a year and is especially responsible for the implementation of the canonical visitations and the convocation of the general chapter.

Gaudium et Spes: Pastoral Constitution on the Church in the Modern World endorsed by the Second Vatican Council and promulgated in 1965. It explained the relationship of the church to the concerns of contemporary society.

General Chapter: The legislative body of the Federation of St. Scholastica. Composed of the prioresses and elected delegates from the 22 autonomous priories, it meets for one week every four years.

Lumen Gentium: Dogmatic Constitution on the Church endorsed by the Second Vatican Council and promulgated in 1965. It provides a theological statement on the nature of the church, its organizational structure, and the relationships among its members.

Mother President: The title formerly given to the elected superior of the Congregation of St. Scholastica. Currently the title is "Sister" in the Federation.

Motu Proprio Ecclesiae Sanctae: The decree of Paul VI promulgated in 1966 giving specific directives to religious communities for the implementation of the document *Perfectae Caritatis* on the renewal of religious life.

Opus Dei: Literally, the work of God. The common prayer for monastic communities prescribed by St. Benedict in his Rule. It consists basically of the recitation of the Psalms and the reading of Scripture in choir at appointed hours of the day.

Perfectae Caritatis: The Second Vatican Council Decree on the Appropriate Renewal of Religious Life, promulgated in 1965. It directed religious communities to recapture their original spirit and to attune it to the needs of contemporary society.

Prioress: In a community of Benedictine Sisters, the elected superior of the priory. She takes the office corresponding to that of the abbot in St. Benedict's *Rule.*

Priory: The independent monastery of Benedictine women whose members constitute a distinct permanent community.

Rule of Benedict: A rule for those who wish to live in monastic community under the direction of an abbot, written, by Benedict of Nursia in 6th century Italy. It has had a very strong influence in the development of monastic life in the western world to the present day.

Sacred Congregation for Religious: A department of the Vatican which has responsibility for maintaining contact and communication between the Roman Catholic Church and its religious orders.

Sacrosanctum Concilium: The Constitution on the Sacred Liturgy endorsed by the Second Vatican Council and promulgated in 1963. It provided a theological statement on the nature of worship and called for changes in the forms of the Church's worship.

Sister Formation Movement: A grass-roots effort in the United States during the decade of the 1950's and early 1960's to upgrade and integrate the spiritual and professional training of younger religious women who were working in the apostolate.

Subsidiarity: Delegation of authority.

Vatican II: The assembly of Roman Catholic bishops convened by Pope John XXIII which met in four sessions from 1962-65 to consider the nature of the Roman Catholic Church and its relationship to the modern world.

Vows: Promises made to express a life-long commitment to God in a particular way of life. The Rule of Benedict specifies three vows: obedience, stability in a particular community, and conversion to the monastic way of life. Modern communities normally profess vows of poverty, chastity, and obedience.

Appendix E

FEDERATION OF SAINT SCHOLASTICA (1977)

Mount Saint Benedict Convent
6101 East Lake Road   Erie, Pennsylvania 16511

Mount Saint Scholastica Convent
ATCHISON, KANSAS

Holy Family Convent
BENET LAKE, WISCONSIN

Saint Scholastica Convent
BOERNE, TEXAS

Saint Benedict Convent
BRISTOW, VIRGINIA

Saint Scholastica Convent
CHICAGO, ILLINOIS

Benet Hill Priory
COLORADO SPRINGS, COLO-
RADO

Saint Walburg Convent
COVINGTON, KENTUCKY

Saint Scholastica Convent
COVINGTON, LOUISIANA

Sacred Heart Convent
CULLMAN, ALABAMA

Saint Walburga Convent
ELIZABETH, NEW JERSEY

Mount Saint Benedict Convent
ERIE, PENNSYLVANIA

Saint Lucy's Convent
GLENDORA, CALIFORNIA

Sacred Heart Convent
LISLE, ILLINOIS

Saint Benedict Convent
MEXICO CITY

Our Lady of Sorrows Convent
OAK FOREST, ILLINOIS

Red Plains Priory
OKLAHOMA CITY, OKLA-
HOMA

Mount Saint Mary Convent
PITTSBURGH, PENNSYL-
VANIA

Saint Gertrude Convent
RIGELY, MARYLAND

Holy Name Priory
SAINT LEO, FLORIDA

Saint Joseph Convent
SAINT MARY, PENNSYL-
VANIA

Saint Joseph Convent
TULSA, OKLAHOMA

Queen of Heaven Convent
WARREN, OHIO

287

Notes

PART I

1. *Declarations and Constitutions of the Congregation of St. Scholastica*, Atchison, Kansas, 1953. No. 22-29.
2. *Choir Ceremonial for the Benedictine Sisters of the Congregation of St. Scholastica*, Atchison, Kansas, 1948; cf., pp. 7-8; also, pp. 14, 19.
3. *Declarations and Constitutions of the Congregation of St. Scholastica*, Atchison, Kansas, 1953, No. 17-18.

PART II

1. A glossary found in Appendix D explains "general chapter" and other technical terms.
2. *Revision of the Declarations To the Rule of Our Holy Father St. Benedict*. Proposed by the General Chapter of the Congregation of Saint Scholastica. To be effective from July 1966 to June 1968. In-house publication. Archives of the Federation of St. Scholastica. Atchison, Kansas.
3. All primary source material cited in this section is held in the archives of the Federation of St. Scholastica.
4. The Conference of Major Superiors of Women, the official ecclesiastical association of the elected leadership of women's communities in the United States, has been known since 1971 as the Leadership Conference of Women Religious.
5. The Federation underwent a membership decline of about 20% from 1963 to 1969. Figures vary in individual priories.
6. *Visitation Manual*. Federation of St. Scholastica. Erie: Benet Press, 1975.
7. Untitled work. Benedictine Sisters. Congregation of St. Scholastica. Renewal Chapter 1968-69. In-house publication. Archives of the Federation of St. Scholastica.
8. *Ecclesiae Sanctae II*, 1966. Norms for Implementing the Decree *Perfectae Caritatis*. No. 6.
9. *Call to Life*. Federation of St. Scholastica. Erie: Benet Press, 1975.
10. *Perfectae Caritatis*. No. 3.
11. *Ecclesiae Sanctae* II. No. 1 and 2.
12. The Benedictine abbot primate, resident in Rome, is the focus of unity and identity for Benedictine communities worldwide. Elected by the Congress of Abbots, he is responsible for representing Benedictine interests before the Holy See and for convoking the Congress of Abbots. Rembert

Weakland of St. Vincent's Archabbey, Latrobe, Pa., was elected abbot primate in 1967.

13. The clergy had often used the term "good sister" in referring to women religious, but sisters considered it both paternalistic and condescending.

14. Community customs books varied only on minor points in the member priories of the Congregation. Copies of typical customs books are available in all community archives.

PART III

1. Archives of the Federation of St. Scholastica. Atchison, Kansas.

2. For a discussion of the circumstances surrounding Vatican I, see *The Vatican Council 1869-1870*, by Cuthbert Butler, O.S.B.; ed. Christopher Butler. Westminister, Md: The Newman Press, 1962.

3. An account of American Benedictine women's early history can be found in *With Lamps Burning*, M. Grace McDonald, O.S.B., St. Joseph, Minnesota: St. Benedict's Priory Press, 1957, pp. 1-55.

4. The non-applicability of the 1901 norms to houses of Benedictine women was immediately evident to some concerned Benedictines in the United States. Abbot Innocent Wolf of St. Benedict's Abbey, Atchison, Kansas, who was assisting in the efforts of American Benedictine women to gain Roman recognition, wrote on 8/27/07 to Mother Aloysia Northman, prioress at Mount St. Scholastica, Atchison, "The Norms of the S.C. of 28 June, 1901, are really for *New Institutes*, as the title already says, whilst the Benedictine Sisters are following the Holy Rule. . . . The "Norms" may nevertheless be a guide in many things, to what is indicated in them as being the will of the Pope expressed through the S.C. . . . What the "Norms" say about . . . the works, Rule, Religious, Monastery, etc.—concern new orders or *Institutes* and not our Sisters." (Mount St. Scholastica Archives, Atchison, Kansas.) Some of the consequences of subsequent imposition by Rome are detailed elsewhere in this section of the study.

5. Two juridical issues were at stake. First, American Benedictine women were not making solemn vows. The bishops of the United States had been advised in 1864 by the Roman Congregation of Bishops and Regulars that with rare exceptions no religious women in the new country would be permitted to pronounce solemn vows. On 6 December, 1859, Roman authorities had denied a particular request that women being professed as Benedictines in the United States should make solemn vows as was customary at St. Walburga, the founding community. (Photostat copy of the 1859 decree, Mount St. Scholastica Archives, Atchison, Ks. For a discussion of the 1864 decision, see *The Catholic Encyclopedia*, "Nuns," 1907.) Second, American Benedictine women did not observe the details of papal enclosure, which severely controls access to and egress from the nuns' quarters by any persons other than authorized clergymen. The circumstances controlling this omission

were practical ones. Papal enclosure was a luxury not available on the American frontier. (Details are provided in McDonald, *With Lamps Burning,* ch. 4, 5, 7.) More importantly, the Rule of Benedict and the monastic way of life flowing from it antedated the juridical requirements of papal enclosure by many centuries. In both cases, what were historically secondary developments in the Benedictine way of life were being used as norms in 1922 for determining Benedictine authenticity.

6. Working as school teachers was itself a mark of continuity with the parent community. St. Walburga's Convent in Eichstatt had taken up school education for girls in 1836, as one of the conditions for the restoration of the convent after a generation of virtual suppression by the government. This establishment of a school was mandated by King Ludwig I of Bavaria with the concurrence of the local bishop. See McDonald, *With Lamps Burning*, p. 6; also, *Spring and Harvest* by The Nuns of St. Walburg, trans. M. Gonzaga Englehart, O.S.B., St. Meinrad, Ind.: The Grail, 1952, pp. 33-38.

7. For details, see *The Americanist Heresy in Roman Catholicism 1895-1900*. Thomas T. McAvoy, CSC, Univ. of Notre Dame Press, 1963.

8. Ellis, John Tracy, ed. *Documents of American Catholic History*. Milwaukee: Bruce Publishing Co., 1956, pp. 553-562.

9. *Gaudium et Spes*, 7 December, 1965. Chapter 1 on the dignity of the human person. Also no. 41-42.

10. McAvoy, *The Americanist Heresy*, p. 296.

11. Baska, Regina, O.S.B., *The Benedictine Congregation of St. Scholastica—Its Foundation and Development: 1880-1930*. Washington, D.C.: Catholic University of America, 1935.

12. Minutes of August 23, 1966, meeting of the prioresses of the Congregation of St. Scholastica at Milwaukee, Wisc.; copy at Mount St. Benedict Convent, Erie, Pa.

13. A 435-item *Participant Profile* was devised and administered early in 1976 to gather the personal assessments of the historic decade from those women who as chapter delegates had shaped the course of post-Vatican II renewal. See Appendix A.

14. *Sacrosanctae Concilium*, 4 December, 1963. No. 21, 23, 37.

15. *Perfectae Caritatis*, 28 October, 1963. No. 2, 3.

16. *Declarations and Constitutions*. Congregation of St. Scholastica, Atchison, Kansas, 1953.

17. Morran, M. Audrey, O.S.B., "A History and Chronology of the Benedictine Institute of Sacred Theology." Unpublished M.A. thesis, 1964. St. John's University, Collegeville, Minn., p. 32.

18. Graduate school file: "BIST: Origin, Formation, History." St. John's University, Collegeville, Minn., see also Morran, p. 32.

19. For a discussion of the larger context of this development, see Langdon Gilkey, *Catholicism Confronts Modernity*. New York: Seabury Press, 1975.

20. For the educational profile of the renewal chapter delegates, see Part II of this study.

21. *Ecclesiae Sanctae II*, 6 August, 1966. Introduction to the Norms for Implementing the Decree *Perfectae Caritatis*. But see also no. 15 of that document, where attention to all the conciliar documents is recommended.

22. *Lumen Gentium*, 21 November, 1964. No. 4.

23. The theological discussion of the period is exemplified in Jerome Hamer, *The Church is a Communion*. New York: Sheed and Ward, 1964, and in Karl Rahner, *The Dynamic Element in the Church*. New York: Herder and Herder, 1964. See also Avery Dulles, *Models of the Church*. New York: Doubleday, 1974.

24. See, for example, Vorgrimler, Herbert, ed. *Commentary on the Documents of Vatican II*. Volume I: *Dogmatic Constitution on the Church*. New York: Herder and Herder, 1966, pp. 234, 239-40.

25. Many canon lawyers and historians of religious life have noted in retrospect that the 1901 norms for women's institutes had suppressed vitality by imposing uniformity for more than half a century. See for example, J. Beyer, "The New Legislation for Religious" in Bassett, William and Peter Huizing, ed. *The Future of Religious Life* (Concilium, Volume 97). New York: Seabury Press, 1974-75, p. 71.

26. *Lumen Gentium*, no. 27.

27. *Lumen Gentium*, no. 45.

28. *Call To Life*. Federation of St. Scholastica. Erie, Pa.: Benet Press, 1974, p. 17.

29. *Call To Life*, p. 17.

30. *Call To Life*, p. 17.

31. *Call To Life*, p. 18.

32. *Call To Life*, pp. 60-61.

33. *Perfectae Caritatis*, no. 14.

34. *Perfectae Caritatis*, no. 9.

35. *Perfectae Caritatis*, no. 1. See Thomas Aquinas, *Summa Theologiae*, II-II, q. 184 and 186 (Vol. 47: *The Pastoral and Religious Lives*. Translation and notes by Jordan Aumann, O.P., Blackfriars, 1973.) See also Friedrich Wulf's commentary on the formulation of the text of *Perfectae Caritatis* in Vorgrimler, Herbert, ed., *Commentary on the Documents of Vatican II*. Volume II. New York: Herder and Herder, 1966.

36. *Rule of Benedict*, ch. 58.

37. For example, documents of professions made in 1873 record four promises: poverty, chastity, obedience, and amendment of my life according to the Rule—but contain no explicit reference to the characteristic Benedictine vow of stability. In 1876 a document records the traditional Benedictine formula of stability, conversion of my life, and obedience. . . . That formula persists until 1925, when the Roman decision to treat American Benedictine women as a "new Institute" results in the hybrid combination of five vows. By 1967, the traditional Benedictine triad had reappeared. (Mount St. Scholastica Convent Archives, Atchison, Kansas.)

38. *Declarations and Constitutions*. Congregation of St. Scholastica, No. 121.

39. James R. Cain documents the judgment that enclosure legislation reflects the historical bias against women. See "Cloister and the Apostolate of Religious Women," *Review for Religious*, vol. 27 (1968), p. 262, 280. For an extended history of cloister legislation for women into the 20th century, consult Cain's series of articles, vol. 27 (1968), pp. 243-280; 427-488; 652-671; 916-937; and vol. 28 (1969), pp. 101-121. See also Schaff, V.T. *The Cloister*. Canon Law Dissertation Series no. 13. Catholic University of America. Cincinnati, Ohio, *St. Anthony Messenger*, 1921, pp. 34-56.

40. Thomas Aquinas. *Summa Theologiae*, II-II, q. 184, art. 5.

41. Thomas Aquinas. *ST*, I-II, q. 108, art. 3 and 4; see also, I-II, q. 84, art. 1 and 2.

42. Thomas Aquinas. *ST*, I-II, q. 108, art. 4; II-II, q. 184, art. 7.

43. *Rule of Benedict*, ch. 58; 1 Corinthians 7, 25-35; Matthew 19:12.

44. *Rule of Benedict*, Prologue and ch. 1.

45. *Rule of Benedict*, Prologue, ch. 73, 2, 71-72, passim.

46. Baska, Regina, O.S.B. *The Benedictine Congregation of St. Scholastica*, pp. 132-137.

47. The concept of solemn vows is itself a medieval ecclesiastical development which adds nothing intrinsic to the inner meaning of the religious act. A solemn vow is a juridical category. By ecclesiastical authority, it imposes the consequence of making invalid any actions contrary to the vow, such as entering into a binding contract. The notion implies a social situation where ecclesiastical jurisdiction prevails over civil jurisdiction for some groups of persons. The post-Vatican II revision of canon law proposes to eliminate the concept of solemn vow. For a discussion of the evolution of the concept of solemn vows, see Matthew Kohmescher. *Additional Vows of Religion in General and in Particular the Vow of Stability in the Society of Mary*. (University of Fribourg dissertation, 1957.) Dayton, Ohio: Marianist Publications, 1957.

48. Baska, Regina, O.S.B., *Benedictine Congregation of St. Scholastica*, pp. 133-137.

49. The 1880 Constitution drafted by Bishop Louis Fink, O.S.B., had said simply that one of the works of the general chapter of the proposed congregation would be to "endeavor to increase the usefulness of the sisters in regards to the education of others, and in helping to supply the needs of the church." (Section XXXIII, no. 2. Mount St. Scholastica Convent Archives, Atchison, Kansas.) In the 1922 Constitution, in order to meet the requirements of the 1901 norms, this reference to the activity of the communities had been narrowed considerably to "the education of the young, both in their academies and in the parish schools." *Declarations and Constitutions of the Congregation of St. Scholastica*, Atchison, Kansas, 1922, no. 1.

50. *Ecclesiae Sanctae*, II, 6 August, 1966, no. 1.

51. *Perfectae Caritatis*, no. 9.

52. *Gaudium et Spes*, 7 December, 1965, no. 12ff; 23ff; 33ff.

53. *Gaudium et Spes*. Pastoral Constitution on the Church in the Modern World, 7 December, 1965. No. 17, 22, 26.

54. *Declarations and Constitutions.* Congregation of St. Scholastica, 1922, no. 1.

55. *Declarations and Constitutions.* 1930. No. 116.

56. *Declarations and Constitutions.* 1930. No. 115.

57. *Declarations and Constitutions.* 1930. No. 4, 61, 90.

58. *Declarations and Constitutions.* 1930. No. 5.

59. The attitudes and behaviors cited are referred to throughout the document. See, for example, no. 18, 155.

60. Literature on the impact of dualism in Christian spirituality is extensive. For an introduction to the topic as it related to men and women, see Rosemary Ruether, "Misogynism and Virginal Feminism In the Fathers of the Church" in Ruether, ed., *Religion and Sexism*, Simon and Schuster, 1974, pp. 150-183.

61. The four texts cited are from the statement of the Benedictine charism in the 1974 document *Call To Life*, pp. 4-6.

62. A foundational statement for this broadened understanding of the presence of the risen Christ is no. 7 of the Constitution on the Sacred Liturgy, 4 December, 1963.

63. In 1976, nine out of ten delegates rejected the notion that the sexual revolution in western society had cast doubt on the values and normality of celibate life and had influenced the discussions and attitudes of the renewal chapters.

64. *Call To Life*, p. 27.

65. The fifth major section of this work, "These Are Not Her Only Children," sets out the personal issues in community renewal in detail.

66. *Call To Life*, p. 28.

67. *Call To Life*, p. 18.

68. *Call To Life*, p. 29.

69. *Call To Life*, p. 41.

70. *Call To Life*, p. 42ff for the series of quotations.

71. See the discussion of attitudes toward pre- and post-Vatican II religious life in "These Are Not Her Only Children," part five of this study.

72. *Call To Life*, pp. 13, 35.

73. *Call To Life*, pp. 52-53.

74. *Call To Life*, pp. 4-6.

75. *Sacrosanctum Concilium.* Constitution on the Sacred Liturgy. 4 December, 1963. No. 2. See also *Lumen Gentium*, No. 3.

76. See note 52.

77. John 17; 6:47-54, 67-69.

78. Thomas M. Gannon and George W. Traub. *The Desert and the City.* Toronto: Collier-Macmillan Canada, Ltd. 1969, pp. 23-25.

79. *Gaudium et Spes.* 7 December, 1965. No. 23.

80. *Call To Life*, p. 6.

81. *Call To Life*, pp. 6, 52.

82. *Call To Life*, p. 5.

83. See, for example, Robert Ledogar, "The Question of Daily Mass,"

Worship, May, 1969, pp. 258-280. Also, Burrell, D. 'Many Masses and One Sacrifice—A Study of the Thought of Karl Rahner," *Yearbook for Liturgical Studies* (1961), Miller, J., ed. pp. 103-117; Karl Rahner and A. Haussling. *The Celebration of the Eucharist*. New York: Herder and Herder, 1968.

84. *Rule of Benedict*. Ch. 4:13; ch. 49.

85. *Rule of Benedict*. Ch. 4:71; ch. 13.

86. *Call To Life*. p. 53, No. 43, 44.

87. *Rule of Benedict*. Ch. 4:14-20.

88. *Call To Life*. p. 53, no. 46.

89. Cultural anthropologist Victor Turner suggests that monasticism is characteristically "normative communitas" within a larger hierarchically ordered social system. See "Communitas: Model and Process" in *The Ritual Process*. Ithaca, New York: Cornell University Press, pp. 131-165.

90. *Call To Life*. p. 9.

PART IV

1. Letter of January 10, 1966. Archives of Federation of St. Scholastica. Atchison, Kansas.

2. Letter of April 14, 1966. Archives, FSS.

3. Letter of Mother Mary Susan Sevier, O.S.B., June 17, 1966. Archives, FSS.

4. Letter of Mother Mary Susan Sevier, O.S.B., to the prioresses of the Congregation, February 6, 1967. Archives, FSS.

5. Letter of Mother Mary Susan Sevier, O.S.B., to the prioresses of the Congregation, February 2, 1967. Archives, FSS.

6. This was evident in the books and articles being published and in the informal discussions of the sisters. At the 1968 meeting of the Conference of Major Superiors of Women, Sister Marie Augusta Neal in her report on the results of the Sisters Survey of 1967 observed that the imposition of the practices of monastic life on the active religious orders was in some part a cause of the dilemma they were then experiencing.

7. Further explanation and specific examples of this conflict will be given in the following analysis of the Opinionnaire on Benedictinism.

8. The Opinionnaire on Benedictinism is included in the appendix. Data is on file in the Archives, FSS.

9. In preparing the Opinionnaire on Benedictinism, the committee did not intend to include all possible elements of monastic life. They attempted rather to list those which seemed most essential to Benedictine life according to the following commentaries on the Rule and works on Benedictine spirituality: C. Butler, *Benedictine Monachism*, (London, 1919); P. DeLatte, *The Rule of St. Benedict*, (Latrobe, 1950); C. Peifer, *Monastic Spirituality*, (New York: Sheed and Ward, 1966); B. Steidle, *The Rule of Benedict, A Commentary*, trans. by U.J. Schnitzhofer, (Canon City: Holy Cross Abbey, 1966); H

VanZeller, *The Holy Rule, Notes on St. Benedict's Legislation for Monks*, (New York, 1958); M. Wolter, *The Principles of Monasticism*, (St. Louis, 1962).

10. Steidle, p. 63, 225-26, 228-29.

11. *New Catholic Encyclopedia*, Vol. IV, (New York: McGraw Hill Book Co., 1967), p. 264.

12. *Spring and Harvest, St. Walburg's Shrine: Symbol and Center of Nine-Hundred Fruitful Years*, by the nuns of St. Walburg's, Eichstatt, Bavaria; trans. by Sister Gonzaga Englehart, O.S.B., (St. Meinrad: The Grail, 1952), p. 36-37.

13. *Declarations on the Rule of our Holy Father St. Benedict and Constitutions of the Congregation of St. Scholastica*, 1922, No. 104.

14. *Norms for the Appropriate Renewal of Religious Life in Vatican II, The Conciliar and Post-Conciliar Documents*, edited by Austin Flannery, O.P., (Collegeville: Liturgical Press, 1975) p. 631, #32. All subsequent quotations from the documents of Vatican II are taken from this edition and cited in the text by paragraph number.

15. *Perfectae Caritatis*, No. 9; see also *Ecclesiae Sanctae* II, No. 32. Further discussion of the equation of monasticism with enclosure can be found in Part III of this study, "I Fail To See The Logic of this Approach."

16. See, for example, The Rule of Benedict: 4, 50, 51, 53, 67.

17. The distinctive Benedictine tradition of vows is discussed in greater detail in Part III of this study, "I Fail To See the Logic Of This Approach."

18. These circumstances are discussed earlier in Part III of this study.

19. *Benedictines*, XXVI: 3-4 (Fall-Winter, 1971), p. 47-70.

20. See the Vatican II Constitution on the Sacred Liturgy, *Sacrosanctum Concilium*. No. 10.

21. *Gaudium et Spes*, No. 22, 34.

22. *Gaudium et Spes*, No. 34; see also No. 40 and 45 for the following citations.

23. *Benedictines*, XXVI: 3-4 (Fall-Winter, 1971), pp. 71-88.

24. Paul VI, "Exhortation on the Renewal of Religious Life," (June, 1971).

25. *Call To Life*, (Erie: Benet Press, 1974).

26. The basic elements of community had been identified in the 1971 Chapter document, "Christian Fellowship in a Prophetic Faith Community," *Benedictines*, Fall-Winter, 1971, pp. 71-87.

27. Steidle, op. cit., p. 256.

28. Acts 2:46; also the Rule of Benedict, Ch. 8-20, Ch. 2 and 3.

29. Acts 2:45-46; also the Rule of Benedict: Prologue, Ch. 2, 4, 32, 48, 49, 54, 55, 58, 71.

30. Acts 2:45-46; also the Rule of Benedict: Prologue, 2, 4, 20, 27, 35, 36, 47, 52, 53, 63, 64, 66, 71.

31. Rule of Benedict, Ch. 2 and 3; see also Ch. 64.

32. Rule of Benedict, Ch. 1; see also Ch. 72.

33. Rule of Benedict, Prologue.

34. Rule of Benedict, Ch. 72, 74.
35. Rule of Benedict, Ch. 20; see also Ch. 9-10 and 16.
36. Rule of Benedict, Ch. 58; see also the Prologue.

PART V

1. The data on which this study is based were gathered through a 453-item *Participant Profile* developed by the authors of this study and distributed in 1976 to all the women who were delegates to the General Chapters of Renewal from 1966-74. A copy of the *Participant Profile* is Appendix A of this work.

2. For a discussion of cognitive dissonance and its effects, see, for example, Zimbardo, Philip and Ebbe B. Ebbesen, *Influencing Attitudes and Changing Behaviors.* Addison-Wesley Publishing Co., Massachusetts, 1970. Also, Insko, Chester A., *Theories of Attitude Change.* Appleton-Century Crofts, New York, 1967; and Young, Paul T. *Motivation and Emotion*, John Wiley and Sons, Inc., New York, 1961.

3. For a discussion of group judgments, see Davis, James H. *Group Performance.* Addison Wesley Publishing Co., Massachusetts, 1969. See also, Asch, Solomon E. *Social Psychology.* Prentice-Hall, Inc., New York, 1952; and Cathcart, Robert S. and Samovar, Larry A., *Small Group Communications: A Reader*, Wm. C. Brown Company, Iowa, 1972.

4. For a detailed account of the organization and work of the general chapters, see Part II of this study, "All They Need Is Courage."

5. Dispensation records for the Federation of St. Scholastica. Federation Archives, Atchison, Kansas.

6. Presentation to the General Chapter by Brother Ronald Fogarty, C.M., June, 1969.

7. Role conflict is treated by Gullahorn, John T. and Jeanne E., "Role Conflict and Resolution" in Dean, Dwight G., ed. *Dynamic Social Psychology.* Random House, New York, 1969, pp. 418-433. See also "Self-Esteem and Responsibility" in Horrocks, John E. and Jackson, Dorothy W., *Self and Role*, Houghton Mifflin Company, New York, 1972, pp. 123-33.

8. See Part III of this study, "I Fail To See The Logic of This Approach."

9. Aspects of the pre-Vatican II religious life of American Benedictine women are described in Part I of this study, "We Are Asking For More Voice."

10. Copies of customs books, which vary only slightly from house to house, are available in community archives.

11. The concept of mental health is discussed, for example, in Jahoda, Marie, *Current Concepts of Positive Mental Health*, Basic Books, Inc., New York, 1958. Also, Maslow, A.H., *Toward a Psychology of Being*, Van Nostrand, New Jersey, 1962; Smith, M. Brewster, *Social Psychology and Human Value*, Aldine Publishing Co., Chicago, 1969; Goffman, Erving, *Asylums*, Doubleday and Company, New York, 1961.

298 *Notes*

12. Declarations and Constitutions of the Congregation of St. Scholastica. 1953, No. 155.

13. For a discussion of dependency and conformity, see Lang, Kurt and Lang, Gladys Engel, *Collective Dynamics*. Thomas Y. Crowell Company, New York, 1961; Kiesler, Charles A. and Kiesler, Sara B., *Conformity*, Addison-Wesley, Massachusetts, 1970, and Rokeach, Milton, *The Open and Closed Mind*. Basic Books, Inc., New York, 1960.

14. The need for group structure is treated in Kaufman, Herbert, *The Limits of Organizational Change*. The University of Alabama Press, 1971. See also, Rogers, Everett M. and Shoemaker, F. Floyd, *Communication of Innovations*, 2nd edition, The Free Press, 1971. Also, Sherif, Muzafer and Sherif, Carolyn W., *Social Psychology*, Harper and Row, Publishers, New York, 1969; and Hinton, Bernard and Reitz, H. Joseph, *Groups and Organizations*. Wadsworth Publishing Company, Inc., California, 1971.

15. Self-image and self-esteem are discussed in Horrocks and Jackson, *Self and Role*. See also, Smith, M. Brewster, *Social Psychology and Human Value* and Brandon, Nathaniel, *The Psychology of Self-Esteem*, Bantam Books, New York, 1971.

16. See Part III of this study, "I Fail To See The Logic of This Approach."

17. Conformity is treated extensively in Adorno, T.W. et al., *The Authoritarian Personality*. New York: Harper, 1950. See also, Kiesler and Kiesler, *Conformity*; Beisecker, Thomas D. and Donn W. Parson. *The Process of Social Influence*. Prentice-Hall, New Jersey, 1972.

18. For a discussion of depersonalization by institutions, see Goffman, *Asylums*; also, Kantor, Rosabeth Moss, *Commitment and Community*. Harvard University Press, Massachusetts, 1972.

19. See, in this study, Part II "All They Need Is Courage" and Part IV "This Is the Crux of the Problem."

20. See, for example, Allport, Gordon W. *The Nature of Prejudice*. Addison-Wesley Publishing Co., Inc., Massachusetts, 1954.

21. See Kutner, B., Carol Wilkins, Penny R. Yarrow, "Verbal Attitudes and Overt Behavior Involving Racial Prejudice," *Journal of Abnormal and Social Psychology*. 1952 (47), pp. 649-652.

22. See note 17 above.

23. See, for example, Sherif and Sherif, *Social Psychology*; Eisenstadt, Samuel, "Social Institutions," in *Encyclopedia of Social Science*, ed. David I. Sills, Macmillan Co.. New York, 1968: Hamilton, Walton, H.. "Institution" in *Encyclopedia of the Social Sciences*, ed. Edwin R.A. Selignam, Macmillan Co., New York, 1932; and Gardner, John, *Self-Renewal*, Harper and Row, New York, 1965.

24. On motivation, see Katz, Elihu and Lazarfeld, Paul F. *Personal Influence*, Free Press, New York, 1966. Also, Sherif, Muzafer, *The Psychology of Social Norms*, Harper Torchbooks, New York, 1966; and Kiesler and Kiesler, *Conformity*.

25. The relationship between conformity and beliefs is treated in Rokeach, *The Open and Closed Mind*. See also, Katz, Elihu and Lazarfeld, Paul, *Personal Influence*, Free Press, New York, 1966; Kiesler and Kiesler, *Conformity*, and Freedman, J.L., Carlsmith, J. Merrill, and Sears, David O., *Readings in Social Psychology*, Prentice-Hall, Inc., New Jersey, 1971.

26. Neal, Marie Augusta, S.N.D., "Cultural Patterns and Behavioral Outcomes in Religious Systems: A Study of Religious Orders of Women in the U.S.A.," unpublished research; Leadership Conference of Women Religious, Washington, D.C.

27. The relationship of central purpose and clarity of goals to the effectiveness of groups and institutions is treated in a brief but comprehensive manner in Weick, Karl E., *The Social Psychology of Organizing*, Addison-Wesley Publishing Company, Reading, Massachusetts, 1969, and Torrance, E. Paul, *Mental Health and Constructive Behavior*, California: Wadsworth Publishing Company, Inc., 1965.

28. Morkin, Sister M. Louis, O.S.B. and Siegel, Sister M. Theophane, O.S.B., *Wind in the Wheat*, A History of the Benedictine Sisters of Erie, 1956; Archives, Mount Saint Benedict Convent, Erie, Pennsylvania, 16511.

29. See note 14 above.

30. For a study of religious orders and institutional life cycle see Cada, Lawrence J., S.M. and Fitz, Raymond L., S.M., "The Recovery of Religious Life" in *Review for Religious*, September, 1975.

INDEX

Americanism, 76-78.

Apostolate, 100, 135, 139-140, 162, 198-199, 217, 225-226, 234. *See also* Ministry.

Asceticism, 121-123, 136, 151, 159, 186, 187.

Attitudes, Pre-Vatican II: 170-174, 177; Post-Vatican II: 174-180.

Authority, 89-93, 111-112, 154-155, 192-194, 223-224. *See also* Government.

Baltimore, Third Plenary Council (1884), 76.

Baska, Sister Regina, O.S.B., 4, 78.

Belief Pattern, 214-227.

Benedictine Charism, 88-89, 94-99, 100-103, 104, 108-114, 115-117, 118-119, 122-124, 131-132, 139, 145, 154, 186, 235.

"Benedictine Community: Eucharistic Ecclesiola," 144-148.

Benedictine Institute of Sacred Theology, 82, 84.

Benedictine Men, 20, 21, 95-96, 99, 137.

Benedictine Women, American, apostolic work, 100, 135, 139-140, 162, 198-199, 232-234; canon law, 75-76, 99, 100, 223; community, 109-114, 235-238; current problems, 228-242; eschatology, 114-124, 219-220; historical influences, 74-78; history, 228; ministry, 123-124, 162, 198-199, 225-226, 232-234, 235; opinionnaire on Benedictinism, 131, 138, 277-282; personal holiness, 101-109; renewal issues, 101-124, 216-219; theological training, 81, 84; vows; 95-100, 155-158. *See also* Federation of St. Scholastica Religious.

Benko, Matthew, O.S.B., 35, 36.

Beuron (Monastery), 133.

"Blue Book." *See* Federation of St. Scholastica, Constitutions.

Boniface VIII (Pope), 137.

Botz, Paschal, O.S.B., 19, 34-35, 83.

Boyle, Mother Cornelia, O.S.B., 35.

Brugelman, Mother Athanasius, O.S.B., 44.

Call to Life, 20, 29, 49-50, 53-54, 60, 62, 91, 92, 106-108, 109-114, 119, 123-124, 150-163, 235.

Canon Law, Code of 1918, 75-76, 99-100, 223, 283.

Celibacy, 98, 157-158, 190-192.

Cenobitic Community, 97-98, 109-114, 115-117, 133, 140-141, 145-150, 154-155, 236-239, 283.

Chapter, 283, 61. *See also* Government, Chapter, General.

Chapter, General, 284; committees, 38-41, 52, 130-132; consultants, 41-42, 53, 274-276; decision-making process, 168-169; definition, 283; delegates, 30-33, 36, 55-56, 63-69, 83-84, 168-169, 174-175, 267-273; pre-chapter sessions, 33-39, 53; *1967*, 131; *1968*, 31, 37; *1969*, 37; *1971*, 38; *1973*, 49; renewal chapters, 169-173, 201-202, 267-273; *1966*, 47, 129-130; *1968-69*, 22-23, 31-32, 35-36, 37-38, 41-42, 47-48, 129-130; *1971*, 41, 49, 148; *1974*, 33, 41; structure, 29, 33-34. *See also* Federation of St. Scholastica.

Chapter of Faults, 13, 187, 284.

Chittister, Sister Joan, O.S.B., 49.

"Christian Fellowship in a Prophetic Faith Community," 148-150.

Church, American, 76-78; *Lumen*

301